"This is a timely book! David Gill has drawn on a variety of sources—popular writings, ethical handbooks, biblical scholarship (including profound insights from the Jewish community) and historical lessons—to produce one of the best studies of the Ten Commandments to come our way for quite a while "

RICHARD J. MOUW, *President and Professor of Christian Philosophy, Fuller Theological Seminary*

"Instead of simply pointing an accusing finger, *Doing Right* offers a truly refreshing and freeing alternative to today's seemingly ubiquitous ethical decay David Gill's examples, illustrations and humor portray the genuine benefits of conducting business and life according to God's principles and priorities "

LORI RANDLES LAGERSTROM, *Sales Director*

"Together with his *Becoming Good,* David Gill's *Doing Right* completes a masterful two-volume exposition of ethical character and practice *Doing Right* provides a carefully researched and clearly expounded analysis of the Decalogue, full of practical wisdom and fresh insight into the wondrous connections between loving God and loving neighbor "

KENNETH R. CHASE, *Associate Professor of Communication and Director, Center for Applied Christian Ethics, Wheaton College (Illinois)*

"*Doing Right* is a thoughtful, scholarly, humorous and loving exploration of God's model of relationships outlined in the Ten Commandments I was captivated by David Gill's theme that treats negative boundaries as only the *beginning* of what must ultimately become positive mandates to love This is an ethic that takes seriously our fallenness but offers hopeful ways to bring healing, justice and freedom to ourselves and others "

REBECCA KLINT TOWNSEND, *MD*

"To our peril we've reduced the discussion of the Ten Commandments in the United States to a fight over a two-ton monument in the rotunda of the Alabama Supreme Court The God who has set us free in Jesus Christ has a road map that will lead us in the way of freedom *Doing Right* is an outstanding book that calls us back to the importance of the Decalogue for anyone who desires to live a good life "

TIM SHAW, *Associate Pastor, First Presbyterian Church of Berkeley*

"Anyone who thinks that an introduction to Christian ethics based on the Ten Commandments might be a bit dry could not be more wrong David Gill's *Doing Right* is written with a sprightly, punchy and energetic style, with a winsome sense of humor, great command of a fascinating and unusual body of biblical and theological research, and an everyman touch honed by years of teaching ethics in nonacademic settings "

DAVID P. GUSHEE, *Graves Professor of Moral Philosophy, Union University, and coauthor* Kingdom Ethics

"*Doing Right* challenges us to *think* deeply, biblically, courageously and wisely about the right thing and then pushes us to *act* more rightly and justly I love Gill's emphasis on ethics as a 'team sport' we need to embrace and live out these principles in community, as a collective body of people seeking God's will "

KIM DAUS-EDWARDS, *Chief Transformational Officer, Equip Business Missions, and coauthor,* Customer Community *and* Beyond Spin

"*Doing Right* is a clear, engaging primer on the Christian moral life With perceptive cultural analysis and lots of down-to-earth examples and advice, David Gill offers fresh insight on the Ten Commandments and their ability to guide us today "

STEVEN BOUMA-PREDIGER, *Jacobson Professor of Religion, Hope College*

"*Doing Right* provides a concise description of what a moral life looks like Using Jesus as the cartographer, David Gill supplies the reader with an ethical map, a practical guide to the principled life "

TERRY NEIFING, *Licensed Clinical Social Worker*

"The fruit of decades of brooding on the Decalogue, David Gill's masterpiece draws deeply on a rich Jewish and Christian tradition He shows how the 'Ten Words' are not merely prohibitions--and that for our good--but describe a lifestyle of love, justice and freedom that is good not just for people of faith but critical for the health of society Two things separate this book from many others on the subject First, he refuses to separate the so-called first table (commandments one to five) as only relating to God, and the second table (six to ten) as concerned exclusively with neighbors Thus he shows how the whole Decalogue, as Jesus said, is fulfilled in love to God and neighbor Second, Gill painstakingly applies these lifestyle standards to the warp and woof of our everyday life--which is exactly what the Author had intended! The questions at the end of each chapter are worth the price of the book "

R. PAUL STEVENS, *David J Brown Family Professor of Marketplace Theology and Leadership, Regent College, Vancouver, BC*

"Wisdom and compassion, truth and gentle humor mingle on the pages of *Doing Right,* bringing life to a subject that often seems stony, cold and chiseled "

SUSAN S. PHILLIPS, *Executive Director, New College Berkeley*

"If you haven't already memorized the Ten Commandments, you will! David Gill's *Doing Right* helps us discover the deeper wisdom of the Ten Commandments and encourages us to lead our lives according to God's design "

DAVID GILMOUR, *Owner, Paradise Foods, and President, Marin Leadership Foundation*

"*Doing Right* is an extremely insightful and highly readable work David Gill provides wise and practical applications of the Ten Commandments to contemporary moral issues, including those occurring in the workplace This book is a must-read for anyone who is interested in understanding what it means to live faithfully in all areas of life "

KENMAN WONG, *Professor of Business Ethics, Seattle Pacific University*

"David Gill brings fresh insight into well-worked material Doing Right is engaging, compelling and preachable!"

JAMIE CROOK, *Senior Pastor, University Covenant Church, Davis, California*

"David Gill's insights on the Ten Commandments, especially his explication of how our obligations toward God flow into our obligations to each other, should be a part of every teaching on the Decalogue Doing Right shows the marks of a person who loves the law of God and who has taught it for years "

GEORGE THOMAS, *Professor of Global Studies and Sociology, Arizona State University*

"In this important new book David Gill shares the fruit of a quarter century of reflection on foundational Christian ethics and life in the marketplaces of ideas and commerce Those who imagine that the Ten Commandments are irrelevant for contemporary life are in for a refreshing surprise! I have observed Dr Gill's transformative teaching on the lives of both traditional students in the classroom and lay Christians in churches and am delighted that his fresh, insightful and faithful instruction is now being shared with a much wider audience I do not know a better guide to thinking Christianly about the ethical challenges of everyday life "

W. WARD GASQUE, *President, Pacific Association for Theological Studies*

"David Gill writes Doing Right with courage and integrity courage to take on the tough issues of our day and integrity not to treat them with simplistic answers Page after page, he shows us how biblical principles will guide us to do the Right Thing "

DAVID BATSTONE, *Executive Editor,* Sojourners, *and author,* Saving the Corporate Soul & (Who Knows?) Maybe Your Own

"In Doing Right, David Gill probes analytically for the deeper meaning of the Ten Commandments, expands each command with thick, specific exegesis of Jesus' teaching, learns from incisive Rabbis and Reformed scholars, shows decisive implications for our doing, and contrasts real flashes of wisdom from these sources with dangerous foolishness in current culture Here is my commandment Buy this book, read it, and do almost all it teaches "

GLEN STASSEN, *Professor of Christian Ethics, Fuller Theological Seminary, and coauthor,* Kingdom Ethics

Other Books by David W. Gill

The Word of God in the Ethics of Jacques Ellul (1984)

Peter the Rock Extraordinary Insights from an Ordinary Man (1986)

The Opening of the Christian Mind (1989)

Should God Get Tenure? Essays on Religion and Higher Education (editor, 1997)

Becoming Good Building Moral Character (2000)

Doing Right

PRACTICING

ETHICAL PRINCIPLES

David W. Gill

WIPF & STOCK · Eugene, Oregon

Wipf and Stock Publishers
199 W 8th Ave, Suite 3
Eugene, OR 97401

Doing Right
Practicing Ethical Principles
By Gill, David W.
Copyright © 2004 by Gill, David W. All rights reserved.
Softcover ISBN-13: 978-1-6667-4727-0
Hardcover ISBN-13: 978-1-6667-4728-7
eBook ISBN-13: 978-1-6667-4729-4
Publication date 5/3/2022
Previously published by InterVarsity Press, 2004

This edition is a scanned facsimile of the original edition published in 2004.

For my students

at New College Berkeley

and North Park University,

with gratitude

Contents

Preface

Just as I entered the University of California at Berkeley as a freshman in 1964, the free speech movement began In the highly charged environment of Berkeley in the sixties, I had my first of three "ethics conversion" experiences my primary interest as a Christian in the world changed from apologetics to ethics I saw in us Christians an eagerness to *argue intellectually* for Christian faith but a troubling incapacity to *demonstrate ethically* our faith in daily life (e g , in politics, work, finance or racial relations)

At that stage I thought of ethics mainly in terms of facing dilemmas, making difficult decisions and acting on them with courage My mission was to search for a more specifically Christian *content* (which seemed to me relatively unexplored), but I didn't much question the *definition* and *form* of the enterprise itself Jacques Ellul and John Howard Yoder reinforced my sense that any ethics called "Christian" should be centered on Jesus Christ This seems obvious, but it was rarely articulated with any clarity or force and was still more rarely practiced

In 1980, I had my second "ethics conversion" experience As a novice professor, I asked Professor Klaus Bockmuehl of Regent College how he organized his introductory course on Christian ethics He replied that his basic course was an exposition of the Ten Commandments I thanked him, but inwardly I reacted, *How on earth could an exposition of the Old Testament Decalogue be an adequate introduction to* Christian *ethics*?

I thought of myself as a "New Testament Christian " I was raised in a church committed to dispensationalism (an interpretive system that accentuates the differences between the epoch of the Mosaic law and other biblical epochs, including the Pauline "day of grace" in which we live) While I memorized a lot of biblical texts in my dispensationalist youth, the Ten Commandments were never on the required list Through the sixties and seventies I moved away from dispensationalism and toward the Anabaptist tradition of radical discipleship, which focused on the Sermon on the Mount, but I remained wary of Old Testament ethics

Nevertheless, since I admired Professor Bockmuehl, I began to study seriously the Ten Commandments For the first time I noticed the high respect granted the Ten Commandments (and the law in general) by Jesus, Paul and the whole New Testament I began to see that, contrary to what I had thought earlier, God's grace and redemption preceded the people's moral responsibility *as much in the Old Testament as in the New* I began to understand Karl Barth's emphasis on the unity of biblical teaching—that the law and the gospel were not in permanent opposition "The Law is nothing but the necessary *form of the Gospel, whose content is grace   The Law is in the Gospel* as the tablets from Sinai were in the Ark of the Covenant "[1]

Luther's *Large Catechism,* with its wonderful meditations on the Ten Commandments, also helped convert me to a Christian ethics grounded in both testaments, one that treats the Decalogue as a central text, as much in harmony with the gospel as the law This second "ethics conversion" was a personal revolution, and I've been working on this material, teaching it in many contexts and promising a book about it for over twenty years

However, not long after my discovery of the Ten Commandments, I had my third "ethics conversion" experience Influenced by Stanley Hauerwas, Peter Kreeft and Alasdair MacIntyre, I became convinced that moral principles and rules have no chance of truly guiding us unless they are sustained by a certain quality of character Doing right is extremely difficult if the agent deciding or acting lacks the necessary

---

[1] Karl Barth, "Gospel and Law," in *Community, State and Church* (Gloucester, Mass Peter Smith, 1968), p 80 Barth first published this essay in 1935

sort of character To do the right thing, we need not only principles and rules to guide us, but also the capacity and inclination, the personal attributes and skills, to understand and carry out such directives

Becoming Good Building Moral Character (InterVarsity Press, 2000) is my study of character ethics, an analysis of the virtues of a Christian moral agent It is the foundation for, and companion to, this present book, *Doing Right Practicing Ethical Principles,* which studies the decision and action side of ethics These books can be read and studied separately, but a full understanding of Christian ethics requires attention to both topics

Part one of *Doing Right,* "Prepare," sets the stage for our study of Christian ethical principles Part two, "Practice," maps out specific ethical guidance by way of a study of the Decalogue My discussions quote a lot of Scripture, which will not surprise those seeking a biblically grounded approach to ethics A greater surprise may be the way my argument engages, at almost every turn, several other expert commentators on the Decalogue *Doing Right* is, I believe, a very original study But as you will see, it has emerged out of an intense conversation with several outstanding authors

Doing Right remains, of course, *a* Christian ethic, not *the* Christian ethic It is also intended as a *primer* on Christian ethics, as an *introduction* written for thoughtful people with little or no background in moral philosophy or theology My intended audience is men and women (and their pastors and teachers) who read and think, who are raising children and grandchildren, who are working in schools and businesses, who are trying to find and pursue an ethically exemplary life even when it is difficult

Doing Right is intended primarily to instruct and challenge Christians, people who choose to be followers of Jesus Christ And yet, I am convinced—more each year—that the biblical ethic matches up not just with a Christian belief system but with basic human experience in a very profound way I hope *Christian readers* will appreciate my approach because it rings *true to Scripture,* I hope both *Christian and non-Christian readers* will like my approach because it rings *true to human experience*

Those wishing to probe Christian ethics in greater depth may want to read the books cited in the footnotes Many of today's specific topics in ethics are discussed in this book, but a general introduction like this can never discuss particular problems as fully as they deserve [2] Inevitably, ethics takes us into controversial territory Some of my arguments will be controversial and perhaps unconvincing I am sure there is something here to offend everybody' I honestly do not enjoy offending anyone or opening myself to misunderstanding or harsh criticism But I also have no illusions that I am providing the final answers on any controversial matters Nor do I claim to be personally any more ethical than anyone else [3] I find myself personally judged and convicted by the ethical principles about which I write [4]

My hope is that my discussions will prod us forward in our struggles to understand and do the right thing I want us to think deeply, biblically, courageously and wisely about these issues I want us to nurture, in our own communities, ethical reflection, discernment and action I hope that we will not just *think* but *act* more rightly and faithfully

---

[2] Often the best way to get started on any given topic is to consult a good dictionary, such as David J Atkinson et al , eds , *New Dictionary of Christian Ethics and Pastoral Theology* (Downers Grove, Ill InterVarsity Press, 1995), or James F Childress and John Macquarrie, eds , *The Westminster Dictionary of Christian Ethics,* 2nd ed (Philadelphia Westminster Press, 1986)

[3] I can bench press more than most professors in their late fifties, and I can dance the fox trot better than most regular churchgoers I think those are my only distinctions

[4] I also have a great appreciation of God's grace and forgiveness Without this, moral self-scrutiny would be paralyzing Christian ethics is about goodness and grace much more than about evil and judgment

Acknowledgments

For the development of my understanding of ethics, I am indebted first of all to my parents, Walter and Vivian Gill I learned three things from them about ethics first, right and wrong, good and evil, are much more important in life than money or most other things and are worth thinking and talking about a lot, second, God and Scripture provide a rich, interesting and reliable guide for understanding right and wrong, and, third, ethics is serious, demanding, challenging and provocative on the one hand, and fun, exciting, reassuring and forgiving on the other

Among my other teachers, Jacques Ellul was the most influential [5] While I don't end up at the same place as Ellul does on all matters, at almost every turn I have been stimulated by his ideas I actually discussed early drafts of several chapters of this book with him in the spring of 1985, when I was on sabbatical study leave in Bordeaux Two of Ellul's main ethical mentors, Søren Kierkegaard and Karl Barth, have also loomed large in my ethics education

Regarding the Ten Commandments, Rabbi André Chouraqui, Rabbi Avroham Chaim Feuer, Rabbi J H Hertz and, to a lesser extent, Martin Buber, Laura Schlessinger and Stewart Vogel are Jewish commentators whose valuable insights you will encounter regularly in my text Prot-

---

[5] I did my Ph D dissertation on Ellul David W Gill, *The Word of God in the Ethics of Jacques Ellul* (Metuchen, N J Scarecrow, 1984) For more information about Ellul, see the International Jacques Ellul Society website at <http //www ellul org>

estant Reformers Luther and Calvin have had an immense influence
on my understanding of the Decalogue The opinions of biblical scholars Brevard Childs, Dale Patrick, Bruce Birch, Walter Kaiser, William
Barclay and Walter Harrelson come into the conversation from time to
time Harrelson and Rupert Davies, a British Methodist scholar, get
pummeled a little by me for selling the Decalogue short (You can be
the judge of whether I am too hard on them) I quote them to show you
some very different ways to think about the Decalogue Pastors Earl
Palmer, Bill Hybels and, above all, Alan Redpath offer some wonderful
insights in this conversation The late ethicist Lew Smedes also has
some good insights, which I have quoted

The best book I ever have read on the Ten Commandments (and I
have read dozens) is unquestionably *Le Decalogue Une morale pour
notre temps* (Labor & Fides, 1985) by Alphonse Maillot, a French Reformed pastor and theologian A close second (and way ahead of third
place) is *Signposts to Freedom The Ten Commandments and Christian Ethics* by Czech theologian Jan Milič Lochman (Augsburg, 1982)
Both Maillot and Lochman provide page after page of blazing insights
It is a shame that Lochman's book is now out of print and that Maillot
has never been translated into English (All translations of Maillot's *Le
Decalogue* and Chouraqui's *Les Dix Commandements* in this book are
my own) With the passing of Maillot in December 2003 and Lochman
in January 2004 we have lost two giants, as I hope you will see as you
encounter their ideas in my quotations

The foregoing list of my teachers and sources is very diverse and
eclectic, not narrow or ideologically pure My goal is always to learn as
much as possible from the whole church and the whole world What
you are about to read, though, are my own ideas, hammered out in the
interaction between such study and my life experience I have taught
the ideas in *Doing Right* hundreds of times in many different settings
(mostly to Christians, but in some interesting secular contexts as well)

Throughout this book project and its predecessor, *Becoming Good,* I
have been grateful for the great support and direction I have received
from my editor, Jim Hoover Much of the "road-testing" of this material
took place in my courses at New College Berkeley and North Park University, in graduate student groups associated with InterVarsity Christian Fellowship, and in various churches, among which Santa Barbara

Community Church, the Evangelical Covenant Churches of Berkeley and Davis, and the First Presbyterian Churches of Berkeley, Burlingame and Evanston were especially memorable

As *Doing Right* neared its final form, several friends read it and gave me their suggestions for improvement I especially want to thank my friend and colleague, Old Testament Professor Anthony Petrotta, for his careful reading of my text John and Marj Erisman, Andrew Cole, Steve Smith, Charles Jenner, Andrew Hoffman and Al Erisman also gave me helpful feedback I subjected my wife, Lucia, to regular requests for feedback as the penultimate text was crafted I haven't always followed all of the advice I received, but often I did, and always I appreciated it My advisors are not to be blamed for the weaknesses, mistakes and eccentricities that remain

This book is dedicated with gratitude to my students at New College Berkeley from 1978 to 1990 and my students at North Park University from 1992 to 2001 I began writing this book in 1985 when New College Berkeley graciously gave me a sabbatical leave to study with Jacques Ellul in Bordeaux, France After many interruptions, I finished the penultimate draft fifteen years later, in 2000, while again on sabbatical in Bordeaux, this time thanks to North Park University I am grateful to both schools for their encouragement and support Four years later still, I am finally crossing the last *t* and dotting the last *i*

PART ONE

Prepare

Mapless Travelers and Christian Cartographers

More than once in my life I have wandered around unnecessarily for long periods of time on foot or in my car because I was utterly confused and lost Why? Because I have a personality defect that makes me think I can somehow sense where to go or perhaps remember my way from a previous visit But this is pure self-delusion I have no such sense of direction, and my memory for directions is conclusively unreliable

There are only two possible solutions to my problem The first is to be sure I always have someone with me who knows where we are and how to get where we need to go The second is to get a good map or clear directions for my travel Fortunately, my wife has a great sense of direction and a good memory for such things As long as I keep my instincts and comments to myself (alas, not always possible) and follow her advice and intuition, we get where we need to go Unfortunately, she is not always available, and I am either too cheap to buy a map or too hasty to get directions So I waste time going in circles

Once in a great while my mapless, unguided travel results in an unexpected discovery Much more often it wastes my time and gasoline (and contributes unnecessarily to air pollution and traffic congestion) Sometimes I have been late and missed the beginning of a great performance (Once I had to watch the first half of an expensive opera on a television monitor in the lobby "Sorry, no latecomer seating!") Sometimes my mapless travel follies make other people wait for me (This is

great for their disposition and general happiness and for our relationship, as you can imagine) I've never harmed anyone, but you can
imagine that speeding drivers who are lost or running late might seriously injure someone in their haste

This saga of maps and travel provides a helpful metaphor for ethics
and life Ethical guidelines are just as essential for finding your way in
life as good maps and directions are for finding your way geographically The Bible is full of the language of pilgrimage and migration toward the promised land Walking in the way and the truth is a common
metaphor Map and travel imagery has the additional virtue of empha-
sizing the dynamic, open, developmental character of the Christian
life—in contrast to the static, abstract and dispassionate character of
most ethics (and theology) literature

But are maps really so important? Isn't this just a matter of taste
and preference (anal-retentive map followers vs free-spirited mapless troubadours)? Perhaps if we lived in small towns with one street
and five or ten houses, we wouldn't need maps But our ethical world
today is vastly more complex, crowded and dangerous Traveling
without a moral map can result in crashes and injuries, in getting lost
in dangerous and lonely places, in aimless, meaningless, profitless
wandering around, and in too much gratuitous pollution We need
better ethical guidance because there is far
too much cruelty, sadness, dishonesty, violence, suffering and injustice in our world—
not just in some distant places, but in the
cities and neighborhoods where we live Ethics is about avoiding harm and overcoming
evil with good This is why we need to find
an ethics map

**Ethical guidelines are just
as essential for finding
your way in life as good
maps and directions are for
finding your way
geographically.**

Our problem is not solved, however, if we
grab a defective map Have you ever had this experience? I have sometimes been frustrated by maps that fail to show the existence of some
street, or that show two roads crossing but don't warn you that you may
not turn from one onto the other, or that show an old name for a road
that has long since been renamed, or that fail to indicate that a road
surface is gravel and mud

So it is with today's ethical maps There are lots of faulty or inadequate ones to lead us astray Hollywood puts out maps that show the road of irresponsible self-indulgence as the way to happiness (There are a lot of wrecks when people use this map) Many governments now put out maps urging citizens to take the lottery road to arrive at wealth and happiness (a bald-faced lie financed with tax money) Businesses put lots of money into maps directing us onto the consumer superhighway to arrive at satisfaction The National Rifle Association promotes a map urging gun-ownership as the main road to political freedom and personal safety and security We need better maps than these

Another school of thought urges each of us to draw a personal ethical map as we wish Apart from the personal dangers of living in such a fabricated dream world, there are just too many people on the road for each of us to insist on making and following our own personal maps If personal autonomy (self-determination) is allowed to trump all other values, we become nearly powerless when seeking any common resolution of the big issues we must face together We need to find an ethical map that respects, protects and values the individual while providing us with good guidance in matters of common concern

WITHOUT A GOOD, RELIABLE MAP

- **you can get lost in very dangerous places**
- **you can waste a great deal of time and resources**
- **you may never reach the destination you want**
- **others can be endangered or hurt by your haste and mistakes**

A Moral Map Is a Network of Guidelines

Saying that we need a better map to guide life's ethical movements means that we need a better network of guidelines for our actions Ethical guidelines are *action guides,* indicating not so much what we *are* as what we should *do,* how we should *act* and what is the *right* thing to *do* [1] These ethical action guides are *ought* statements *imperatives*

---

[1] What makes something *morally* right or wrong has been hotly debated by philosophers, of course, but one fundamental characteristic is that *wrong* harms and hurts lives, while *right* protects and nurtures lives There are right ways to pronounce French vowels, grill salmon, change the oil filter on your car and set the table, but these are not matters of ethical or moral correctness because the threat of harm is inconsequential (although some experts would say that my French accent is in fact a moral issue because it threatens actual harm to the ears and sensibilities of my hearers)

concerning what we *must* do, which are *prescriptive* rather than descriptive in tone Terms like *commandment, duty* and *obligation* underscore this emphasis

What gives ethical guidelines their oughtness? Why are the Ten Commandments not just the Ten Suggestions? Why isn't Immanuel Kant's "categorical imperative" just the "categorical option"? The short answer is some more map talk "If you want to get to destination *X*, you must turn right on road *Y* and proceed 3 4 miles," and so on Thus, if you want to know and please God, you ought to obey his commandments, or, if you want to be consistently rational, you ought to do what Kant says Ethical principles are linked with, and dependent on, purposes

There are many terms for such moral action guides (e g , rules, precepts, axioms, counsels), each of which carries various nuances or shades of meaning These guidelines are often organized into *codes* of some sort, such codes are, in turn, components in larger moralities, moral philosophies or ethics [2] Such ethics and moralities are, in their turn, components in philosophies or theologies of life We will mainly confine ourselves to four terms as we try to map out the guidelines for a Christian ethic *principle, rule, law* and *commandment*

Principle comes from the Latin *principium,* meaning "beginning " A principle is thus a fundamental starting point truth on which others are based It is a guideline or rule of conduct at a very fundamental level

Rule comes from the Latin *regula,* meaning a straight piece of wood, such as a ruler A rule is thus a guideline established to *regulate* action, a criterion or standard by which the rightness (or straightness) of an action can be measured Rules can be very broad and general or very narrow and specific

Law comes from the Latin *lex,* meaning a rule (or system of rules) of conduct laid down and established by an authority, political or otherwise It is not unusual to encounter the phrase "moral law," which sometimes implies a law above the law *Law* has also been a common

---

[2]There are no basic (or justified) differences in the meanings of these two families of words *Ethics* terms come from Greek roots, *morality* terms are of Latin origin Historically, they referred to the same subject matter, and in the literature, both ancient and modern, there are no certain or consistent differences I will use ethics and morality terminology interchangeably

English translation of the Hebrew *torah,* referring sometimes to the Decalogue, sometimes to all 613 laws in the Pentateuch, sometimes to the Pentateuch as a whole and sometimes to the whole Old Testament *Torah,* however, must be understood not just as a collection of regulations, but in the broader sense as teaching, instruction and guidance

Command (or *commandment*) comes from the Latin *commendatus,* meaning "to commit to one's charge " A commandment is thus an order or mandate from an authority This notion of a commander entrusting or charging someone to do something is a central feature of Christian ethics [3]

Cover Principles and Area Principles

We should make an important distinction between action guides that are broad, inclusive and general in their field of application, and others that are narrow, specific and limited The first type is like the Golden Rule ("Do to others as you would have them do to you," Mt 7 12 par Lk 6 31) or the principle of utility ("Do what results in the greatest good for the greatest number") Examples of the second would be "Do not murder," "Do not give a patient a deadly drug even if they ask for it" (from the Hippocratic oath), and "Be kind to children and the elderly " Such rules pertain to certain situations or sectors of life

Some ethicists call the general statements *principles* and the more specific ones *rules* However, there are no compelling etymological reasons to require this distinction, nor is there anything like a consistent customary usage (e g , Golden *Rule*) I think it is better to use *principle* and *rule* interchangeably (unless a specific nuance is made clear in context) and to distinguish instead between *cover* principles (or rules) and *area* principles (or rules) The Golden Rule, the principle of utility, the categorical imperative and the love command (see chapter two) are four examples of what I will call *cover principles* They cover everything, every situation They are general In the travel metaphor, these cover principles could be called "rules of the road" they apply to every itinerary at all times Cover principles help us to have a coherent, integrated, unified moral perspective Cover

---

[3]The primary Old Testament term for the Ten Commandments, however, is not *commandment* but *word* (Hebrew *dabar*), i e , the "Ten Words" from God

principles remind us of the overarching purpose and intent of our
area principles

Area principles include prohibitions such as those against murder,
theft and lying, or those enjoining kindness, generosity and truth telling Area principles help to make the demands of our general, cover
principles more concrete, practical and specific In the travel metaphor, I think of these area principles as "itineraries," guidance for how
best to explore a certain region If you want to see Paris, Michelin's
green tourist guide will give you twenty-five walking itineraries, pretty
much covering the whole city I will argue in this book that the Decalogue provides ten such moral itineraries for exploring human life

If we press to a level of still greater detail and particularity, some
rules can be so specific that even designating them as area guides is too
broad (e g , "do not use a photo-
copy of a copyrighted song unless the composer has been compensated") We might call this
the level of *situation rules* All of
our action guides together form
a kind of hierarchy, a pyramid,
with the most general cover
principles at the top, the area
principles in the middle and the
specific situation rules on the
bottom The love commandment
is a cover principle at the top of
the Christian ethics hierarchy,

> **Cover principles** are broad, general,
> inclusive action guides that apply to all
> situations for example, "Do to others as
> you would have them do to you," or "Do
> what results in the greatest happiness for
> the greatest number."
>
> **Area principles** are narrower in focus
> for example, "Do not murder" (which
> applies to human life), "Do not steal"
> (which applies to property), or "Speak the
> truth in love" (which applies to speech).

the Ten Commandments are a set of area principles in the middle, and
the hundreds of specific, contextual moral injunctions of Scripture are
at the bottom of the hierarchy

Improvisation, Spontaneity and Principles

Let's leave the map and travel metaphor for a moment and think about
sports Principles function in the moral life like plays function for competitors in an athletic contest (such as football) Players could, of
course, compete in games *only* by improvisation, they could make up
plays in the huddle or in the middle of the action If they played in this

unplanned way, they would probably have a real adventure and their personal self-determination would be fully respected However, they would almost certainly be soundly defeated by the opposition' Learning ethical principles and rules is like learning life's playbook

Allow me another metaphor the jazz ensemble Improvisation is a basic element in the beauty and joy of jazz But jazz musicians improvise on a standard or on a theme It is not total chaos Playing only the notes on a musical score might be wooden and lifeless, but having no musical score at all would be meaningless noise

So in sports and music, *and in the moral life,* it is important to preserve those elements of instinct, intuition, feeling and improvisation To reduce every action to nothing more than interpretation and compliance with a principle or rule would diminish life in a terrible way On the other hand, if our imagination is not creatively related to some sound rules and principles, our life risks becoming chaotic, meaningless and perhaps even destructive

Principles Don't Stand Alone

Sound principles, as crucial as they are, do not stand alone Let's briefly note a few key relationships

Principles and purposes. Maps derive their value and persuasiveness from the destination or goal of the traveler (arriving at place X or exploring neighborhood Y) In a similar way, ethical principles and rules guide us toward the achievement of our life goals and purposes Without a clear, convincing and inspiring "end," moral principles will remain unclear, and irrelevant People are motivated to behave ethically only when they value the end that such ethical guidance serves [4] We will never convince others to be more ethical without *first* convincing them that a changed life could serve to bring their lives richer meaning, purpose and direction This is an absolutely crucial point We cannot, for example, resolve specific ethical issues among rivals (whether children, spouses, churches, ethnic groups or nations) unless the contending parties embrace a common purpose or goal A great deal of our ethics (e g , in business, health care and politics) fails at

---

[4] This is as true for Kant and other deontologists as it is for frankly teleological theorists If one does not value rationality, logic and detached universality as ends, Kant's categorical imperative is totally unconvincing

precisely this point Later in this chapter we will consider the purpose and goal of Christian ethics

Principles and character. Ethical principles are also linked to personal character Ethics of character or virtue ("becoming a good person") is like physical conditioning for athletes Without adequate physical conditioning, the best-designed football plays will fail to lead to victory Travel, even with good maps, will not be successful without acquiring the capacities to read (maps and signs), to drive cars (of various types), to speak foreign languages (if foreign travel is intended) and so on A map by itself doesn't get you where you want to go

Without character, principles and rules are impotent Many of us profess allegiance to moral principles, and yet these principles do not guide our behavior when the going gets tough We do what we know is wrong, and we fail to do what we know is right We lack the strength of character to recall, interpret and apply our own principles when a challenge comes our way Character traits, virtues, vices and habits define our capacity, inclination and potential to do the right thing [5]

Principles and community. Individual moral agents also need *communities* if they are to succeed in following their principles Ethics and morality is a *team* sport, not an individualistic enterprise like singles tennis or marathon running [6] It is as impossible to be victorious in the moral life (i e , to achieve our highest good, our mission and purpose) as an ethical Lone Ranger as it is to defeat an opposing football team all by yourself [7] Travel is possible for individuals, of course But having one or more people with you to help with the driving or the directions and to encourage you not to give up when you feel hopelessly lost is a much better way to travel

Community relates to ethical principles in at least two ways First, our communities (family, friends, influential others) help us *learn* and *discern* our principles and rules This is their educative function Sec-

---

[5] In *Becoming Good* I develop a fuller account of character shaped by the Pauline virtues of faith, hope and love and by Jesus' eight Beatitudes in the Sermon on the Mount As I said in the preface, I actually began writing *Doing Right* several years before I wrote *Becoming Good,* but I then became convinced that it made no sense to write about principles and action if I didn't first address the character issue
[6] Of course, the singles tennis player and distance runner need practice and workout partners, coaches, trainers and fans, so these metaphors are not strictly accurate
[7] Oops' Even the Lone Ranger had Tonto Nobody does it all alone

ond, our communities provide us with *care* and *support* when the going gets tough in our pursuit of a principled existence A lack of community can paralyze our ability to carry through a good decision in today's complex and challenging times (We will return to the role of the church as a critical factor in Christian ethics below)

Principles and practices. Principles require practices, principles need to be applied to life If a given principle goes unpracticed, we are left to ask whether we really are committed to it Moral value is achieved in situations where a principle is applied, not just proclaimed, here progress is made along the road toward life's purpose and goal Maps are to use, not just to mount on the wall As our principles are practiced, we understand them more fully, and they become more fully embedded in our moral perspective and identity If they aren't practiced, our principles become mere abstractions It is one thing to affirm a principle at a theoretical level and quite another to practice it in daily life

Worse than such abstraction is hypocrisy when high principles are espoused but one lives in contradiction to them We don't practice what we preach We might be moralistically high-minded on matters that cost us little It's easy to proclaim and practice principles guarding our own personal liberties, it's not so easy to proclaim and practice principles of equality or of compassion for the poor It is easy for many Christians to proclaim and practice rigorous principles prohibiting homosexual activity, not so easy (it appears) to practice similar rigor concerning divorce and remarriage

Practicing our ethical principles means allowing them to range proactively across our life like searchlights Thus, if one of our principles is "Do not kill," why defer its guidance and practice until a tough case of violence rises up? Why not allow this principle to question our whole life? Is there anything in my lifestyle, my activities or my attitudes that contributes to violence and killing in the world? Is there anything in my business (or my political party or my church) that contributes in this negative way? Am I doing anything in a positive way to head off the causes of killing and violence, or am I blind and apathetic in this violent world, excusing myself from moral self-scrutiny just because I don't shoot people?

Principles and cases. Inevitably, of course, ethical crises and di-

---

STEPS IN FACING ETHICAL CASES, DILEMMAS AND QUANDARIES

1 **Recognize** (Ask yourself, *Is this an important ethical problem or not?*)

2 **Analyze** (If it is an important ethical problem, it deserves your careful consideration)

3 **Resolve** (Do the best, most responsible thing you can.)

---

lemmas will arise We will face tough cases where there is a conflict of values or principles (within an individual or among different people) and where we are uncertain about the right thing to do So what shall we do? First, we must be clear about our ethical *principles* and values Not only will that help us, it may be something we can contribute to others, like sharing a reliable map with some lost travelers Second, we must have an effective *method* for resolving ethical crises and quandaries No method can guarantee a perfect process or outcome, but with care, we can minimize damages and maximize good outcomes, both in the short- and long-term My proposed method outlines three processes in facing the ethical dilemmas of our lives recognition, analysis and resolution

We begin by determining whether the matter that concerns us is truly an important ethical problem Sometimes this is not at all clear The best way to recognize a legitimate ethical crisis is to ask some questions [8]

- Would Jesus do this? Would Jesus question it?

- Does it violate clear biblical teaching about right and wrong?

- Does it go against basic Christian teaching and tradition?

- Does it violate your (or another's) conscience?

- Would you like this done to you or your loved ones (per the Golden Rule)?

- Could someone be seriously harmed?

- Would this practice continue if it were publicized? (Most unethical acts flourish in secrecy "People [love] darkness rather than light because their deeds [are] evil," Jn 3 19)

- Is it illegal? (Ethics is always more than mere compliance with laws,

---

[8]This set of questions is tailored to *Christian* ethics In a general business setting, the questions would be phrased a little differently

and laws themselves have on occasion been unethical, but breaking the law is often a tip-off that something is wrong)

If you answer yes to some or all of the preceding eight questions—that is, the situation has tested positive for an "ethics infection"—we must go on to stage two and carry out the best analysis we can under the circumstances There are three aspects needing careful analysis First, clarify the ethical principles and values at stake What is crucially and clearly important to God here? We must weigh these competing values and later justify our proposal by appealing to these principles Second, clarify the relevant facts of the case Many apparent ethical dilemmas are resolved by this step alone Third, clarify the options we have for action and the possible outcomes of each This step is not easy, especially predicting consequences, but we must not barge ahead without considering the possible benefits and harms of our actions

In all of this analysis, we are required to investigate carefully and prayerfully, to do good research, to think critically and to humbly depend on God to guide us What the crisis also begs for is some real creativity and imagination, especially in the face of hard ethical challenges Can we find or invent a win-win solution that will honor the ethical principle, minimize damage and harm, and maximize positive outcomes? So often when bad, unethical things are done, the way we handle them bungles things even worse Finally, we should, as much as possible, get advice from others Share the burden, the thinking and the responsibility There is safety and wisdom in community-derived ethical discernment Don't try to be an individualistic hero if you have the slightest chance to work with others when confronting an ethical crisis

Some ethical crises will blow over and disappear, but others will not, we must bite the bullet and act to resolve them as faithfully and courageously as possible The time comes when we must bring to a close our analytical, imaginative and consultative process and choose the best, most responsible option we can come up with We must act, even though we know we are not perfect In the short-term, we hope the crisis can be resolved by appealing directly to the principal offender If this doesn't work, we bring another person or two into the process, trying to resolve it without going public And if that doesn't work, public whistleblowing may be necessary (i e , going over or around the offending individual or organization to authorities inside or outside the con-

---

**ETHICAL PRINCIPLES DO NOT STAND ALONE.
THEY ALSO REQUIRE**

- a compelling mission and purpose
  to serve
- strength of personal character
- a community for discernment and
  support
- proactive, practical application in
  daily life
- a faithful, effective method to resolve
  crisis cases

---

text and forcing the issue until
the offense is stopped and the
harm is addressed) [9]

But an ethics challenge is not
fully addressed until we follow
through on those immediate actions with ongoing, deeper reforms of the structures, procedures and circumstances that
caused or allowed that ethical
problem to occur in the first
place To fail to do this thorough
work is to invite further crises If
it is possible to follow through with the ethical offenders themselves—
to help them see what went wrong and avoid making the same mistake
again—so much the better for all concerned

Picking Our Principles: Christian Cartography

We all operate, even if thoughtlessly or inconsistently, by some de facto
principles A careful observer could figure out what ethical principles
and rules are implicit in our choices and actions We inherit some basic values and principles from our family, church and friends, and we
absorb others from the influence of the surrounding culture Sometimes our ethical commitments are a fairly trivial, casual, thoughtless
affair, based mostly on uninformed feelings and preferences But this
can hardly be a very satisfactory way to live, especially for Christians
who are called to "take every thought captive to obey Christ" (2 Cor
10 5)

Thus, we must consider what makes an ethical principle "Christian " Cartography is the art and science of mapmaking How should
we approach the task of Christian moral cartography, mapping out an
authentically Christian ethics? Many erroneous and counterfeit moralities have been attributed to Christianity over the past two millennia

---

[9]Remember Jesus' instruction on how to deal with an erring brother First go to him
privately, then go with one or two others if the first visit wasn't productive Only if
you fail at this second stage should you publicize it to the whole church (Mt 18 15-
20)

Though it is sad and shameful to have to review the parade of allegedly Christian crusaders, inquisitors, racists, sexists, imperialists, holy warriors and quietist dropouts, we should not be completely surprised by such a motley crew [10] All good causes in history—including all religions, political movements and social reform efforts—have been exploited, betrayed, diverted and co-opted at various times Fellow travelers, hucksters and opportunists lurk around the edges of every good movement and organization waiting for their chance Too often they manage to get into the driver's seat

Still, the proper response to our spotty Christian moral history is neither to make excuses nor to assign blame, but to try again I want to argue that the construction of an authentic Christian ethic—the design of a Christian ethical map—proceeds from four sources [11] From highest to lowest priority (or from the center to the periphery), these are Jesus Christ, the Bible, the church and the world We have to leave room for a range of opinion and judgment here, but we cannot accept everything that appropriates the label of "Christian" ethics

An Ethics Centered on Jesus Christ

The primary, foundational, central authority in Christian ethics is the person of Jesus Christ, whom Christians affirm as Savior, Lord and God Jesus Christ is our ethical mapmaker and guide, he is the Lord, Master and Captain of our moral life If we want to know the right thing to do—or what justice is, or what love requires, or what is good—we look to Jesus Christ as our central authority When other guidance is unclear, Jesus is our clarifying center

Tragically, even among Christians, Jesus Christ has often *not* been

---

[10] A very helpful study of this painful past is Jacques Ellul, *The Subversion of Christianity* (Grand Rapids, Mich Eerdmans, 1986) The bad stuff should not blind us to the awesome good done by Christians throughout the centuries Most of the time, I am convinced, Christian faith has brought real improvements to individuals and to communities and nations

[11] Metaethics (Greek for "after ethics") is the branch of moral philosophy that studies questions of justification (the grounding of moral norms and values), the definition of moral terminology and the logic of moral arguments This chapter is my metaethics, although I am more concerned about justifying (and clearly defining) my approach to the people who will be using it than comparing it to some standard set up in the philosophers' guild

the Lord and center of ethics Some excuse this rejection by saying
that we cannot know the real, true, historical Jesus and, thus, we cannot base our ethics on what is illusive Others have argued that Jesus'
mission was purely spiritual and inward, that he never intended to
teach anybody ethics Still others think that Jesus taught some ethics,
but not for us, that is, his ethics apply only to first-century Palestine,
or to a future millennium, or just to monks and saints, not to ordinary
people like you and me

But Jesus *must* be at center of Christian ethics Christians are followers and disciples of Jesus Christ We are not Paulians, Mosesians,
Lutherans or Darbyites, but Christians [12] We believe in the incarnation, we believe that God himself assumed human form in Jesus of Naz-
areth Jesus knows God and Jesus knows humanity Jesus is the "one
who in every respect has been tested as we are" and yet never yielded
to sin He alone can be the understanding captain of our ethical ship
(Heb 2 8-18, 4 14-16)

Jesus is the Word of God, the message and representative of God, revealed in our human flesh and history Jesus is the Messiah, the focal
point of the whole Bible, the "exact imprint of God's very being" (Heb
1 3), the one in whom "all the fullness of God was pleased to dwell" (Col
1 19) on our earth God has revealed himself at many times, in many
places, in many different ways But *only* in Jesus is God's self-revelation
exact, elsewhere it is true but *inexact* Only in Jesus did *all the fullness*
of God dwell, elsewhere it is *partial* (Jn 1 1-18, Lk 24 27, 44)

Jesus Christ gets the first and last words on what is right and wrong
He completely fulfilled the law and was always guided by Holy Spirit
With him the kingdom of God truly arrived and the will of the Father
was truly done, on earth as it is in heaven The church is called the
body of Christ—a powerful image that implies our serious effort to
know and to carry on what Jesus was and did in his own bodily history

The agenda for Christian ethics is set primarily and fundamentally
by God Of course, people should freely bring their problems and questions to God But we also should bring a pen and blank sheets of paper
to make notes on what God thinks is ethically important The empha-

---

[12] This is to say nothing of potential nonbiblical centers such as Immanuel Kant, John
Stuart Mill, Karl Marx, Adam Smith, Adolf Hitler or Uncle Sam For authentic *Christian* ethics there can be only one center Jesus the *Christ*

sis on a God-centered ethics would be hard to accept, except that God has come alongside us, in our human history, in Jesus Christ It is Jesus who anchors and reveals an ethics from above Jesus Christ is still very much alive and seeks a *living* relationship with people The ethical traveler relates not just to a map but to the Mapmaker In a Christian ethic, our participating in evil is more fundamentally a breaking of God's heart and a breach of faith

The person of Jesus Christ is always the central guide in Christian ethics

with our Ruler than a breaking of the rules (though it is that as well) Christian ethics proceeds in prayer, worship and a daily life in relationship with God

Guided by Scripture

We do not know about Jesus Christ and the transcendent God he incarnates, however, except through a book, the Bible, the map for Christian ethics Actually, to refer to the Bible as a map is too weak The Bible is not just a map, it is an atlas! The Bible includes *many* different maps, many different views of life's terrain and abundant ethical directions to help us navigate our way toward the goal While it is a huge atlas with many contributors over several centuries, Christians believe there is but one overall editor-in-chief and one clear thematic center to our atlas

Some people think that Scripture cannot suffice as our ethical guide (or that major parts of it must be rejected) Sometimes this is because it seems irrelevant the differences between the cultural and political world of the Bible and our own seem too great [13] Some biblical scholars have been reticent to do any more with the biblical text than probe (though sometimes rather speculatively, on meager evi-

---

[13]Rupert Davies says boldly, "We can abolish at a stroke the myriad regulations laid down in the Pentateuch, and in subsequent rabbinical and Christian rule-books Life continually bursts the bounds of ethical manuals, and it is absolutely useless to go through the Old and New Testaments in order to find a rule which we can apply in a modern situation " *Making Sense of the Commandments* (London Epworth, 1990), p 25 It boggles the mind to read this kind of stuff Davies, with one wave of the hand (he provides no convincing reasons), dismisses the Golden Rule and everything else

dence) for its historical development For some, the purpose of the
Bible seems to be religious rather than ethical For others, biblical
ethics seems contradictory—egalitarian but then hierarchical, peaceful but then warlike Some reject biblical ethics because it seems negative and legalistic, too full of "you shall not" statements Worst of all,
to some, much of the Bible seems self-evidently immoral, they are
disturbed by tribal and religious wars of extermination, polygamy, the
oppression of women, the toleration of slavery, the shrill condemnation of homosexuals, arbitrarily restrictive dietary laws and the counsel to passivity before tyranny, violence and injustice Furthermore,
many of the Bible's loudest defenders throughout history seem self-
serving, angry, judgmental, hypocritical, ignorant, unethical and
downright dangerous[1] So there are lots of reasons and excuses not to
look for a biblical ethics

I agree that many of these are serious and important issues, but I argue that Scripture must remain the second great source and authority
in Christian ethics for several reasons The main reason is that source
number one (Jesus) urges and requires us to take Scripture seriously
(And, by the way, he was never guilty of teaching or practicing the
problems mentioned in the previous paragraph If we keep Jesus as the
center of our ethics, the foregoing list of problems rapidly diminishes)
Jesus constantly quoted Scripture, explained it and treated it as a
source of authoritative guidance (Lk 24 27) He saw the Old Testament
as an illuminating explanation and prophecy of his own life He promised the Spirit's guidance for the future leaders of the church, who
would write the New Testament (Jn 14 25-26, 16 12-15)

One of the latest texts in the New Testament expresses the early
church's attitude "All scripture is inspired by God and is useful for
teaching, for reproof, for correction, and for training in righteousness,
so that everyone who belongs to God may be proficient, equipped for
every good work" (2 Tim 3 16-17) While there have been differences
of opinion over the centuries, the Christian church has accepted and
set apart this book as the written Word of God Luther, for example,
was passionate about the importance of studying Scripture "Time and
paper would fail me if I were to recount all the blessings that flow from
God's Word   Shall we frivolously despise this might, blessing,
power, and fruit   ? If so, we deserve not only to be refused food but

also to be chased out by dogs and pelted with dung "[14] John Coleman Bennett, one of the outstanding liberal Protestant leaders of the twentieth century, also called for a renewed Christian ethic that would be based on "the Bible with Jesus as the center "[15]

What does Scripture do for our ethics?[16] How does it contribute to our mapmaking? When received as the Word of God, it nurtures and sustains our relationship to Jesus Christ (our primary ethical authority) and also places us in relationship to Israel and the church, "people of the book" formed and shaped by the authority of the Bible Reading the Bible reinforces our family tradition, our story and our identity, and it shapes our personal character and values

The Bible provides many specific ethical laws, commandments, counsels, criteria, principles and norms, which in turn help us draw a moral map and then interpret and apply it Of course, the ethic of Scripture is conveyed not just by its explicit principles and rules but by its stories, poems, proverbs and parables, by apocalyptic and prophetic visions, by Gospel and letter writing, even by genealogical lists and census reports There is more to a good atlas than austere lines, street names and numbers

Scripture is not always clear to its readers or self-interpreting To avoid getting lost or misunderstanding, we must remember the first principle for the interpretation of biblical ethics Jesus is the center, the apex, the clearest revelation of what is right and good When other parts of the Bible are unclear or hazy (e g , on war, children, women, slavery, money), we look to Jesus to find clarity Second, we must be careful to distinguish major points from minor ones, and what is clearly and frequently taught from what is rarely and obscurely taught in the Bible We should concentrate on the classic texts, the ethical summaries and master themes, not the rare and obscure texts We must also understand the historical context and flow of the biblical teaching—that God participated in specific historical-cultural con-

---

[14]Martin Luther, *The Large Catechism,* trans Robert H Fischer (1529, Philadelphia Fortress, 1959), p 4

[15]John Coleman Bennett, *The Radical Imperative* (Philadelphia Westminster Press, 1975), pp 29ff

[16]On Scripture and ethics, see Bruce C Birch and Larry L Rasmussen, *Bible and Ethics in the Christian Life* (Minneapolis Augsburg, 1976)

texts, sometimes as a "still small voice" (1 Kings 19 12 KJV) The Bible is not an account of abstract, detached moral perfection, it provides guidance for people in contexts that are often messy and fall far below God's intention (e g , polygamy, war) Third, as we will discuss in the next section, our understanding of Scripture should always be informed by what Israel and the church have believed it to mean

The Bible, with Jesus at the center, is the atlas of Christian ethics.

Informed by the Church

The third source of Christian ethical guidance is the community of faith other people who share a relationship with God as we know him in Jesus and Scripture This is the primary Christian response to the point that principles need community, which I made earlier This means, of course, the church, the *koinōnia* (Greek for "community"), but community also comes in the form of families, households, small groups and friendships Individualism may be valued in some philosophical traditions and in American cultural myths, but it is blatantly out of place in the ethics of Jesus and Scripture Ethical pilgrims not only need a Bible to navigate their way through the world, they need also some partners—not only the atlas but a Society of Atlas Readers All authentic Christian ethics is *koinonia* ethics Why is this so important?

Humanity was created as *cohumanity* in the image and likeness of the triune God ("Let *us* make man in *our* image   In the image of God he created *them*," Gen 1 26-27, italics added) The only time God declares that something is not good in creation is when he says, "It is not good that the man should be alone" (Gen 2 18) The Ten Commandments are given to a *people* liberated from Egypt, not just to Moses or to an individual pilgrim escapee The Sermon on the Mount, and all other major biblical ethical instruction, is given to groups, not isolated individuals We are given no reason to think that individuals will ever be able to understand and carry out this guidance without help from others

Jesus sent his disciples out two by two, not one by one (Mk 6 7) He promised his presence "where two or three are gathered in my name" (Mt 18 20) Paul asks (in 1 Cor 12 21), how can members of the church say they have no need of other members? "[Do] not think of yourself more highly than you ought to think," Paul says at the beginning of his major ethical passage (Rom 12 3-8) Remember that you are only one member of the body of Christ and you need the others (1 Cor 12 12-26)

The Bible itself did not just drop out of the sky, nor does it copy, translate or reprint itself It does not interpret and apply itself without human participation The Bible is found in the church, the people of God, the dwelling place of God's living, holy Spirit The church is (in one of its major functions) the Society of Atlas Readers, gathering to study and preserve this central text God is present not just in Jesus Christ and in the pages of Scripture, but in the church, its members and activities Certainly, God calls us to responsibility and helps us as unique individuals known by him Being isolated is never a sufficient or valid *excuse* for failing to do God's will But community and partnership are the normal ethical context

How does the church help us? It directs its members to God and to Jesus Christ, the center and source of our ethics By its teaching and storytelling, by its affirmation or criticism, community shapes our identity and character and builds up our knowledge of God's moral guidance Community acts as a pilot project and testing ground for our understanding of what is right (e g , our views of decision making, racial reconciliation or the care of the poor) Our community is a model and witness, for better or worse, to the world Remember that Jesus prayed that his followers would be united in love so that the world would believe (Jn 17 20-21, cf Jn 13 34-35) Our relationships together bear witness to a world in need of salt and light

Community in its various forms is absolutely essential for *discerning* the right thing to do "In an abundance of counselors there is safety" (Prov 11 14) The complexity and scope of today's ethical challenges can overwhelm isolated individuals Being part of a prayerful, thoughtful community will vastly improve our likelihood of accurately interpreting both our situation and the appropriate guidance from Scripture This is more than just a matter of common sense Jesus granted authority to his church to bind and to loose, a metaphor for moral decision making (Mt 16 19) [17]

---

[17]See John Howard Yoder, *The Priestly Kingdom* (Notre Dame, Ind University of Notre Dame Press, 1984), pp 26-28

Community is essential also to *support* us during the application of what we have discerned as ethically right Figuring out what to do is extremely difficult, but carrying it out can be even harder We need each other This is such a core point in Christian ethics that we could say that it is wrong to advise a difficult course of action and then fail to be there to support those burdened with applying our counsel

The church—past and present, near and far, with the Bible as its atlas and Jesus as its center—helps teach and interpret Christian ethics

Our agenda, then, is to create (or discover) and sustain meaningful community—from friendship and household to church We will benefit greatly by taking some steps to enrich and expand our community input, deepening our knowledge of our own historical tradition and broadening our knowledge of people in other geographical and cultural settings We need community in both large and small groups, among both experts and nonexperts, with both old and young [18]

Practiced in the World

God's world contributes to our Christian ethical mapmaking in two basic ways First, the world of nature and society *around us* can bear witness to what is true, right and good Second, our own nature and conscience *within us* can bear witness to that ethical truth In both cases we must be careful, for we can easily misinterpret and misapply these witnesses But remember, this is the *fourth* source of mapmaking guidance, subordinate to the three sources above it Paul argues that "his eternal power and divine nature, invisible though they are, have been understood and seen through the things he has made" (Rom 1 20) By carefully looking at humanity, society and nature as a whole, we can learn some ethical basics Paul also says that the law of God is "written on [the human] heart " Thus, our interior conscience bears witness to God's moral guid-

---

[18]On the role of community in Christian ethics, see James M Gustafson, *Christian Ethics and the Community* (Philadelphia Pilgrim, 1971)

ance in some way (Rom 2 15) Paul concludes, of course, that these two
sources have been unable to produce righteousness and goodness in our
lives But the thrust of his argument is that *by themselves* they are inadequate, not that we have no use for them at all They can teach us something true, even if it is not sufficient

Calvin argued that the Ten Commandments teach what is known or
knowable "by that internal law, which   is in a manner written and
stamped on every heart For conscience   acts as an inward witness
and monitor, reminds of what we owe to God, points out the distinction between good and evil " The written law, Calvin says, is necessary
because of our "dullness and contumacy" and our "lethargy "[19]

We cannot forget that God created the whole world, not just the
Garden of Eden, and that he made it "very good " Adam and Eve were
banned from Eden, but they were not banned from the rest of the
world, which God also created and called "good " Though the world is
fallen and our sight is dim and susceptible to deception, still "The
heavens are telling the glory of God, and the firmament proclaims his
handiwork" (Ps 19 1) Adam and Eve sinned and erred by seizing the
fruit of the tree of the knowledge of good and evil (the "ethics tree") In
so doing they gave up a direct knowledge of goodness through an un-
hindered, uncorrupted relation with the God who pronounces that his
creation is good, but remember that God also created that ethics tree
from which they ate What they received, even if second best, was still
a certain kind of divinely created "knowledge of good and evil "

And God is still at work in human life and culture For example, God
adopts human language The Ten Commandments begin, "God spoke
all these words" (Ex 20 1) God's revelation is contextualized in human
language and culture God did not speak and write in a special other-
worldly language, he communicated in the language of a particular,
fallen, human culture And Jesus took on flesh just like yours and
mine, not some special kryptonite superflesh

While retaining a critical and mature judgment, we should be open
and receptive to what God might be saying to us through the world
around us The world may be messed up, but it is still *God's world,* and
therefore it is far from worthless We may personally be very messed

---

[19]Calvin *Institutes of the Christian Religion* 2 8 1

up human beings, but we are still made in *God's image* and likeness If
God can speak through Balaam's donkey, he can certainly speak
through anything in his world or any of us [20]

**God's creation—the world, its peoples
and cultures, its learning and
experience—also contributes to Christian
ethical guidance**

Whether Christian or not, all
people continue to bear the image and likeness of God Yes, the
world and humanity are sinful
and fallen, but *so too is the
church,* and yet we can still sense
God's presence within it We
need to weigh critically the
world's witness on the scales of
Scripture and Jesus, and then to
accept what is good The world's
philosophy and science, its arts
and humanities, even its religions and myths must not be arbitrarily dis-
missed God has spoken to us (and still speaks) in many different ways

The world is the arena in which our Christian ethics are to be practiced This very practice helps us to understand God's guidance God's
ethical guidance "fits" with our life experience in a profound way Theories, as someone has said, relate to reality (the facts) like shoes relate
to feet A wide variety of shoe styles and designs are possible, but there
are limitations, at least if we want shoes we can actually walk in An el-
egant appearance has some importance, but the true test of a shoe is
whether our feet are comfortable and protected as we walk over a period of time through varied terrain and weather So too with our ethical
systems and theories Can we actually live with them? Are they practical? Do they make sense of our life and help us through all kinds of sit-
uational terrain and weather? Our initial reaction to God's guidance is
often shock It may seem to us absurd to forgive, or to be generous, or
to protect marriages so aggressively, or to resist covetousness, and so
on But a deeper examination, and a bit of practical testing of the concepts, will show that what appeared at first to be foolish is profoundly
wise Nature and experience confirm the truth

---

[20]See Num 22 21-34 This is surely one of the most comforting of all stories for those
occasions when we feel inadequate and uncertain that God can use us

Three Reasons to Travel: Three Purposes of Christian Ethics

Why travel? What could motivate us to get out a map or guidebook and use it? What are the results and benefits that make it worthwhile? Some people travel to escape boredom, criticism or danger Others travel for more positive reasons, perhaps in search of great natural beauty (such as the fjords of Norway) or art and architecture (in Paris or the Alhambra in Granada), or to meet people and experience other cultures (through music, art, food, language) All of these positive reasons are what motivate me to travel I buy a Michelin *Green Guide* and start planning a trip because I want these results Travel is also hard work and is often expensive, if it were not for good reasons such as these, I might stay home

We need to raise the same question about Christian ethics Why study it? What are the reasons that motivate us, the benefits and payoffs that make it worthwhile? Why should we work at developing the Christian ethical map and then using it to guide our daily lives? What will our efforts accomplish? Earlier, I argued that just as our desired destination makes a map important, so too a life mission makes ethical principles important I want to propose a threefold mission served by Christian ethics

1. It's good for you. First, a Christian ethic can guide you in ways that you and yours will truly be blessed This is not the only or the main reason, but it remains valid and important Jesus said, "I came that they may have life, and have it abundantly" (Jn 10 10) He promised that all who lose their life will gain it back again (e g , Mk 8 35) "Your reward is great in heaven," Jesus promises, but even in this lifetime we will be "blessed" as Jesus' Beatitudes describe (Mt 5 12) Being "blessed" (Gk *makarios*) does not just mean feeling happy (having positive emotional feelings), blessedness is a state of well-being It's *good for you* to be meek, merciful, pure in heart and so on (Mt 5 3-11)

The Old Testament makes the same point Love God and keep his commandments "so that you may live" and experience God's "steadfast love" (Deut 4 1, 5 10), so that your "days will be long" and it will "go well" with you "all the days of your life" in a "land flowing with milk and honey" (Deut 6 2-3) "Do what is right and good in the sight of the LORD, so that it may go well with you   The LORD commanded us to observe all these statutes, to fear the LORD our God, for our lasting good, so as to keep us alive, as is now the case" (Deut 6 18, 24)

The Christian life does entail, of course, some sacrifice and long-suffering Christianity does not bring automatic health, wealth and happiness, nor does it insulate us from the difficulties of life and death But neither does any other philosophy or religion in this world Christianity is profoundly realistic about the trials and tribulations of human life and offers a way of coping with them—by

---
Being good and doing right the Christian way do not bring us a life without pain, struggle or failure, but they are the best ways of understanding and coping with such challenges, and often bring joy, friendship, contentment, meaning, comfort, freedom and hope

---

bringing resurrection and hope into our broken world Even in the hardest of times, even when we walk through the valley of the shadow of death (Ps 23 4), the best map to follow is the biblical Christian one No one understands human life like its Creator, and no one understands human pain, alienation and struggle—and how to overcome them—like our Redeemer

2. It's good for our neighbors. Second, when we travel by the Christian ethical map, we bring blessing and benefit to our neighbors and the nations around us Jesus taught an ethic that would create "salt" (which preserves against deterioration) and "light" (which provides conditions for vision and growth) in the world He did not just offer personal blessing for his followers The promise to Abraham was that through his descendents "all the families of the earth shall be blessed" (Gen 11 3) Israel was chosen by God to be a light to the nations, not just a self-contained private enclave

You must observe [the Ten Commandments] diligently, for this will show your wisdom and discernment to the peoples, who, when they hear all these statutes, will say, "Surely this great nation is a wise and discerning people'" For what other great nation has a god so near to it as the LORD our God is whenever we call to him? And what other great nation has statutes and ordinances as just as this entire law that I am setting before you today? (Deut 4 6-8)

The Christian ethical map does not lead to selfishness, even though following it is in our best interest and is good for us It is a map that is also good for the world, for our neighbors both near and distant, contemporary and future

3. God is pleased. Third, following the Christian ethics map leads to God's glory and blessing Jesus says that when people see our good works they will "give glory to your Father in heaven" (Mt 5 16) Near the end of his earthly pilgrimage, Jesus himself could say in his prayer, "I glorified you on earth by finishing the work that you gave me to do" (Jn 17 4) For us too, doing God's work—following his ethical map—brings glory and pleasure to God

> **The Christian ethical life is not just good for its practitioners, it is also good for its neighbors, near and far. Doing the right thing in a Christian ethic blesses and helps others**

At its foundation, Christian ethics depends on, assumes and sustains a covenant relationship with God "I will be your God, and you shall be my people" (Jer 7 23) A personal relationship with God underlies the whole ethic Christian ethical action guides are not just abstract rules or autonomous principles We relate more to a Commander than to commandments We are called to *love* God, *seek* God, *live* with God, *talk* with God, *glorify* and *please* God Christian ethical guidelines are directions on how to arrive at that place where God is glorified

> *The primary motivation of our ethical efforts should be to please God.* **But this does not mean being faithful to a Christian ethic is not at the very same time good for our neighbors and good for us**

For Reflection and Discussion

1 What are the strengths and weaknesses of the map metaphor for ethics? What other images, metaphors or explanations might help us understand what ethics is and does in our lives?

2 What are some of your basic ethical principles and rules? Where did you get these from? How have you grappled with ethical dilemmas or crises in the past?

3 What ethical teachings of Jesus or the Bible do you know best? Can
   you describe an ethical problem that Jesus or the Bible helped you
   resolve?

4 What is the best community-building strategy for Christians facing tough ethical challenges so that they won't feel alone in these
   battles?

2

Opening the Atlas of Christian Ethics

Now that we have looked at the sources, authorities, motivations and consequences of constructing and using a specifically Christian ethical map, we turn to its content Earlier, a distinction was made between *cover* principles and *area* principles Cover principles *summarize* the overall, collective impact of narrower area principles, and they also *guide* the interpretation and application of those narrower rules and principles These great cover principles are like rules of the road, guidelines that apply *everywhere* we travel, at all times, in all conditions

I propose that we think in terms of four interrelated, overlapping rules of the road love God, love your neighbor as yourself, act justly and righteously, and liberate and redeem Each of these four great guidelines is a major theme in biblical Christian ethics, and, together, they are comprehensive enough to account for the ethical truth of Scripture

Cover Principle 1: Love God
The Shema, repeated twice daily by pious Jews through the centuries, begins, "Hear, O Israel The LORD is our God, the LORD alone You shall love the LORD your God with all your heart, and with all your soul, and with all your might" (Deut 6 4-5) The Shema was the source of Jesus' great love commandment, which, he explained, summarizes both the Law and the Prophets (Mt 22 34-40, Mk 12 28-34),

and the gospel of eternal life "You shall love the Lord your God with all your heart, and with all your soul, and with all your strength, and with all your mind" (Lk 10 27) To say that this commandment *is* the law *and* the gospel, and to say that we should express such love with *every faculty and power* we possess, is about as broad and inclusive as a claim can be

> Every decision and every action born out of genuinely Christian ethics must be understood as an expression of love to God What should we do in this or that circumstance? Do what represents and exhibits love to God

What is the right thing to do? We should do whatever authentically expresses love to God, our Creator and Redeemer Augustine famously said, "Love God and do as you please," to emphasize how powerful a guide such love for God can be All ethical principles and guidance on the Christian map should be understood as ways of loving God

The Ten Commandments are ten ways of loving God, that is their first and primary meaning Glorifying and pleasing God is one of the three great *ends* we pursue, loving God is one of the central *means* of doing that

What is love? The basic movements can be summarized under the symbolism of the *cross* and the *table* Cross-love is the love that serves, sacrifices, forgives and obeys It is sometimes difficult, costly and painful Jesus taught this love by service (washing the feet of his disciples), forgiveness and sacrifice (giving his life on the cross) Table-love, on the other hand, is the mutual enjoyment of friends, such as when we gather to feast around the table Table-love is union, community, togetherness and celebration The cross of Christ is the great symbol of sacrificial, serving, forgiving love The marriage supper of the Lamb in the afterlife (anticipated in this life by our love feasts, potlucks and Eucharistic celebrations) is the great symbol of the mutual love of reconciled friends

Our first cover principle (or rule of the road), "Always do what expresses love to God," includes both cross-love and table-love Jesus served and sacrificed *for* God, and Jesus pursued close community *with* God All Christian ethical principles need to be seen as ways of serving and sacrificing for God and ways of drawing near to God in a close and living relationship

Cover Principle 2: Love Your Neighbor

The second rule of the road is, "Always do what expresses love to your neighbor." *Everything* that is right in Christian ethics is in some important way an expression of love to your neighbor. The list of ways to express love to your neighbor is not a second, different list from that of how to express love to God. It is the same list but with a different angle of vision. Love for neighbor (like love for God) means both cross-love and table-love, both sacrificial servanthood and celebrative communion.

The second part of Jesus' great love command, "You shall love your neighbor as yourself," is given as a summary of both the law *and* the gospel. It is actually a quotation (Lev 19 18) from Israel's famous Holiness Code (Lev 17—26). Jesus also taught what is sometimes called the "new commandment." "Love one another. Just as I have loved you, you also should love one another. By this everyone will know that you are my disciples, if you have love for one another" (Jn 13 34-35). "This is my commandment, that you love one another as I have loved you. No one has greater love than this, to lay down one's life for one's friends. I am giving you these commands so that you may love one another" (Jn 13 35, 15 12-17). Jesus taught that this love should extend to strangers and enemies, not just to our friends (Mt 5 38-48).

Jesus modeled this love for others. He fed the hungry and healed the sick. He reached out to children, to lepers, to women, to Samaritans. He ate and drank with publicans and sinners and provided good wine when a marriage celebration was running short.[1] He taught those who were ignorant. He prayed for others. He washed their feet. He healed even the ungrateful. Above all he gave his life on the cross—for his enemies and accusers as well as his friends. If we learn anything from Jesus, it is this matter of neighbor-love—both cross-love and table-love.

The apostles continued the same emphasis as Jesus. Paul says, "Owe no one anything, except to love one another, for the one who

---

[1] Many are shocked by the wide-range of this expression of neighbor-love. Wine-lovers! (Re-)publicans! Sinners! Who then could ever be excluded? I jest a bit, of course, but, truly, the range of our Lord's outreach was astonishing. We must be inspired to express this anew in our place and time.

loves another has fulfilled the law The commandments   are
summed up in this word, 'Love your neighbor as yourself' Love does
no wrong to a neighbor, there-

**What is the right thing to do? It is the
thing that expresses love to our
neighbors, to other people, near and far,
friend and enemy Every authentically
Christian ethical act is good for our
neighbor in some important sense.**

---

fore, love is the fulfilling of the
law" (Rom 13 8-10) In another
of his letters, Paul repeats this
thought "For the whole law is
summed up in a single commandment, 'You shall love your
neighbor as yourself'" (Gal
5 14) Note carefully that Paul
does not say "the second half" of the law, he specifies that the *whole*
law, *all* of the commandments, are ways of loving your neighbor as
yourself

The apostle James refers to "You shall love your neighbor as yourself" as the "royal law" (Jas 2 8) Peter writes, "Above all, maintain
constant love for one another, for love covers a multitude of sins" (1
Pet 4 8) John's emphasis on love is well known "Let us love one another, because love is from God, everyone who loves is born of God and
knows God Whoever does not love does not know God, for God is
love" (1 Jn 4 7-8) So neighbor-love is at the heart of the apostolic
teaching, not just a special emphasis of Jesus

Cover Principle 3: Do Justice

Jesus also teaches us our third cover principle "Always do what is
righteous and just " (The two English terms, "righteousness" and "justice," translate one Greek term, *dikaiosyne* It is a mistake to separate
the concepts) "Blessed are those who hunger and thirst for righteousness, for they shall be filled   Unless your righteousness exceeds that
of the scribes and Pharisees, you will never enter the kingdom of
heaven" (Mt 5 6, 20) "Strive first for the kingdom of God and his righteousness" (Mt 6 33) What Jesus *was* and *did* can be summarized in
terms of righteousness and justice "Surely this was a righteous man,"
said the centurion at his death (Lk 23 47 NIV) "We have an advocate
Jesus Christ the righteous," wrote John (1 Jn 2 1)

Jesus and justice are intimately bound together in our ethics
Jacques Ellul has written,

All the characteristics of God's righteousness are united and embodied in the life, the death, and the resurrection of Jesus Christ Jesus Christ has become the righteousness of God There can be no justice whatsoever, even relative, outside Jesus Christ Jesus Christ as the righteousness of God exercises this justice One could say that his whole life is this exercise [2]

The prophet Micah famously put it, "Do justice, love kindness, and walk humbly with your God" (Mic 6 8) The prophet Isaiah said God's people "will be called oaks of righteousness I the LORD love justice The Lord GOD will cause righteousness and praise to spring up before all the nations" (Is 61 3, 8, 11) In the New Testament, Paul urged Christians to present their bodies to God as "instruments of righteousness" and said that "the kingdom of God is righteousness and peace and joy in the Holy Spirit" (Rom 6 13, 14 17)

What exactly are righteousness and justice? The biblical terms refer fundamentally to an attribute of God's character God is completely right, just and fair "The LORD is righteous, he loves righteous deeds" (Ps 11 7) God "speaks," "judges" and "acts" righteously (Is 45 19, Ps 119 160, 164, 1 Pet 2 23, Rev 19 2) [3] The content of God's justice and righteousness is the content of God's character The agenda of justice is the agenda of God

God's justice agenda includes a concern for individual rights, especially those of the poor and downtrodden Lew Smedes writes that "justice is fundamentally a matter of rights" and that the Decalogue is a "digest of human rights "

> In the decalogue we find a series of five basic human rights laid down Each commandment which forbids me to injure you implies that you have a fundamental right not to be injured by me or anyone else Every "Thou shalt not" signals a right [Justice means *respect*,] a sense for the other person's right to be

---

[2] Jacques Ellul, *The Theological Foundation of Law* (New York Seabury, 1969), p 42
[3] On justice and righteousness, see Karen Lebacqz, *Six Theories of Justice* (Minneapolis Augsburg, 1986), Alasdair MacIntyre, *Whose Justice? Which Rationality?* (Notre Dame, Ind University of Notre Dame Press, 1988), Stephen C Mott, *Biblical Faith and Social Change* (New York Oxford, 1982), and Christopher J H Wright, *An Eye for an Eye The Place of Old Testament Ethics Today* (Downers Grove, Ill InterVarsity Press, 1983)

who he is, to have what he properly has coming to him, and to be
allowed to do what he is called to do [4]

> All genuinely Christian ethical decisions and actions are actions of justice and righteousness They exhibit what is right and fair in the eyes of the Creator of all people—not just a tribal, national or personal notion of what is fair and right.

Fairness is also a common synonym today Justice and fairness mean that people get what they deserve or what is due to them (equal pay for equal work, punishment that fits the crime, etc) The Golden Rule, "Do to others as you would have them do to you" (Mt 7 12), is basically a rule about fairness—a method by which to figure out what is fair, what expresses an equality between your interests and mine [5]

How does justice relate to love? For Augustine, love is the great master theme, and justice refers to the proper distribution of love For others, justice and love are like the left and right hands of God Justice is hard and demanding, love is soft, generous and forgiving Smedes argues that "justice is love's minimum demand " Love "enlarges the scope of justice," "enriches justice" with mercy and "gets direction from justice "[6]

Every ethical decision and movement in the Christian life must be guided by the cover principle of justice We must ask ourselves, *How can I do what is just and righteous in the eyes of God?*

Cover Principle 4: Liberate and Redeem

Our fourth cover principle is, "Always act in ways that express and produce freedom " Jesus began his public ministry by identifying with Isaiah's prophetic statement "The Spirit of the Lord is upon me, be-

---

[4]Lewis B Smedes, *Mere Morality What God Expects from Ordinary People* (Grand Rapids, Mich Eerdmans, 1983), pp 15, 32, 55 I agree with Smedes in general, but I would say that we have ten basic rights, not just five, and that they are first of all ten rights or claims that God has on us, and, derivatively, they are ten rights of all people made in God's image

[5]Of course the Golden Rule can be about love as much as justice in that you could wish others to love as you would love But even in this application, the point is to choose a treatment for others that is equivalent to what I want for myself It is a great formula for fairness between people

[6]Smedes, *Mere Morality,* p 55

cause he has anointed me to bring good news to the poor He has sent me to proclaim release to the captives and recovery of sight to the blind, to let the oppressed go free, to proclaim the year of the Lord's favor" (Lk 4 18-19) Jesus also said, "If the Son makes you free, you will be free indeed" (Jn 8 36)

In healing people from disease and bondage to demons, Jesus broke peoples' chains and set them free Jesus set people free from physical restrictions, but he also broke the chains of social convention (by his interaction with women, children, publicans, sinners and all manner of outsiders), the bonds of religious legalism and formalism, and enslavement to sin and its consequences In his resurrection, Jesus destroyed the fatality of death and the grave Jesus was all about *redemption* (buying people's freedom when in captivity) and *freedom* [7] The apostles also urge freedom "For freedom Christ has set us free Stand firm, therefore, and do not submit again to a yoke of slavery" (Gal 5 1) "As servants of God, live as free people, yet do not use your freedom as a pretext for evil" (1 Pet 2 16)

God's action in human history is redeeming and liberating, not enslaving or in any way diminishing of our true life and liberty God's ethical laws, commandments and principles assume that we have been redeemed and set free by God Their point is *always* to *keep us free* No less in the Old Testament than the New, God sets us free first and only then asks for obedience to his law God's redemptive gift always comes first, his ethical guidelines are intended to ward off future slavery and keep us free Every one of the Ten Commandments is a "signpost to freedom " None of them are chains or handcuffs to restrict our freedom or fun or fulfillment

We have not fully understood Christian ethics until we see it as a guide to freedom not just for ourselves but also for others. Authentic Christian ethical guidance steers us away from bondage and toward freedom.

The gospel of redemption and freedom is the inner content of the law and commandments The Christian ethical map brings *freedom*

---

[7] On freedom, see Jacques Ellul, *The Ethics of Freedom* (Grand Rapids, Mich Eerdmans, 1976)

for me—freedom from bondage to my appetites, to principalities and powers, to traditions and institutions Set free from such slave masters, I am invited to invent ways of loving God and caring for others This also brings *freedom to others* around me For example, if I live by the command not to steal, my neighbor's property is safe, and she does not need to fear for her security The poor may be helped toward economic freedom if the command not to steal guides me to respond creatively and redemptively to the needs of others The Christian ethical map also guards and respects the *freedom of God,* refusing to put God in any boxes—legalistic, philosophical, moralistic or otherwise

---

FOUR COVER PRINCIPLES IN CHRISTIAN ETHICS

1 Always do what expresses love to God.
2 Always do what expresses love to your neighbor
3 Always do what is righteous and just
4. Always act in ways that express and produce freedom

In every ethical arena, with every ethical principle and in the face of every ethical challenge, we must figure out how to express and produce freedom If we can't find the freedom, we have missed something crucial

Opening the Atlas of Ethics

For good reasons, the best-known moral guidelines in the Bible are the Ten Commandments (or Decalogue, from the Greek terms for "ten" and "words") The Decalogue is a list of principles that guide our judgments about right and wrong in the ten key areas of human life In light of the controversy over calling biblical ethical guidelines and commandments "principles," let me cite four very different figures who use such language (I have added the italics for emphasis)

Sixteenth-century Genevan Reformer John Calvin, in his *Institutes of the Christian Religion,* said about each of the commandments that we should seek to be "guided by the *principle* of the commandment—viz , to consider in the case of each what the purpose is for which it was given "[8] Twentieth-century Anglican William Barclay wrote that the Ten Commandments are "a series of *principles,* not a body of de-

---

[8]Calvin *Institutes of the Christian Religion* 2 8 8

tailed rules and regulations "[9] Rabbi André Chouraqui writes, "We attempt to discern the *fundamental principles* of the Decalogue at the sources of the human and of all morality, religious or otherwise "[10] Finally, Old Testament scholar Bruce Birch says, "The Decalogue appears not so much as a legal code itself as the *foundational principles* of the covenant on which subsequent legal codes may be based The Decalogue seems more intended to lay out *broad principles* and general moral presumptions which require further legal application and refinement in particular contexts "[11]

The range of applicability of each of these ten principles is less than that of our four cover principles [12] And yet they remain broad, deep and comprehensive If God-love, neighbor-love, justice and freedom provide four rules of the road for all of life's travels, we might think of these ten area principles as itineraries—guides for our visits to ten sectors of life

With all ten together, we have coverage of all of the major aspects and domains of human life They provide a holistic perspective, dealing with speech, action and attitude They deal with both our vertical relation to God and our horizontal relation to people "There is a comprehensiveness to the commands which sets the Decalogue apart from other series "[13] Smedes says,

> The moral commandments of the decalogue are not barked at us by a capricious heavenly staff sergeant As I view them, they match the configurations of life as God created it Each commandment seems to cordon off a sector of life and pinpoint the moral nucleus of that sector[ ] family life,   marriage,   com-

---

[9]William Barclay, *The Ten Commandments for Today* (Grand Rapids, Mich Eerdmans, 1973), p 13

[10]André Chouraqui, *Les Dix Commandements Aujourd'hui* (Paris Robert Laffont, 2000), p 26

[11]Bruce C Birch, *Let Justice Roll Down The Old Testament, Ethics and Christian Life* (Louisville, Ky Westminster John Knox Press, 1991), p 168 This is an excellent overview and introduction to Old Testament ethics

[12]Except for the first commandment, which, as we shall see, is in one important sense all-inclusive in its coverage

[13]Brevard S Childs, *The Book of Exodus A Critical, Theological Commentary* (Philadelphia Westminster Press, 1974), p 400 This work is an outstanding critical-historical study of the Exodus text

munication   If we think of any community as a network of
these sectors, we can see that the commandments are survival
guidelines for the human community [14]

Unfortunately, many Christians are biblically illiterate and don't
even know the Ten Commandments I have often asked my college students or church groups, "Who knows the Ten Commandments well
enough to recite them?" Fewer than 1 percent raise their hands This
is hardly a promising statistic for the salt of the earth' Such ignorance
of the Ten Commandments (and other classic biblical texts) is embarrassing, tragic and, frankly, insulting to God

French Reformed pastor and theologian Alphonse Maillot also de-
plores the

> negativity with which the Decalogue is still considered in many
> Christian churches It is no longer read in worship Many think
> that the word "Decalogue" necessarily signifies legalism   We
> forget .   that legalism was not created by the Decalogue but by
> people   who forgot the liberating character of the Decalogue
> promise, future, joy [15]

Czech theologian Jan Milič Lochman agrees "To interpret the Ten
Commandments legalistically and moralistically is to misunderstand
them not just from the standpoint of the New Testament but also from
that of the original context of the Decalogue itself "[16]

Others, including some biblical scholars, may know the commandments but reject them as inapplicable [17] This rejection is usually based
on a terrible myopia By contrast, radio talk-show host Laura
Schlessinger has written,

---

[14]Smedes, *Mere Morality,* p 15

[15]Alphonse Maillot, *Le Decalogue Une morale pour notre temps* (Geneva Labor &
Fides, 1985), p 7

[16]Jan Milič Lochman, *Signposts to Freedom The Ten Commandments and Christian
Ethics* (Minneapolis Augsburg, 1982), p 17

[17]Speaking of scholarship that tends to diminish the originality, meaning or importance of the Decalogue, Brevard Childs says, "Certainly it remains a haunting question for anyone who has followed this history of exegesis whether one can really
describe it as a history of steadily increasing insight   To the extent to which the
scholar now finds himself increasingly estranged from the very substance which he
studies, one wonders how far the lack of content which he discovers stems from a
condition in the text or in himself " *Book of Exodus,* p 437

The first time we entered a synagogue, I had to leave because I was overwhelmed when they took out the Torah and held it up for the congregation I stood in the parking lot, not quite understanding why I was crying my eyes out It seemed to be incredible that I was part of a four-thousand-year history of something so magnificent and special the world's introduction to God's relationship with people [18]

If we do not feel something like this sense of awe and wonder before the Ten Commandments, we have not yet truly heard them

So our first assignment is to memorize the Decalogue, at least in its short form [19]

Why We Choose the Ten Commandments as Our Guide

Jesus and the Decalogue. Jesus has often been represented as rejecting or replacing the law in a decisive way because he called his disciples to a simple, radical faith Certainly he rejected the *legalism* of the Pharisees, but he did not reject the *law* In the Sermon on the Mount, he said,

Do not think that I have come to abolish the law or the prophets, I have not come to abolish but to fulfill For truly I tell you, until heaven and earth pass away, not one letter, not one stroke of a letter, will pass from the law until all is accomplished Therefore, whoever breaks one of the least of these commandments, and teaches others to do the same, will be called least in the kingdom of heaven, but whoever does them and teaches them will be

---

[18]Laura Schlessinger and Stewart Vogel, *The Ten Commandments The Significance of God's Laws in Everyday Life* (New York HarperCollins, 1998), p xxi It is astonishing that this book—a fairly severe interpretation of the Ten Commandments—made it onto the bestseller lists for many weeks

[19]In this book I employ the numbering of the commandments used by the Reformed and Greek Orthodox traditions, which I believe is the most logical and convincing approach (and for which John Calvin also cited the authority of the ancient church father Origen) Jewish tradition treats the Exodus prologue, "I am the LORD your God, who brought you out of the land of Egypt" (Ex 20 2), as the first commandment and then has "no other gods" and "no images" together in the second commandment The Catholic and Lutheran tradition has "no other gods" and "no images" together in the first commandment and "no misuse of God's name" as the second (instead of its being third, as it is in both Jewish and Reformed traditions) The Catholics and Lutherans still end up with ten commandments because they make "do not covet your neighbor's wife" the ninth and "do not covet your neighbor's goods" the tenth

called great in the kingdom of heaven (Mt 5 17-19)

The Sermon on the Mount is the most illuminating passage on Jesus and the Decalogue The first two of the six "antitheses" of Matthew 5 ("You have heard it said,   but I say   ") are not really *antitheses* at all but *intensifications* of the sixth and seventh commandments The commandments are not set aside but rather "filled full" of greater significance than ever For Jesus, the Ten Commandments clearly stand higher than all other laws and traditions "It is evident that Jesus regarded the Decalogue as the revealed will of God and in this respect did not differ from the Judaism of his age To the rich young ruler (Mt 19 18ff) who sought eternal life, Jesus simply quoted the ten commandments as the expressed

---

THE TEN COMMANDMENTS

"And God spoke all these words. I am the Lord your God, who brought you out of Egypt, out of the land of slavery" (Ex 20.2)

1   You shall have no other gods before me
2   Do not make for yourself any image
3. Do not misuse the Lord's name.
4   Remember the sabbath day Labor and work for six days.
5. Honor your father and mother
6   Do not murder
7   Do not commit adultery
8   Do not steal.
9. Do not bear false witness.
10 Do not covet

---

will of God "[20] If being a Christian means being a follower of Jesus Christ, we must adopt his position and not presume to know better

Paul and the apostles. Paul is the biblical author cited most often by Christians wishing to declare their independence from biblical law Paul certainly emphasized that righteousness before God comes by faith, not by observing the law "All who rely on the works of the law are under a curse   No one is justified before God by the law, for 'The one who is righteous will live by faith' " (Gal 3 10-11) For Paul, the law has a clear pedagogical value in showing us our shortcomings and our need of a Savior "If it had not been for the law, I would not have known sin I would not have known what it was to covet if the law had not said, 'You shall not covet'" (Rom 7 7)

But is this the end of the law's importance in the Christian life? "Do we then overthrow the law by this faith?" asks Paul "By no means! On

---

[20]Childs, *Book of Exodus*, p 429

the contrary, we uphold the law" (Rom 3 31) "For the law of the Spirit of life in Christ Jesus has set you free from the law of sin and of death For God has done what the law, weakened by the flesh, could not do by sending his own Son   so that the just requirement of the law might be fulfilled in us, who walk not according to the flesh but according to the Spirit" (Rom 8 2-4) With the power of the Spirit, the law is able to guide us in our new life It is only when we are walking in the flesh— apart from God—that we cannot live out the principles of God's law This is Paul's *theory* of the law, his *practice* of quoting and affirming the commandments is also a decisive endorsement (cf Rom 13 8-10)

The other New Testament writers have not raised the same kind of problem for Christians seeking to understand the Decalogue I will only quote the apostle John, who writes, "The love of God is this, that we obey his commandments And his commandments are not burdensome, for whatever is born of God conquers the world" (1 Jn 5 3-4) Thus, we are urged not only by Jesus (though that should be enough), but also by Paul and the apostolic church to make the ethical guidance of the *torah* central We must understand the law as being in *harmony* with the gospel of grace and faith, not in permanent *opposition* [21]

---

[21] John Nelson Darby, the creator of the theological system called *dispensationalism,* was an "antinomian" (meaning "against law") Darby argued that the law "is a principle of dealing with men which necessarily destroys and condemns them This is the way the Spirit of God uses law in contrast with Christ, and never in Christian teaching puts men under it Nor does Scripture ever think of saying, You are not under the law in one way, but you are in another, you are not under for justification, but you are for a rule of life " "On the Law," quoted in Walter C Kaiser Jr , *Toward Old Testament Ethics* (Grand Rapids, Mich Zondervan, 1983), pp 145-46 Darby's dispensationalist assumptions permitted him to sidestep our Lord's teaching about the importance and meaning of the law How he evaded Paul's clear affirmations is harder to comprehend

Alan Redpath, former pastor of Moody Memorial Church in Chicago and dean of Capernwray Bible School, says—about those who think the Ten Commandments were just given to the Jews and have a limited national and dispensational impact and no place in the "age of grace"—that "such teaching is not only highly dangerous but totally unbiblical   In the Ten Commandments and the Sermon on the Mount we find the terms for citizens of God's kingdom   The Ten Commandments are not merely from an Old Testament dispensation, they are the blueprint for all happiness Obedience to them always brings harmony with the purpose of God and in relation to other people too, for holiness and happiness are inseparable " *Law and Liberty A New Look at the Ten Commandments in the Light of Contemporary Society* (Old Tappan, N J Revell, 1978), pp 11, 23, 55

The Decalogue in ancient Israel. Christians often carry a mental image of our Jewish forebears toiling away under the accusing finger of the law, weighed down by their guilt and the heavy hand of the law. Only when Jesus came, we think, was freedom or joy possible. This image is mistaken. No doubt, there were guilt-ridden, burdened Jews back then, just as there are guilt-ridden, burdened Christians today. But there were also, then as now, people walking in the joy of God's law.

> We are urged not only by Jesus (though that should be enough) but also by Paul and the apostolic church to make the ethical guidance of the *torah* central. We must understand the law as being in *harmony* with the gospel of grace and faith, not in permanent *opposition.*

The prophets, of course, often scolded Israel for failing to walk in God's ways, and for them the commandments are clearly a central measuring standard. "Will you steal, murder, commit adultery, swear falsely, make offerings to Baal, and go after other gods that you have not known, and then come and stand before me in this house, which is called by my name, and say 'We are safe'—only to go on doing all these abominations?" (Jer 7 9-10) "There is no faithfulness or loyalty, and no knowledge of God in the land. Swearing, lying, and murder, and stealing and adultery break out, bloodshed follows bloodshed" (Hos 4 1-2). Such indictments often echo the Ten Commandments or provide a partial list of its concerns.

Psalms is an essential place to examine Jewish attitudes toward the law. Not only do the psalms reflect their authors' joy (and guilt and fear and anguish), they served as Israel's worship and hymn collection. They are the sentiments not just of the psalmists, but of congregational life. Psalm 119, the longest chapter in the Bible, is an extraordinary song about the greatness of God's law.

> Oh, how I love your law!
>> It is my meditation all day long. (Ps 119 97)
>
> Your decrees are my heritage forever,
>> they are the joy of my heart. (Ps 119 111)
>
> Your decrees are wonderful,
>> therefore my soul keeps them
> The unfolding of your words gives light,

it imparts understanding to the simple
With open mouth I pant,
because I long for your commandments (Ps 119 129-31)

So much for suffering and groaning under the accusing finger of the law!

Even in the Old Testament, the gospel was at the heart of the law, and the Decalogue was the essential core statement of the law "The Decalogue is clearly regarded as foundational by the biblical communities and within the biblical witness "[22] "It is not without reason," Luther wrote "that the Old Testament commands men to write the Ten Commandments on every wall and corner, and even on their garments

It is obvious once again how highly these Ten Commandments are to be exalted and extolled above all orders, commands, and works which are taught and practiced apart from them "[23]

The Decalogue in its context. Often repeated individually or in partial lists throughout the Bible, the complete list of the Ten Commandments is given in just two places Exodus 20 1-17 and Deuteronomy 5 6-21 The historical, literary and religious context clearly suggests that these ten are different and higher in rank than the other 603 laws or commands in the Torah After struggling and suffering as slaves in Egypt for hundreds of years, the children of Israel were led to freedom by Moses (Ex 1—14) As they began a wandering pilgrimage across the Sinai Peninsula to the Promised Land (Ex 15—18), God appeared and made his covenant with them at Mount Sinai (also called Mount Horeb) in the form of the Ten Words

There are two features of the story that emphasize the singular, special status of these Ten Words First, they were *spoken directly by the voice of God* to the people, not through an intermediary "The LORD spoke with you face to face" (Deut 5 4) Second, they were *written directly by the finger of God* on the tablets "The tablets were the work of God, and the writing was the writing of God, engraved upon the tablets" (Ex 32 16) "The LORD gave me the two stone tablets written with the finger of God, on them were written all the words that the LORD had spoken to you at

---

[22]Birch, *Let Justice*, p 168

[23]Martin Luther, *The Large Catechism*, trans Robert H Fischer (1529, Philadelphia Fortress, 1959), p 54

the mountain out of the fire on the day of the assembly" (Deut 9 10)

This covenant was inscribed on two stone tablets, which were probably duplicates, each written "on both sides" (Ex 32 15) The tradition of referring to the first four or five commandments as the "first table" and the second five or six as the "second table" is a little misleading here It is more accurate to refer to the "two sides" of each table Why would two copies be made of this two-sided engraved stone covenant? This would provide one copy for each party to the agreement—one for God and one for the people—just as we get a copy of any contracts we sign Both copies were to be stored in the Ark of the Covenant (Deut 10 2), in the holy of holies of the Tabernacle around which Israel camped This was God's dwelling place among the covenant people

---

WHY THE TEN COMMANDMENTS ARE SPECIAL

- They were written by the finger of God
- They were spoken by the voice of God within people's hearing
- Two copies were made, one for each party to the covenant
- They were kept in the Ark of the Covenant, in the holy of holies

---

You may recall that the covenant (the Decalogue) was broken even before Moses got back down from the mountain The impatient Israelites created a golden calf, Aaron declared a festival to Yahweh, and the celebration began Moses was not pleased! "I saw that you had sinned against the LORD your God   So I took hold of the two tablets and flung them from my two hands, smashing them before your eyes" (Deut 9 16-17) But God graciously gave them a second chance "The LORD said to me, 'Carve out two tablets of stone like the former ones, and come up to me on the mountain, and make an ark of wood I will write on the tablets the words that were on the former tablets, which you smashed, and you shall put them in the ark'" (Deut 10 1-2) The clear lesson from this story is that God's covenant remains valid even when we fail to observe its provisions This is the good news, the gospel

The Decalogue and us. As I confessed earlier, I did not always appreciate the Ten Commandments, but I have come to agree with Luther "This much is certain anyone who knows the Ten Commandments perfectly knows the entire Scriptures In all affairs and circumstances he can counsel, help, comfort, judge, and make decisions in both spiritual and temporal matters."[24] Twentieth-century theologian Karl Barth said that the Decalogue "is the foundation statute of the divine covenant of grace and valid for all ages" and for "all the situations of our lives."[25]

How the Decalogue Guides Our Christian Ethic

The prologue (or preamble) to the Ten Commandments provides an essential point of entry for understanding these guidelines (Ex 20 1-2, cf Deut 5 4-6) As Jan Milič Lochman writes, "Our understanding of the whole Decalogue and all its details directly depends on correctly understanding this preamble If we go astray here, if we miss this entrance, we are committing ourselves from the very beginning to a direction where our understanding of the individual commandments is imperiled or even made quite impossible."[26]

The author: "the Lord God spoke." "Then God spoke all these words" (Ex 20 1) Earlier, I used the phrase *an ethic from above* to stress that it is God who has taken the initiative to establish this ethic No doubt the people copied them and handed them on through history *Raiders of the Lost Ark* was a fun film, but the truth is that the Ark of the Covenant is lost forever and with it the original stone tablets Still, with Israel and the church, we believe that "*God* spoke all these words."[27]

In the prologue and first two commandments God speaks in the first person "*I* am the LORD your God   You shall have no other gods before *me*   *I* the LORD your God am a jealous god" (Ex 20 2-5) Rabbi Avroham Chaim Feuer says that the Hebrew term used here for *I* emphasizes God's uniqueness and exclusiveness "I, and I alone, am

---

[24]Luther, *Large Catechism*, p 5

[25]Karl Barth, *Church Dogmatics* 2/2, trans Geoffrey W Bromiley (Edinburgh T & T Clark), pp 685, 708

[26]Lochman, *Signposts*, p 21

[27]Well, most of the church believes this Rupert Davies writes, "The Code of Hammurabi and no doubt other codes were available for inspection, and the result of studying them and the needs of Israel was the publication of the original form of the code contained in Exodus 20 " *Making Sense of the Commandments* (London Epworth, 1990), p 2 So much for "God spoke all these words " My objection is not at all to a serious, critical exploration of the historical relationship of the Decalogue to other codes, but to the complete absence (especially in the teaching of a church leader) of any sense that there might just (also) be a God who had something to do with it Frankly, it is also an insult to Israel to imply that its greatest moral and legal achievement was just borrowed and cobbled together from surrounding nations

God "[28] In the third, fourth and fifth commandments God is referred to in the third person "You shall not make wrongful use of the name of the LORD your God   The LORD will not acquit   The seventh day is a sabbath to the LORD your God   The LORD made heaven and earth," and so on (Ex 20 7-11) All ten of the commandments are equally words spoken by God, but the first two have a special force in establishing a personal relationship between God and the people Our Christian ethic must continue to be understood as *personal address from the living God*

The audience: "the people listened." Who is the intended (and potential) audience for the moral instruction of the Decalogue? These guidelines assume that there is a living relationship between the audience and the speaker and that this audience recognizes the speaker as its own Lord, God and Liberator The Ten Commandments *are* the *covenant* between God and the people "He declared to you his covenant, which he charged you to observe, that is, the ten commandments" (Deut 4 13) The stone tablets are "the tablets of the covenant that the LORD made with you" (Deut 9 9) The covenant establishes a relationship ("I will take you as my people, and I will be your God," Ex 6 7) and defines ten terms of that relationship

The covenant people (the audience) was liberated as a group, as a community, and it is now addressed as a group assembled before the speaker The Ten Commandments are to be heard and understood in the community of faith, not by isolated individualists Nevertheless, the Hebrew language here addresses a *singular* (not plural) "you," thus placing each individual in responsibility and privilege before God All such individuals are part of the community, but they have individual identity and responsibility Martin Buber has written, "The soul of the Decalogue   is to be found in the word 'thou '   Only those persons really grasped the Decalogue who literally felt it as having been addressed to themselves "[29] Feuer powerfully states,

God addressed Israel in the second person singular form as if he

[28]Avroham Chaim Feuer, *Aseres Hadibros The Ten Commandments, A New Translation with a Commentary Anthologized from Talmudic, Midrashic and Rabbinic Sources* (Brooklyn, N Y Mesorah, 1981), p 25 I am indebted, big time, to my late friend Katharine Temple for this wonderful little book

[29]Martin Buber, *On the Bible Eighteen Studies* (New York Schocken, 1968), p 106

were speaking to only one individual   This usage teaches every Jew to feel 'The Ten Commandments and the entire Torah were addressed directly to *me*', I personally am responsible for the Torah and I cannot excuse myself by saying it is enough if others observe the commandments   Moreover   it is not sufficient to be a practicing Jew only   in the company of others who observe [30]

Still, the community aspect must not be lost "No matter how repeatedly the individual alone is addressed," writes Buber, "it is nevertheless not the isolated individual who is meant "[31] Walter Harrelson summarizes the balance well "The second person singular form of address does not exclude the community as a whole, rather   it includes the community Each Israelite is to find the commandments binding, but the commandments fall upon the community of the covenant and thus upon all of its members "[32]

There is also an extraordinarily democratic reach to this audience The book of the covenant, the Holiness Code and other laws were mediated through Moses, but the Ten Commandments were spoken, directly and unmediated, in the hearing of *all* the people "The Decalogue is not addressed to a specific segment of the population, to the priestly class, or a prophetic office within Israel, but to every man It has no need of legal interpretation, but is straightforward and immediately manifest in its meaning "[33]

Earl Palmer captures well this revolutionary development

Before this moment Moses alone has a direct relationship with Yahweh The people can only listen dutifully to what Moses, their leader   has to say to them about his discoveries of God's guidance Now we see how that is permanently altered by an event in which God places between himself and Moses a permanently etched self-disclosure of his will   Moses is no longer absolute, rather, from that day onward there is a check and a balance

---

[30]Feuer, *Aseres Hadibros,* p 26

[31]Buber, *On the Bible,* p 107

[32]Walter Harrelson, *The Ten Commandments and Human Rights* (Philadelphia Fortress, 1980), p 51

[33]Childs, *Book of Exodus,* pp 399-400

alongside every sentence and every act that comes from him [34]

Thus, our own practice of the principles of the Christian ethic must be both an individual and a community affair Individuals—and this means *all* individuals in the community—cannot evade responsibility for seeking and doing the right thing Nevertheless it is a terrible mistake to attempt this individualistically, without a community of friends and fellow pilgrims In Deuteronomy, households are encouraged to discuss the commandments and their meaning to recite them to each other and talk about them, at home and on the road, when they rise and when they lie down (Deut 6 6-9) Christian ethics is always *koinonia* ethics, ethics for people in community relationships

Finally, we must ask whether the Decalogue has any relevance outside the community of faith Many theological traditions have believed that there are *three* uses of the law to convict people of sin and bring people to Christ, to provide the basic structure of political justice in the world, and to guide the Christian life Actually, that third use of the law (guiding the Christian life) has been more hotly debated, at least in Protestantism, than the second (political) use

Maillot describes the place where we must begin our reflection "The Decalogue is for those who have heard the word of the 'Lord who delivers', we do not have the right to impose it on others   It is not for those who are staying in Egypt " More expansively, however, Maillot writes, "For whom is the Decalogue valuable? For those who listen to it' It is not a folkloric document of value to certain people in the past, nor a universal chart diluted by generality, limited by anonymity, it is a word that addresses me and to which I must respond "[35]

Challenging us even more boldly, Chouraqui writes,

> The reach of the Ten Commandments is not limited to the three Abrahamic religions The place of their proclamation is a desert The desert belongs to no one an object found in its dry, stony terrain belongs to whomever bothers to bend down and pick it up The Ten Words address themselves to humanity as a whole in that they summarize in a few sentences the human condition and

---

[34]Earl F Palmer, *Old Law, New Life The Ten Commandments and New Testament Faith* (Nashville Abingdon, 1984), p 33
[35]Maillot, *Le Decalogue,* pp 25, 13, 16-17

the conditions on which the survival of humanity depends
The author of the Decalogue is the Creator of the heavens and
the earth [36]

My own position is that the Ten Commandments are primarily intended to be the principles of love, freedom and justice of a worldwide
community of people in a living faith-based relationship with God
The commandments are both a gift and a requirement for God's followers While it is wrong to impose this on others (a relationship with
God can only begin with the free, not coerced, assent of a new disciple), I do believe that these principles correspond to human reality in
a profound way The author of the Decalogue is the Creator of all people, not just of Israel or the church We should offer what we have
learned to whoever cares to hear, and we should not be surprised if
they accept it Scripture hints that this may well happen in the promise that neighboring nations will be
impressed by the justice of these
laws as well as by the personal near-
ness of the lawgiver of Israel's Decalogue (Deut 4 6-8)

The message: "all these words. "
What God spoke (and wrote) were
words (Heb *dabar, devarim*) from
normal human language This ethic
enters into the ordinary culture and
activity of our existence, it does not
hover above our existence in some
special angelic tongue understand-

> **The Ten Commandments are
> primarily intended as guidance for a
> community of people (which means
> everyone, not just the leaders) in a
> living relationship to a speaking God.
> At the same time, the wisdom of the
> core principles of the Decalogue is
> often recognizable and helpful
> beyond the community of faith**

able only by a special elite class Christian ethics is incarnational God
will speak his guidance into our ordinary, daily situation, in language
we can understand

Although the term *commandment* is used often enough in the
broader literary context, the Ten Words are not first of all "commandments" or "orders," but "sayings" and "declarations " Even as a form of
law, the Decalogue is what is called *apodictic law* rather than *case
law* Harrelson points out,

---

[36]Chouraqui, *Les Dix Commandements,* pp 23-24

These are not laws in the ordinary sense of the term *law* The
Ten Commandments are much more akin to statements about
the character of life in community than they are to cases of violation   and   punishment   They provide the policy statements that can help a new member of the community come to
clarity rather quickly regarding what is the shape of life within
our community [37]

Chouraqui argues that the verb tense itself helps us understand the
nature of these "words"

> The Decalogue is a declarative text rather than a legislative proc-
> lamation Let me underscore this in Hebrew, the command-
> ments are not formulated in the imperative but in the imperfect,
> which reveals their educative role Human nature is not changed
> by the proclamation of an order by itself It is necessary to edu-
> cate man in the spirit of this ethical revelation [38]

Negative words? What are we to make of the negative form ("You
shall not") in which most of these words are given? This apparent neg-
ativism has been a stumbling block and turn-off to many people
Brevard Childs tries to salvage the situation by pointing out that with
two commandments stated positively, the Decalogue "serves not only
to chart the outer boundary but also to provide positive content for life
within the circle of the covenant The Decalogue looks both outward
and inward, it guards against the way of death and points to the way of
life "[39] Most people will not find comfort in that low ratio of positive to
negative, however!

From another angle, we should better appreciate the negative form
itself Ellul has argued that saying no is itself the first act of freedom
Barclay explains the negative structure by saying that self-limitation is
the essential prerequisite to community There is no community without such willingly accepted negation and limitation of our self-interest [40] Both personal freedom and community life thus depend on some
negation

---

[37]Harrelson, *Ten Commandments*, pp 12-13
[38]Chouraqui, *Les Dix Commandements*, p 153
[39]Childs, *Book of Exodus*, p 398
[40]Barclay, *Ten Commandments*, p 14

Still further, Harrelson argues that "prohibitions are particularly valuable because they leave open many matters that must be settled in other ways The short, pithy prohibitions do not get into particularity They simply let the community know what kinds of human conduct are in principle ruled out, not allowable, not to be entertained at all "[41] Maillot sees positive freedom as implicit in the negative structure

> The Decalogue presents itself more like a series of prohibitions than a series of precise orders It is curious that a prohibition is much less acceptable to us than an order But it is truly by a fundamental perversion that we get to this point Because the prohibition is often much more open than the order A prohibition is often one hundred permissions [42]

Maillot points out that in the Garden of Eden the one prohibited tree was accompanied by hundreds of other freely available trees "You are free" but "you must not " Do not eat of *that* tree, but eat freely from any of the others (You choose which ones!) The story of Adam and Eve shows the fundamental human problem of failing to see and grasp our great freedom and of becoming obsessed by a single prohibition And, yet, it is the prohibition that enables freedom Driving restrictions, such as one-way streets, are precisely what enable traffic to circulate Thus, Maillot continues, "Let's repeat a law composed of prohibitions is infinitely more vast than a law composed of orders But we have a spirit so bizarre that we do not want to believe it and above all to understand it "[43]

The negative commands are like warning signs posted in front of potential taskmasters ready to enslave us again Your life is free, but it must be navigated amid certain dangers Each of these potential slave masters lurks at a critical and vulnerable point in our existence, we don't walk by these temptations without a struggle They represent the perversions of the ten best things, which is why they have such attractive power

Another way of getting at this is to say that there is a dialectical relationship of positive and negative each *command* contains (or di-

---

[41]Harrelson, *The Ten Commandments,* p 13
[42]Maillot, *Le Decalogue,* p 14
[43]Ibid , pp 14-15

rectly implies) a *permission* Some commentators like to say the *law* contains the *gospel* Barth saw the law and the gospel as two sides to one covenant—a no is paired with a yes, an imperative with an indicative, a must with a may, a threat with a promise, a claim with a gift, a prohibition with a permission, a boundary with a freedom, an obligation with a possibility

John Wesley came to similar conclusions

> There is no contrariety at all between the law and the gospel, there is no need for the law to pass away, in order to the establishing of the gospel Indeed, neither of them supersedes the other, but they agree perfectly well together Yea, the very same words, considered in different respects are parts both of the law and of the gospel if they are considered as commandments, they are parts of the law, if as promises, of the gospel   Every command in holy writ is only a covered promise   God hath engaged to give whatsoever He commands Does He command us then to "pray without ceasing," to "rejoice evermore," to be "holy as He is holy"? It is enough He will work in us this very thing it shall be unto us according to His word [44]

Donald Bloesch also supports this position "Every promise of the gospel contains an imperative and every imperative of the law contains a promise"[45] Walter Kaiser argues that "when an evil is forbidden in one of the commandments, its opposite good must be practiced before one can be called obedient"[46] Smedes argues that love "translates negative rules into affirmative laws *Respect* becomes *care* 'Thou shalt not kill' becomes Do everything in your power to protect, nourish, and nurture your neighbor's life," and so on[47]

Calvin says, "There is always more in the requirements and prohibitions of the Law than is expressed in words " It is "ridiculous," Calvin says, to "attempt to restrict the spirit of the Law to the strict letter of the words " We must "reason from the precept to its contrary   If

---

[44]John Wesley, *John Wesley's Forty-Four Sermons* (London Epworth, 1952), pp 255-56, quoted in Donald Bloesch, *Freedom for Obedience* (San Francisco Harper & Row, 1987), p 115

[45]Bloesch, *Freedom,* p 132

[46]Kaiser, *Toward Old Testament Ethics,* p 83

[47]Smedes, *Mere Morality,* p 62

this pleases God, its opposite displeases, if that displeases, the opposite pleases, if God commands this, he forbids the opposite, if he forbids that, he commands the opposite " For example, Calvin says, "the commandment 'Thou shalt not kill,' the generality of men will merely consider as an injunction to abstain from all injury, and all wish to inflict injury I hold that it moreover means, that we are to aid our neighbor's life by every means in our power " Why are the commandments given in such an elliptical, partial form then? Because

> **It is very important to see each of the Ten Commandments as both a negative prohibition or boundary and a positive mandate or guiding star.**

"the Lord sets forth, by way of example, whatever is foulest and most iniquitous in each species of transgression "[48]

Although this honor roll of commentators can help us see the positive side of what seem initially to be very negative guidelines, it is Jesus himself who best makes the case Immediately after his comment about fulfilling the law (near the beginning of the Sermon on the Mount), Jesus proceeds to an exposition of the sixth commandment, "You shall not kill " After reinforcing the negative side by prohibiting murderous anger and insult as well as action, Jesus concludes by saying,

> So when you are offering your gift at the altar, if you remember that your brother or sister has something against you, leave your gift there before the altar and go, first be reconciled to your brother or sister, and then come and offer your gift Come to terms quickly with your accuser while you are on the way to court with him (Mt 5 21-26)

Thus, what looks like a simple negative commandment ("You shall not kill") actually means that we should not just refrain from violence, but take positive initiative to head it off before it can occur

Narrow words? Another important question about these Ten Words is, how wide or narrow is their range of meaning? Jesus is again our best guide He said that he came not to destroy but to fulfill the law, and that not one jot or tittle—not the slightest stroke of a pen— should be lost from the law The Greek term for fulfillment (*plēroma*) literally means "filled full " Jesus augments rather than limits the law

---

[48]Calvin *Institutes* 2 8 8-10

The "righteousness [that] exceeds that of the scribes and Pharisees" (Mt 5 20), which Jesus calls for, refers to the righteousness enacted and achieved by Jesus' life and death and also to a broader, deeper understanding of justice and righteousness per se Jesus taught a more "fully filled" law concerning murder by saying that it applied to speech and attitude as well as act, and that it meant working positively for reconciliation as well as refraining from violence He taught that refraining from the act of adultery must be accompanied by refraining from improper lust and by taking radical action to remove the true causes of the sin By explanation and practice, Jesus also helped fulfill the sabbath commandment for us

> **Each commandment has a precise, narrow, historical meaning and a wide-ranging meaning that grows directly out of its core principle.**

Luther's *Large Catechism* consistently follows this pattern [49] For example, honoring mother and father is the narrow command The broader implications for Luther have to do with our attitudes toward all legitimate authorities in our life "Luther's exegesis gave to the Decalogue a profoundly comprehensive role, covering every area of life, which has seldom been matched At the same time he clothed it with such a concrete form of flesh and blood that it carried a tremendous impact in shaping the Christian life "[50] Remember Calvin's statement as well "There is always more in the requirements and prohibitions of the Law than is expressed in words "[51]

Thus, we will also range about, exploring the broader reach of each command We want to understand the fundamental principle embedded in each commandment and then explore what it implies both negatively and positively for our practices

Keeping the tables together? Nearly every commentator on the Ten Commandments has made a distinction between the earlier commandments, which appear to guide our relationship to God, and the later commandments, which guide our relations with other people Usually the neighbor commands are said to begin with the fifth commandment, "Honor your father and mother " I am among the minority

---

[49] Luther, *Large Catechism*, pp 52-54
[50] Childs, *Exodus*, p 433
[51] Calvin *Institutes* 2 8 8

who see commandment five as more of an act of love toward God (parents are God's agents and representatives) than toward our neighbors (of whom our parents are our first ones)

Where my approach is still more unusual is in my argument that all ten are ways of relating to God *and* that all ten are ways of relating to your neighbor I will explain this as we go along, but for the moment I wish to point out that Jesus does not divide the commands into two groups, so as to fit them into his double love command (an incorrect deduction made by later readers) And Paul says very clearly, *twice*, that the *whole* law (not just half of it) is summarized by "love your neighbor as yourself" (Rom 13 8-10, Gal 5 14) [52]

> **Each of the Ten Commandments indicates both a way of relating to God and a way of relating to our neighbor.**

So Smedes errs, I think, when he says he is "imitating Paul, who, when he speaks of the law of God, cites only the second half, the moral part of the decalogue, which deals with human relationships (Rom 13 8-10) "[53] The separation of morality and religion in this way is wrong, one of the lessons of the Decalogue is precisely that we must never separate them It is also shortsighted to interpret the first four commandments as exclusively God-oriented when they have such rich implications for our relationships with people (made in God's image and likeness) Maillot says,

> I regret it when one separates too much the Decalogue into two tables the table of commandments relative to God and the table of commandments relative to the neighbor That is only partially true, and it risks becoming completely false if one were to reintroduce by that bias limited domains of the divine and the human in the life of the Israelites and the Christians [54]

---

[52] Regent College Professor Paul Stevens is the only other person I know of who commonly uses all ten commandments to teach the ways of neighbor love—in his case, the ways of marital love Thus, "You shall give exclusive loyalty to your spouse," "You shall not make false images of your spouse," "You shall honor your spouse's name in public and private," etc *Married for Good* (Downers Grove, Ill InterVarsity Press, 1986), p 87

[53] Smedes, *Mere Morality*, p 15

[54] Maillot, *Le Decalogue*, p 12

Liberation: the past and present of Decalogue-directed lives.
The final introductory perspective embedded in the prologue is the
phrase where God identifies himself as the one "who brought you out
of the land of Egypt, out of the house of slavery" (Ex 20 2) Kaiser
writes that "over 125 times Israel was reminded that 'I am the Lord
your God who brought you up out of the land of Egypt ' "[55] The Decalogue is thus an ethic based on God's mighty act of salvation, redemption and liberation Earlier in this chapter I called this the cover principle of freedom It is clear that the speaker of the Ten Words is the
Creator of all things—the One who spoke worlds into existence But it
is of the highest importance to note that God presents this guidance
not to a people in some kind of new Eden, but to a hurting people on
the run from terrible oppression and misery This is a realistic, historically savvy ethic This is an ethic that takes bondage and evil seriously
and does something about it

The Ten Commandments are based on the gracious, liberating redemption God has already accomplished They are the covenant of a
redeemed people They are intended to carry forward the spirit of freedom and preserve it in our daily lives

> The Decalogue is not, first of all what God requires of his people,
> but rather what he gives them The Decalogue is a grace that God
> gives freely to his people   The covenant is that God delivers
> from Egypt and gives the Decalogue It is God who delivers the
> slaves and gives to these slaves the possibility of living as free
> people He gives the commandment and he gives the obedience
> He gives the freedom, the will, and the action   The Decalogue
> is not first of all a law, but a *charter* It is not first of all the means
> of obtaining a deliverance and a divine favor, it is the conse-
> quence of that [56]

"The reference to the redemption from Egypt is of deepest significance," writes Rabbi J H Hertz "The primal word of Israel's divine
message is the proclamation of the One God as the God of Freedom
The recognition of God as the God of Freedom illumines the whole of
human history for us In the light of this truth, history becomes one

---

[55]Kaiser, *Old Testament Ethics,* p 33
[56]Maillot, *Le Decalogue,* pp 16-17

continuous Divine revelation of the gradual growth of freedom and justice on earth "[57] Lochman points out that "the Decalogue is the *Magna Carta* of the Covenant, the title deeds of the history of Israel's liberation The purpose of 'teaching' the Decalogue was to maintain and exercise this God-given freedom This document of the covenant, essentially is a *charter of freedom* The Ten Commandments are the 'Ten Great Freedoms' "[58]

Walter Harrelson puts it this way

God, the Lord of the covenant, has brought a band of slaves to freedom Now the same God lays upon the freed slaves a set of obligations Each hearer of this list will know without being told that it is sheer folly and perhaps even madness to violate these commandments, for to do so cannot help but bring harm These prohibitions are designed for the good of these freed slaves Life and joy and peace lie ahead for those who quite simply rule out such conduct as is here specified [59]

He goes on to say, "The first thing people need to know is that they can have no real life, no real freedom, no real joy in life save as they lay aside the kinds of actions that destroy the very things they are seeking The Ten Commandments ward off conduct on our part which, if engaged in, will make impossible the love of God and of neighbor "[60]

God, writes Chouraqui,

is above all the liberator of a people reduced to slavery The Ten Words are the law, which will condition the life of this people, assuming the liberty constitutive of their being, their identity, their rights and duties It reveals to them the essentials of a liberating way of thinking that will only be fully understood when human beings have broken the shackles of their servitude, of their idols and, above all, their self-centeredness If he is not free,

---

[57]J H Hertz, ed , *The Pentateuch and Haftorahs Hebrew Text, English Translation and Commentary,* 2nd ed (London Soncino, 1988), p 295 I am indebted to Marlene Kasting for this immensely illuminating, standard Jewish commentary

[58]Lochman, *Signposts,* pp 18-19

[59]Harrelson, *Ten Commandments,* pp 16-17

[60]Ibid , p 188

man cannot be in the image of his Creator Being His first duty is to not succumb to other servitudes   The liberated man will be always and everywhere available to follow the way marked out for him by his Liberator   The Decalogue proposes to humanity the charter of freedom for a people freed from their slavery   The Ten Words are not an end in themselves, but the means of arriving at freedom [61]

> Each of the Ten Commandments is a "signpost to freedom." Each commandment is a warning against potential slavery and a way of bringing freedom to others while experiencing it ourselves

"We have accepted the prohibitive Ten Commandments, in the sweat of our brows and the sorrow of our hearts," reflects Joy Davidman "But the joyous, liberating commandments of Christ we have yet to learn "[62] These are the *same* commandments! We must learn to see their liberating power Maillot stresses, "The Torah is not just holy and righteous, it is *good!* Good for us And it is just this goodness, liberated by the Decalogue expressed in particular in the first command, that I don't often find among the commentators "[63]

> Each commandment is a principle of justice (what is right and fair) and a principle of love It is not either-or but both-and.

Words of justice and love. The cover principle of freedom is thus intimately woven into each part of the Decalogue In closing, let us remember that the commandments are also the ways of love (for God, for neighbor) and justice Chouraqui says, "The essence of the Ten Commandments [is] the law of universal love "[64] The literary context in Deuteronomy makes this very clear with the Shema's command to love God (Deut 6 4-5), the promise of blessing on household, neighbors and even nations (Deut 4 6-8, 40, 5 29, 33, 6 3, 18), and the statement that these are the ways of justice and righteousness (Deut 6 25)

---

[61] Chouraqui, *Les Dix Commandements,* pp 50-53

[62] Joy Davidman, *Smoke on the Mountain An Interpretation of the Ten Commandments* (Philadelphia Westminster Press, 1953), p 131

[63] Maillot, *Le Decalogue,* pp 7-8

[64] Chouraqui, *Les Dix Commandements,* p 147

"These commandments," writes Smedes, "make more specific the two fundamental commandments for the moral life—that we should do justice and act in love Justice and love are absolute, unconditional, unequivocal They are global, universal, all-embracing commands Justice and love cover every conceivable human situation "[65] The commandments spell out and make specific the grand principles of justice and love, as they do freedom and redemption

For Reflection and Discussion

1 How do you react to the author's emphasis on love, freedom and justice as cover principles? Can you identify other cover principles you think should be included?

2 How many of the Ten Commandments can you recite from memory? Do you agree that all Christians should know them by heart?

3 Do you think that all (or part or none) of the Decalogue is relevant to nonbelievers? Why? What is your opinion of the controversies over posting the Ten Commandments in public places?

4 What are the biggest obstacles to making the Decalogue our code of ethics in life?

---

[65] Smedes, *Mere Morality,* p 15

PART TWO

Practice

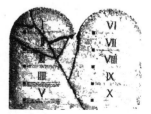

3

Nobody but You
Uniqueness and Exclusivity

If the first commandment is an area principle, as I have suggested, what is the area? If it is a sort of itinerary for life's moral journey, where does it take us? One answer is that this first itinerary guides us straight to the highest place on the landscape, a vantage point from which every other itinerary can be seen If the first day's itinerary in the famous Michelin guide to Paris took you to the Eiffel Tower, that would be something like what I am saying When you are in Paris, you can get re-oriented fairly quickly just by spotting the Eiffel Tower, no matter where you are From the top of the tower, you can see the layout of the whole magnificent city The first commandment plays that kind of role in relation to the nine that follow it It takes us straight to the Lord God, the source and center of everything Later we will examine two corollary implications of this first principle, one having to do with human relationships, the other having to do with ethical reform and growth

The first commandment is stated as a simple, straightforward prohibition "You shall have no other gods before me" (Ex 20 3 par Deut 5 7) [1] What does this mean? What is the fundamental principle embed-

---

[1] As I explained above (see n 19 in chap two), Jewish tradition views this as the second commandment with "I am the Lord your God" (what I call the prologue) as the first For both Jewish and Catholic/Lutheran traditions, "no other gods" is combined in one commandment with "no images," what the Reformed tradition views as the second commandment and which will be discussed below in chapter four

ded in this statement? In what ways does this command exhibit the
love of God, love of neighbor, justice and freedom?

Some other possible ways of translating this command include
"there shall be for you no other gods," "over against me," "before my
face," "between me and you" and "beside me" This message is repeated over and over through Scripture

> You shall worship no other god, because the LORD   is a jealous
> God (Ex 34 14)

> Take care that you do not forget the LORD, who brought you out
> of the land of Egypt, out of the house of slavery The LORD your
> God you shall fear, him you shall serve, and by his name alone
> you shall swear Do not follow other gods, any of the gods of the
> peoples who are all around you, because the LORD your God, who
> is present with you, is a jealous God (Deut 6 12-15)

> The LORD your God you shall follow, him alone you shall fear, his
> commandments you shall keep, his voice you shall obey, him you
> shall serve, and to him you shall hold fast (Deut 13 4)

> There shall be no strange god among you, you shall not bow
> down to a foreign god (Ps 81 9)

Jesus warned that we cannot serve two masters We cannot worship God and Mammon, for example (Mt 6 24) He refuted Satan's
temptation by citing Deuteronomy 6 13 "Worship the LORD your
God, and serve only him" (Mt 4 10) In a great passage (1 Cor 8 4-6),
Paul writes,

> We know that "no idol in the world really exists," and that
> "there is no God but one " Indeed, even though there may be
> so-called gods in heaven or on earth—as in fact there are many
> gods and many lords—yet for us there is one God, the Father,
> from whom are all things and for whom we exist, and one Lord,
> Jesus Christ, through whom are all things and through whom
> we exist

The first commandment guides us to say to the Lord, "You are my
Lord and God I want nobody but you on the throne of my life You
alone, you uniquely, will have this exclusive place in my life "

The Gospel in This Law

The positive side to this commandment—the gospel contained in this law—is the awesome possibility of having the Creator and Redeemer as our personal God This is not merely a commandment to *flee from* other gods, it is an invitation to *run to* the

> The first commandment guides us to say to the Lord· "You are my Lord and God I want nobody but you on the throne of my life You alone, you uniquely, will have this exclusive place in my life "

God of the universe, of the Exodus, of Bethlehem, of Calvary and of the empty tomb "I will be your God," promises the Lord, "and you will be my people" (e g, Lev 26 12, Jer 7 23, 2 Cor 6 16) "The LORD has taken you and brought you out of the iron-smelter, out of Egypt, to become a people of his very own possession, as you are now" (Deut 4 20) "Seek the LORD your God, and you will find him if you search after him with all your heart and soul   He will neither abandon you nor destroy you, he will not forget the covenant" (Deut 4 29, 31)

Jesus' own teaching and example on this topic are overwhelmingly *gospel-oriented* [2] For each of his warnings against false gods, Jesus gives us a hundred encouragements to walk closely with the Lord God—to seek his will, to incarnate his kingdom rule, to feast with his friends, to introduce him to others, to carry out his revolutionary agenda and generally to bask in the warmth of his love and acceptance Jesus chose his disciples not just to help him do a job, but to *be* with him Before his betrayal, he said, "I have eagerly desired to eat this Passover with you before I suffer" (Lk 22 15) "If I go and prepare a place for you, I will come again and take you to myself, so that where I am, there you may be also" (Jn 14 3)

> This is not merely a commandment to *flee from* other gods; it is an invitation to *run to* the God of the universe, of the Exodus, of Bethlehem, of Calvary and of the empty tomb "I will be your God," promises the Lord, "and you will be my people "

Luther says that this commandment "requires that man's whole heart and confidence be placed in God alone, and in no one else   We

---

[2] Is there a lesson here? How about "overcome evil with good"? Following Jesus, we could spend less energy attacking falsehood and more energy demonstrating truth, less time attacking false gods and more time promoting the true One

lay hold of him when our heart embraces him and clings to him "[3]
Calvin says, "The purport of the commandment is, that the Lord will
have himself alone to be exalted
in his people, and claims the entire possession of them as his
own   It is not enough to refrain from other gods We must
at the same time devote ourselves wholly to him "[4]

A truly astonishing angle on this first commandment is provided when we recognize that _God treats us exactly as this commandment tells us to treat him!_ Each of us is known to him by name, he finds us irreplaceable, and we are each the object of his particular love and care.

It is extraordinary that we
can _know_ God and have God
present in our life, but there is
still more there is _loving_ and _being loved by_ God The Shema, the
source of Jesus' great commandment, begins, "Hear, O Israel The
LORD is our God, the LORD alone You shall love the LORD your God
with all your heart, and with all your soul, and with all your might"
(Deut 6 4-5) We can know and love God deeply and intimately, talk
to him, hear him and have him present in our daily lives This is the
answer to life's agonies, problems and mysteries it is the source of
life's meaning and direction Life, forgiveness, hope, consolation, illu-
mination and guidance—all these come when God is on his throne in
our lives

A truly astonishing angle on this first commandment is provided
when we recognize that _God treats us exactly as this commandment
tells us to treat him!_ Each of us is known to him by name, he finds us
irreplaceable, and we are each the object of his particular love and
care He even numbers the hairs on my head He cares for me as a
unique individual, never forgetting me or wishing to replace me He tol-
erates no rivals in my seat at his table When I come to him I know that
he knows me intimately, that he listens to me and cares for me, that he
longs to have me alongside him now, and that he has prepared a place
for me with him in the afterlife God _loves_ us, and the first law of love
is exclusivity God gives it and God asks for it Everything follows from
this first movement

---

[3]Martin Luther, _The Large Catechism,_ trans Robert H Fischer (1529, Philadelphia
Fortress, 1959), p 10
[4]Calvin _Institutes of the Christian Religion_ 2 8 16

Not every commentator is quite so enthusiastic about all this, however Walter Harrelson, for example, questions

whether the commandment has any continuing force for us It is not entirely defensible, in all likelihood, to substitute for "gods" the items of our contemporary life that preoccupy us and divert us from concern for God and fellow human beings, items such as money, position, and security   The imposition of the identifying marks of ancient Israel involves a step that is for many a giant one I was not in Egypt, God has not brought me from slavery to freedom, and there are no rival powers in my life that vie for absolute allegiance

The best that Harrelson can come up with is a rather insipid mystical admonition "To commit oneself to have no other gods is to commit oneself to the one holy Mystery, the truth that all life is dependent at every moment upon the One who grounds all that has being "[5] Can you hear Moses thundering these words?

Of course, ancient Israel was located in a polytheistic culture, and many rival gods vied for the Israelites' attention In our era few are forsaking Yahweh or Jesus for Baal, Molech or Ishtar, but we should not be too quick to assert our freedom from ancient or primitive deities Astrology, paganism, goddess worship, Satanism, witchcraft and shamanism are seeing a revival today Reading chicken entrails cannot be too far behind the discerning of sacred crystals and other hokum many in our "advanced" civilization find attractive Limiting our attention only to such more-or-less self-declared alternative gods and religious experiences is, however, a serious and unwarranted error *Jesus,* remember, was the one who said that Mammon (the god personifying money) was a rival to our worshiping God We will return to this below

We must have a "nobody but you" stance toward God God must have a unique and exclusive place on the throne of our life Let's try then to restate the essential core principle of the first commandment,

---

[5]Walter Harrelson, *The Ten Commandments and Human Rights* (Philadelphia Fortress, 1980), pp 56-57, 61 If this is what Moses said after coming down from the mountain, I think I would have caught the next camel back to Egypt I don't mean to be cruel, but this example helps us understand why people stay home on Sunday mornings and read the *New York Times* rather than attending sermons given by preachers trained in this way of looking at the biblical text

in both its negative and positive forms

How to Recognize a God

Let's probe just a little further by asking ourselves, *What is a "god"? What is the "god-place" in my life? How would I recognize a god in my life if there were one?* The clues come in the statements following the second commandment (and which refer back to both the first and second commandments) "You shall not bow down to them or worship them" (Ex 20 5 par Deut 5 9) A god is not necessarily what we designate or call "god " A god is *whatever we bow down to and worship* It is best described in functional terms In the texts cited earlier the key attitudes and behaviors are *sacrificing* (giving valuable things or gifts to it), *fear* (revering or being in awe of it), *service* (working on behalf of it), *swearing by his name* (invoking its power and authority), *going after* (pursuing or giving time to it), *following and obeying* (doing what it wants) and *holding fast* (clinging to it in devotion) Luther got it right when he said, "That to which your heart clings and entrusts itself is, I say, really your God "[6]

> **Area Principle 1. Never allow anyone or anything to threaten God's central place in your life. Rather, make it your top priority to value and cultivate your relationship with God.**

> **A god is not necessarily what we designate or call "god." A god is whatever we bow down to and worship.**

Our gods are the things (or persons or ideas or powers) before which we *bow down* with our most sincere and profound respect For what do we *sacrifice* time, money and effort? What is at the *center* of our lives, giving us *meaning, purpose* and *direction?* What truly *motivates, awes* and *inspires* us? What preoccupies us and focuses our attention? What defines our values and our philosophy of life? Where do we look for *salvation, healing* and *freedom?* What is it that we leap to defend if it is attacked, belittled or "profaned"? These questions help us identify the gods in our lives

---

[6]Luther, *Large Catechism*, p 9

God's Rivals in the Twenty-First Century

It is not the pantheon of primitive gods and goddesses who are the greatest rivals to the Creator/Redeemer at this moment in history but, rather, god-substitutes like the Nation or Race or Gender [7] Luther warned against letting mammon (money and possessions) or "great learning, wisdom, power, prestige, family, and honor" rival the true God [8] Joy Davidman writes that "greatest among the false gods are these Sex, the State, Science, and Society "[9]

Jacques Ellul's great little sociology of religion, *The New Demons,* argues that the major twin poles of today's sacred are the nation-state and technology [10] The "old demons" (e g , Christendom) have been exorcised from Western civilization, but rather than having a house empty of superstition and religion, several new demons worse than the earlier occupants have taken over It is to the government that we look for care, for solutions, for education in basic values and so on It is in technology that we have faith and hope for medical cures, better food production, longer lives, more meaningful relationships and so on People used to rely on God for healing or for rain Today we rely on biotechnology and irrigation technologies Of course we are not officially required to treat the nation-state or technology as sacred, but we need to be aware of the temptation to do so

Technology and sex often serve today as the unacknowledged "saviors, lords and gods" of our lives, as do power, beauty, health, careers and perhaps even our children and family Celebrities and sports heroes of one kind or another receive the adoration and devotion once directed only to saints Probably the greatest rival to God in our era is the self The gospel of self-satisfaction, personal autonomy and self-determination is wowing and wooing thousands of converts today [11] Mam-

---

[7] Actually, it is not nation, race or gender per se that threaten God's place but rather *nationalism* (and *Americanism* is no better than *Serbianism* or any other form), *racism* (in all forms, covert and overt) and *sexism* (including *genderism* in either of its two potential versions)

[8] Luther, *Large Catechism,* pp 9-10

[9] Joy Davidman, *Smoke on the Mountain An Interpretation of the Ten Commandments* (Philadelphia Westminster Press, 1953), p 26

[10] Jacques Ellul, *The New Demons* (New York Seabury, 1975)

[11] Christian versions of this narcissism (regrettably, often encouraged by televangelists) are the worst of all

mon and material possessions *look* a lot like gods today but, in my view, these are often *means* to serve the self, rather than sacred *ends* in themselves The bottom line is that we should be very cautious about awarding ourselves a pass on the first commandment just because we are not offering prayers and pinches of incense to some little pagan idols in our apartment Rival gods can appear to be neutral or can appear even as angels of light Be careful!

> Probably the greatest rival to God in our era is the self The gospel of self-satisfaction, personal autonomy and self-determination is wowing and wooing thousands of converts today

How and Why We Go Wrong

Doesn't it seem odd that we would have difficulty keeping God in his unique place on the throne of our life? The Lord God is so great, so good, so beautiful God has done so much for us It is amazing that we could ever be tempted to let other gods come between us and God, let alone replace God in our lives So how is it that we go wrong? Deuteronomy 13 describes three ways by which rival gods gain access into people's lives First, false prophets and religious leaders can lead us astray (Recall also that one of Jesus' three great temptations occurred on the pinnacle of the Jerusalem temple) Second, friends and family members can lead us astray Third, the towns, cultures and societies in which we live often steer us toward other gods We need to be careful and vigilant in all three areas

But why are we so vulnerable? The first reason why we are likely to revere rival gods and to wane in our love for God is that we are distressingly prone to do what is selfish and wrong Here is what often happens We know that the true God is holy Just as Adam and Eve hid from God in shame and fear after their sin, and just as Cain hid after killing his brother Abel, we are inclined to hide from God when we sin Rival gods tempt us by not condemning our sins They may even encourage or justify them This is an illusory and vain strategy, however, because we are progressively enslaved not only to our sin but to the false god standing behind it The true God will point out our sin *(ouch!)*, but then he forgives it and rids us of it

The second reason we are vulnerable is that we are finite, weak and ignorant, which makes us susceptible to deceptive promises of power and insight We are attracted like magnets to any show of power Sometimes we are just plain foolish and forgetful of how wonderful our God is, and we are sidetracked into chasing something far less than the best We get bored because we have been distracted from knowing our exciting, adventurous God We get lost and are then vulnerable to whatever god promises to restore direction to our lives We get lonely and are vulnerable to people who invite us to accompany them and their gods

The rivals to Yahweh make big promises to us, and we are suckers for their sales pitches The serpent promised to Adam and Eve, "You will be like God" (Gen 3 5) Satan promised Jesus "all the kingdoms of the world" and their glory if he would just bow down and worship him (Mt 4 8-9, Lk 4 5-7) In an important sense, Satan could have delivered on that promise, but it would have come at a terrible price All too often, however, these rival gods do not and cannot deliver what they promise (e g , happiness for those who fall down and worship money or sex)

Such are our vulnerabilities to rival gods—even though none of these competitors is in the same league as the true God we know in Jesus Christ

> **Rival gods tempt us by not condemning our sins They may even encourage or justify them. This is an illusory and vain strategy, however, because we are progressively enslaved not only to our sin but to the false god standing behind it The true God will point out our sin (ouch!), but then he forgives it and rids us of it**

Justice and Love for God

It may help us to respect and observe this first great principle if we consider it first as a simple matter of *justice* God *deserves* to be in the god place, on the sacred throne of our life God has a right to be our only god, to not be demoted or replaced The Lord God is our Creator and our Maker and the Sustainer of all life—he certainly deserves some kind of privilege given that! He is also our Redeemer, the one who went to the cross for us, reached out to us, liberated us from our bondage and slavery, forgave us our sins, healed us and welcomed us back into his family—some kind of right and privilege should follow all that! It is an abysmal lack of gratitude and fairness for us not to give God the loyalty he rightfully deserves

Then too, we made a deal, a covenant with God he would be our God and we would be his people God keeps his end of this commitment, he is always faithful, we ought also to be faithful and uphold our end of the covenant To do otherwise is a treacherous betrayal of an agreement, a commitment, we made to him God has a *right* to have a unique, exclusive place in our life as God It is a matter of justice "God desires to be all in all to his children, and claims an exclusive right to their love and obedience "[12]

Consider it first as a simple matter of *justice* God *deserves* to be in the god place, on the sacred throne of our life God has a right to be our only god, to not be demoted or replaced

Yet it's even more than a matter of justice Following the first commandment is above all an issue of love Our relationship with God is not just (or primarily) a matter of observing the rights and provisions of an agreement God is love We love him because he first loved us We are called to love the Lord our God with all of our heart, soul and strength— just as he loved us to the point of laying down his life for us at Calvary This commandment is about a love relationship It is about guarding and nurturing fidelity and faithfulness, and it is about warding off infidelity and adultery

Israel accepted God's sovereignty at Sinai and, in return, was designated as his chosen nation This intimate relationship resembles the bond of matrimony between a man and wife A Jew who worships another god is like a spouse willfully engaging in adultery, the betrayed partner—God—is justified in his anger The prophets who admonished Israel for their sin of idol worship often compared the unfaithful nation to a harlot and an adulterous wife (Ez 16 32, 36, 38) [13]

[12] J H Hertz, ed , *The Pentateuch and Haftorahs Hebrew Text, English Translation and Commentary,* 2nd ed (London Soncino, 1988), p 295
[13] Avroham Chaim Feuer, *Aseres Hadibros The Ten Commandments, A New Translation with a Commentary Anthologized from Talmudic, Midrashic and Rabbinic Sources* (Brooklyn, N Y Mesorah, 1981), pp 33, 56

Rabbi André Chouraqui writes that

one of the constants in the biblical ethic and aesthetic is the comparison of the covenant between Elohim and Israel to a marital covenant This leitmotif leads to a presentation of idolatry as a violation of a conjugal link and shows a link between the second and the seventh command that is more than a figure of speech   Conversely, the corollary of the affirmation of an exclusive love, as celebrated in the Song of Songs, is a privileged relationship with the Supreme Being

In sixteen uses of the word *na'af* [adultery] it describes the act of one prostituted   In sixteen others, the adulteration is committed by Israel or other peoples who fill the earth with falsifications and betrayals in relation to their Creator   The prophets have treated at length the theme of the adulterous Israel, unfaithful spouse of Elohim, or the Church, adulterous spouse of Christ The covenant of Adonai/Yahweh with his people is assimilated to a marriage of love which all infidelity dishonors [14]

In a marriage (or in any other intimate friendship) the biggest threat to happiness is always the appearance of a rival on the scene (I do not mean the appearance of another person, per se, but the rise of a rival— someone who might come between the lover and the beloved or take the place of the beloved) The very first principle, the first and primary movement of love, is to establish a relationship in which the other occupies a unique and exclusive place   That is what spouses want and need from each other above all   Such examples from human life and relationships ring true because human beings are made in the image and likeness of God   This is a veritable law of the universe, a law of all life The first and fundamental expression of love is exclusivity, the unique place of the other   The first thing God asks of us is to be our only God

The first and fundamental expression of love is exclusivity, the unique place of the other The first thing God asks of us is to be our only God.

---

[14]André Chouraqui, *Les Dix Commandements Aujourd'hui* (Paris Robert Laffont, 2000), pp 180-82

Profaning Rival Gods and Drawing Near the True One

An important practice for those who follow the first commandment is to actively, deliberately profane any potential rival gods in our life [15] How do we know when saying no (to a rival) really means no? *Profane* means to treat as ordinary or to desacralize If money appears to be a potential object of worship, we can profane it by giving it away more recklessly than usual If technology is treated with hushed tones of awe and reverence or with ecstatic praise, then let us criticize it and point out its weaknesses, let us refuse to depend on it or let it dominate our lives If our gender is being sacralized, let us joke about it Take the names of false rival gods in vain regularly! Mock them Treat them as ordinary and common Above all, do this with your own temptations (Money? Nationalism?) If these suggested practices cause you to fear or be embarrassed, it may be time for some religious self-examination

Profaning real or potential gods can hurt sometimes if we have already given our hearts away to these gods to some degree Often a broken heart is only healed when we fall in love with someone else Our strategy must be to dump the rivals and flee to the arms of God We must also seek—with our intellect, our spirit and our emotions—the presence of God and cling to him We can aggressively seek to "take every thought captive to obey Christ" and to "be transformed by the renewing of [our] minds" (2 Cor 10 5, Rom 12 2) We should not passively moan about what we gave up but instead actively find ways to "glorify God in your body" (1 Cor 6 20) [16]

We Become Like Our Gods

Some very practical issues are at stake here as well When God is on his throne in our life, things happen God is at work within us as our Liberator and Sanctifier, but we are never just passive recipients of his action We play an active role in relation to our chosen gods First, we tend to imitate our gods

It is necessary to begin with God, for the very simple reason that

---

[15]Jacques Ellul, *The Ethics of Freedom* (Grand Rapids, Mich Eerdmans, 1976)

[16]On seeking God there is a huge literature See Richard J Foster, *Celebration of Discipline* (San Francisco Harper & Row, 1978), and J I Packer, *Knowing God* (Downers Grove, Ill InterVarsity Press, 1973)

[humans] necessarily wish to be like the gods in whom they believe, and, therefore, the kind of gods they believe in will make all the difference to the kind of life which they live   It is of the first necessity to get the idea of God right, for a man will quite inevitably become like the god he worships   It is from here that ethics takes its start A man's god dictates a man's conduct, consciously or unconsciously [17]

Again, "A man becomes like the thing he worships If he puts anything in the place of God, he ultimately becomes like it "[18]

Having the God of Israel and Jesus Christ on our throne thus shapes our identity in critical ways It also brings life, freedom from slavery, safety and peace into our experience Putting a rival god in God's place brings death, bondage, danger and conflict There's also an issue of *meaning* here following this command brings meaning and purpose to our life Meaning in life depends on significance and direction Yahweh grants and affirms our significance in a way that other gods do not He is not a tribal or national god but the creator of the universe, who has made men and women in his image and likeness, as "signs" of his reality and being Yahweh-on-the-throne gives direction and purpose, under his leadership we have a high mission and purpose to pursue

Our Gods Determines Our Goods

Alphonse Maillot has written that

this commandment is *the Commandment,* the commandment par excellence, of which all the others are only the consequences or commentaries   Thus, in truth there are not ten commandments but *one* plus *nine One* true, one great, one alone, and *nine* which develop it, explain it, and show its consequences This is why I would repeat my reticence before a too strong distinction between two tables of the Law   just as in the same way it is erroneous to separate too much the two commandments of the Summary of the Law It is fundamentally the same "you shall

---

[17]William Barclay, *The Ten Commandments for Today* (Grand Rapids, Mich Eerdmans, 1973), pp 17-18

[18]Alan Redpath, *Law and Liberty A New Look at the Ten Commandments in the Light of Contemporary Society* (Old Tappan, N J Revell, 1978), p 25

love " God is the one who delivers and Israel is a people liberated in *all* of its existence Fundamentally there is only one
table, that of the new life, that of freedom for Israel It is not
only at worship, not only in my prayers nor only when I read my
Bible that I may not have other gods, but it is in *all* of my life In
my work, in my family, in my political actions, in my relations
with my neighbor, there is no question that I could have another
God, another reference, another criterion than the one who
delivered me from Egypt out of all my slaveries [19]

Many Jewish rabbis and Christian teachers have argued that the remaining nine commandments are merely elaborations of the first
They delineate nine direct implications of having Yahweh as our living
God If God is truly on the throne of our life, then, we will make no
idols, use his name respectfully, remember his sabbath day, honor our
parents, protect life, marriage, property and reputation, and avoid covetousness There are nine implications of having this God in his unique
place As Luther put it, "Where the heart is right with God and this
commandment is kept, fulfillment of all the others will follow of its own
accord "[20]

Two Ways the First Commandment Helps My Neighbor

Remember that Jesus and Paul said that the *whole* law—not just the
"second half"—can be summed up in the statement "You shall love
your neighbor as yourself " So often this point is lost The first commandment represents the first and most important way of loving and
benefiting your neighbor To view this as a religious and not a moral
command is wrong There are two ways in which this commandment
benefits our neighbors

First, it is great for our neighbor that we worship the God of Israel
and Jesus Christ This is the very best thing I can do for my neighbor
because this commitment leverages everything else of importance in
life This is the God who created *everyone* in his own image and likeness This is not a tribal, racial or national god This is not an African,

---

[19]Alphonse Maillot, *Le Decalogue Une morale pour notre temps* (Geneva Labor &
Fides, 1985), pp 22-23
[20]Luther, *Large Catechism,* p 15

European or Asian God This is the Palestinian/Jew *crossroads* God, the God in whose image both male and female have been fashioned Any time *this* God is truly on life's throne, in obedience to the first commandment, my neighbor's dignity and value will be protected If another god gets on the throne, look out neighbor!

This is the God who believes in justice and compassion, in truth and freedom This is the God who delivers people out of bondage into freedom and who offers forgiveness This is the God who demands respect for one's name, who rejects images, who protects life, property, relationships, truth and a pure heart If this is truly my God, and no other gods are between me and him, then my neighbor benefits This is the first way in which the first commandment preserves and nurtures neighbor-love

Second, this command habituates us to a fundamental pattern of how to love somebody Our neighbors (including spouses, housemates, colleagues, strangers and enemies) are made in the image and likeness of God Therefore, as we learn to love God, we learn at the very same time how to love the neighbor made in God's image and likeness The first movement of love is always and everywhere exclusivity and uniqueness

As we said earlier, the greatest threat to marriage is the appearance of a rival The worst thing you can do is to allow a rival to claim part (or all) of the place reserved alone for your spouse So too with our children, friends, clients the first movement of love is to make sure they have—and know that they have—a unique and irreplaceable place before you If they think they are replaceable, all is lost Children need to feel and know that no matter how many other people are in the family, they have a unique place in their parents' life

Employees also need to feel valued by and unique before their employers and colleagues if they are to flourish. Think too of an enemy or

> The first commandment habituates us to a fundamental pattern of how to love somebody. Our neighbors (including spouses, housemates, colleagues, strangers and enemies) are made in the image and likeness of God Therefore, as we learn to love God, we learn at the very same time how to love the neighbor made in God's image and likeness The first movement of love is always and everywhere exclusivity and uniqueness

stranger If your first principle is to see all people as unique, irreplaceable human beings made in the image of God, you will be far less likely
to dismiss their interests or value Are those people on the other side of
the city (or planet) each unique, irreplaceable beings? If so, how can I
turn away from their need? How could I ever treat them as statistics or
consent to economic or political policies that imply they are valueless
sub-humans?

As we proceed through the rest of the Ten Commandments, we will
see more specifically how to express love to our neighbor But even at
this early stage, it is important to let this commandment permeate us
and reform our relationships It begins in our
head and our heart, in our attitude and our
values Then we act on it We need to pray,
"Lord, help me to truly see those around me
as you see them unique, valuable, made in
your image Help me to carve out a special
place for each of them in my heart and my affections, my consciousness and my actions
Help me to value them and protect their place
in my life Help them to know where they
stand with me "

**Corollary 1 1 Never treat
any persons as though
they are dispensable or
without value Rather,
regard and treat all people
as unique individuals of
great worth.**

This is, more often than we might think, really a matter of justice
Our women colleagues, for example, have a right before God to be
granted dignity and value equal to what is given to men This is justice,
not grace! Our spouse and our children deserve to be treated as
unique, valuable individuals, we are not doing them a "favor" when we
do so This is guarding their freedom to be who they are—who God
wants them to be

The Ethics of Mission Control

Let's look at the first commandment and principle from one final perspective All moral principles with any power to actually guide us point
back to, and are dependent on, an initial choice of a god, purpose and
mission Much of today's ethics overlooks this and is little more than
"damage-control ethics", various moral crises, dilemmas, quandaries
and problems spin out of control and beg for careful analysis and creative resolution Unfortunately, at this damage-control stage our op-

tions tend to be narrow This is not a very good way to do ethics

The alternative approach is to develop an "ethics of mission control" No moral principles or rules have persuasive force unless they can be shown to guide to a mutually desired end If we don't buy the mission, we won't buy the principles and rules The architecture of the Ten Commandments follows this "mission-control" pattern The first commandment clearly establishes the mission by placing on our throne the Lord God of justice, love and freedom If God's position is solid and unrivaled, then his agenda of justice, love and freedom will follow, and we will be formed by the other nine specific area principles

The pattern of the Decalogue provides us with an important insight for our participation in organizational, institutional and business ethics Christians should work first at calling attention to the broader, deeper purposes of such organizations, perhaps questioning them and prodding them toward a richer and better content If we can prod colleagues and organizations explicitly toward the justice, love and freedom of God, that's great But even if our companies do not commit themselves explicitly to the service of God in their mission statements, our encouraging them to commit to larger missional ends (like improving the lives of all stakeholders, being responsible in caring for the environment and so on) can help leverage better ethical performance in the details of daily work Any time Christians can encourage others to address the broader questions of the meaning and purpose of life, work and business, they have contributed something significant

> **Corollary 1 2: All ethical progress (reform, growth, maturity) depends on a clear and compelling vision of an end (purpose, mission)**

While there are management texts with cynical titles like *The Management Principles of Attila the Hun,* it is encouraging that some of the best and most popular business books have promoted this sort of mission-control ethics James Collins and Jerry Porras's *Built to Last* argues that the best long-term companies first "preserve the core" and then "stimulate progress "[21] The order is crucial, they say The core mission and fundamental values must be the first priority Max

---

[21]James C Collins and Jerry I Porras, *Built to Last* (New York HarperCollins, 1994)

DePree's books, such as *Leadership Is an Art,* make the same point in other language the leader's chief responsibility is to tell the story that establishes the identity, mission and values of the company [22]

The fundamental point of the first commandment is to guard and nurture our relationship with the Lord as our only God Without that, the rest of the ethic makes little sense Nevertheless, there are two corollaries to this basic principle One teaches us the first law of all human relationships treat the other person as unique The second teaches us a general ethics lesson that has often escaped the ethics experts first get the mission and end purpose straight, then you can spell out a persuasive ethical stance

For Reflection and Discussion

1 What do you think are the most dangerous rival gods today? Do you agree that the worship of the self may be God's major rival today?

2 How do you work at knowing the true God better in your own life and at making sure no rivals get in the way?

3 Do you agree with the author's emphasis on exclusivity and uniqueness as the first movements in love, whether love for God or love for people? Can you give any examples of how this is evident from your own experience?

4 Describe the mission and purpose of a business or organization that you know well Do you agree that the Ten Commandments teach a basic pattern for all ethics, that is, that ethical "goods" (like the other nine commandments) depend on and follow from our choice of "gods" (the first commandment)?

---

[22]Max DePree, *Leadership Is an Art* (New York Doubleday, 1989)

4

Freedom Now
Vitality and Reality

Our second area principle (prohibiting images and idols) is so tightly related to the first one (prohibiting other gods) that the Jewish, Catholic and Lutheran traditions have considered them together as a single twofold commandment I believe the Reformed and Orthodox traditions have been right, however, in viewing this second commandment as distinct from the first, even though they are intimately related The first principle is about *having* and the second is about *making*, the first is about a *relationship* and the second is about an *activity* This activity is either *reducing God* to a thing or *exalting a thing* into a god To return to the travel metaphor with which we began, this "itinerary" guides our exploration of the land of freedom and vitality (life) in all of its stark reality

The second commandment says, "You shall not make for yourself an idol, whether in the form of anything that is in heaven above, or that is on the earth beneath, or that is in the water under the earth " This is followed by a comment that applies to both the first and second commandments "You shall not bow down to them or worship them, for I the LORD your God am a jealous God, punishing children for the iniquity of parents, to the third and the fourth generation of those who reject me, but showing steadfast love to the thousandth generation of those who love me and keep my commandments" (Ex 20 4-6 par Deut 5 8-10)

The first commandment has to do with the exclusivity and uniqueness of God's place in our lives It prohibits our having other gods *of any type*—including idols and images The second commandment prohibits a specific form of "having"—*having by means of making* for myself In Walter Kaiser's summary, the first commandment concerns the *object* of our worship, the second concerns the *mode* of worship and of relating to that object [1] Dale Patrick puts it this way "Images of other deities would be excluded by the first commandment, but a separate prohibition was required to ban images of Yahweh "[2]

The Bible is full of warnings not to make and worship such idols "The LORD spoke to you   You heard the sound of words but saw no form, there was only a voice

Since you saw no form when the LORD spoke to you at Horeb, watch yourselves closely so that you do not act corruptly by making an idol for yourselves, in the form of any figure" (Deut 4 12, 15-16) If the people persist in substituting idols for God, "the LORD will scatter you among the peoples   You will serve gods made by human hands, objects of wood and stone that neither see, nor hear, nor eat, nor smell" (Deut 4 27-28)

The commandments prohibit any creation or worship of images More than fifty of the 613 laws in the Pentateuch are directed against such idolatry [3] Household idols are described in some of the stories in Genesis Immediately after

The first commandment has to do with the exclusivity and uniqueness of God's place in our lives. It prohibits our having other gods *of any type*—including idols and images The second commandment prohibits a specific form of "having"—*having by means of making* for myself The first commandment concerns the *object* of our worship, the second concerns the *mode* of worship and of relating to that object   . "Images of other deities would be excluded by the first commandment, but a separate prohibition was required to ban images of Yahweh."

---

[1] Walter C Kaiser Jr , *Toward Old Testament Ethics* (Grand Rapids, Mich   Zondervan, 1983), p 85

[2] Dale Patrick, *Old Testament Law* (Atlanta   John Knox Press, 1985), pp 44-45

[3] Laura Schlessinger and Stewart Vogel, *The Ten Commandments* (New York   Harper-Collins, 1998), p 31 For some of these additional laws, see Ex 20 22ff, 34 17, Lev 19 4, 26 1, Deut 27 15 Rupert Davies's *Making Sense of the Commandments*

receiving the Ten Commandments—as Moses slowly worked his way down the mountain back to Israel's camp—the Israelites fashioned a golden calf and began a frenzy of worship (Ex 32) Later on, Gideon made an ephod, which quickly became an idol (Judg 8 27) The bronze serpent lifted up in the wilderness by Moses eventually became worshiped as an idol and had to be destroyed by Hezekiah (Num 21 6-9, 2 Kings 18 4) The books of Samuel and Kings describe the recurring temptation of idols in Israel The prophet Elisha had a dramatic encounter with the idolaters on Mount Carmel (1 Kings 18)

The prophets Isaiah and Jeremiah have long diatribes against making idols (Is 2, 40, 44, 46, Jer 10 3-5) The Psalmist joins the attack on idolatry from time to time (e g , Ps 135 15-18) And every Jewish and Christian kid loves the story of Shadrach, Meshach and Abednego's heroic refusal to bow down to Nebuchadnezzar's huge golden statue (Dan 3)

Jesus addresses the temptation of idolatry by calling the Samaritan woman to worship God in spirit and in truth—not by getting fixated on the Samaritan holy mountain (Jn 4 24) He scolded the Pharisees for exchanging God's living reality for unbending human tradition He warned that Mammon (money) could replace God Paul's great sermon in Athens was occasioned by all the idols he observed (in this city of advanced philosophy, no less), including one altar dedicated "to an unknown god" (Acts 17) Paul warned Christians to "flee from the worship of idols" (1 Cor 10 14, cf Gal 5 20) Idolatry is included in most of the lists of vices in the New Testament So even in the New Testament era it was still appropriate for John to write, "Keep yourselves from idols" (1 Jn 5 21)

What Is an Idol or Image?

According to Kaiser, "there are fourteen Hebrew words for idols or images "[4] The first term in the commandment (Heb *pesel,* "idols") refers to carved, hammered or forged objects made of wood, stone or metal

---

(London Epworth, 1990) argues, however, that "we cannot easily ascribe this vast prohibition to Moses, since for a long time after him various images used in religious worship were officially tolerated" (p 39) Davies sees Gideon's ephod and Jeroboam's idolatry as evidence that Israel officially tolerated rather than prohibited idolatry Contra Davies, these episodes are evidence of human weakness and failure *despite* clear policies and principles to the contrary

[4]Kaiser, *Toward Old Testament Ethics,* p 86

Brevard Childs explains that "making a *pesel* refers, first of all, to an image carved from wood or stone, but which later came to include metal figures as well "[5] The second term (Heb *temunah,* "form, shape or likeness"), Kaiser says, "applies to any real or imagined pictorial representation of deities "[6] Childs explains that "to the prohibition of an image is attached a further specification which broadens the prohibition to include every representation The term *temunah* designates the form or outward shape of an object " On the other hand, he cautions, "it does not denote a mental concept as some have suggested from the Job parallel "[7]

The New Testament term for such images and idols is *eidōlon*—a "visible likeness," perhaps even a "phantom" or "shadow " Visible physical images may seem more real and tangible than a spiritual and transcendent God Yet the reverse is really the case it is the idol that is but a shadow of reality

Such idols and images were sometimes based on heavenly bodies, such as those the Babylonians adored, and sometimes on land or marine animals, such as those the Egyptians worshiped In the fiasco just after the Decalogue was given, when the Israelites fashioned a golden calf, Aaron declared, "These are your gods, O Israel, who brought you up out of the land of Egypt'" (Ex 32 4) Aaron declared a feast not to Ashteroth or Baal but to Yahweh (Ex 32 5) Note this carefully the people are celebrating their liberation from Egypt with a feast to Yahweh [8] The basic problem addressed by the second commandment is the attempt to make an image to represent the true God The intent is not so much to replace God as to represent him

Why would they choose a golden calf to represent Yahweh? Jan Milič Lochman points out that the golden calf or bull "is not only the 'embodiment of fertility' but also symbolizes at the same time military power and strength   [and] the worship of 'Mammon ' "[9] Sexuality,

---

[5]Brevard Childs, *The Book of Exodus A Critical, Theological Commentary* (Philadelphia Westminster Press, 1974), p 404

[6]Kaiser, *Toward Old Testament Ethics,* p 86

[7]Childs, *Book of Exodus,* p 405

[8]Often there is something good at the root of our idolatry—perhaps an effort to get close to God But it goes wrong and has a terrible impact across the generations

[9]Jan Milič Lochman, *Signposts to Freedom The Ten Commandments and Christian Ethics* (Minneapolis Augsburg, 1982), pp 36-37

power and possessions—actually three gracious gifts of God—are exalted above their Giver into idols As Bill Hybels speculates,

> perhaps Aaron felt that the bull, the paragon of power and potency, was an appropriate symbol for the true God After all, hadn't God just done some pretty powerful things? He had sent the plagues, He had parted the Red Sea, He had provided manna and quail and water Certainly, reasoned the Israelites, God would not be offended if they portrayed him as a strong and powerful bull![10]

But they reasoned wrongly

Why Are Idol Worship and Image Making Wrong?

How important is it not to bow down to idols and images?

> The Talmud (*Avodah Zarah* 12a) teaches that it is improper to do anything vaguely resembling prostration before an idol Thus, if a thorn lodged in a person's foot or his money was scattered before an idol, he is not allowed to remove the thorn or to gather the coins in such a way that he appears to be bowing toward the idol [11]

Now *this,* as humorous as it may strike us today, reflects a sensitivity to the true importance of this commandment

Rupert Davies and Walter Harrelson, on the other hand, aren't so sure that idolatry is wrong or all that important Davies boldly says, "The conclusion for modern Christians must be that the Second Commandment as it stands has outlived its usefulness as an element in the moral consciousness of the human race "[12] And here is Harrelson's remarkable insight

> Actually, the higher religions (higher by most standards) are the ones that know how to provide a place for representations of the deity in material form Far from being a mark of crude religious

---

[10]Bill Hybels, *Laws That Liberate* (Wheaton, Ill Victor, 1985), pp 24-25

[11]Avroham Chaim Feuer, *Aseres Hadibros The Ten Commandments, A New Translation with a Commentary Anthologized from Talmudic, Midrashic and Rabbinic Sources* (Brooklyn, N Y Mesorah, 1981), p 32

[12]Davies, *Making Sense,* p 44 Davies concedes that the gods constructed by Afrikaanerdom, Nazism and even Victorian Christendom are examples of unacceptable modern idolatry

understanding, the making of representatives of the divine powers is a highly sophisticated religious practice and rests upon a well-developed understanding of how the transcendent world is to find its depiction here on the material earth The Israelite break with the making of images is an extraordinarily radical break with the high and profound religious understandings of Israel's neighbors [13]

But *why* is image making and idol worship so wrong?

Usurping the Creator's place. Idolatry is wrong because of its arrogance and presumption The creature is playing Creator But the Creator *has already chosen* to witness to his own reality— above all in his speech, by revealing himself through his name "I am Yahweh "

The issue turns on Yahweh's testimony to himself set over against man's The prohibition of images is grounded in the self-introductory formula, "I am Yahweh," which summarizes God's own testimony to himself The contrast to this true witness, the substitution of an image—regardless of whether spiritual or crass—is judged to be a false witness, hence a delusion [14]

We are God's creation, God is not our creation

Downward worship. Idolatry directs our worship downward to something not just less than God but less than human Idols are made and controlled by their makers, they are lesser and lower than their creators To think that we should represent the God of the universe by bits of clay or wood is as insulting as forcing a distinguished visiting dignitary to address an important gathering while wearing a clown costume God is great, higher than the heavens, any idol, no matter how large, is puny by comparison

Partial truth at best. Any image is also necessarily partial—and

---

[13]Walter Harrelson, *The Ten Commandments and Human Rights* (Philadelphia Fortress, 1980), p 62 Try to imagine Aaron quoting Harrelson to Moses as the latter returns from the mountain and reaches the golden calf party "Look, Moses, representing the divine powers is a highly sophisticated religious practice and rests upon a well-developed understanding of how the transcendent world is to find its depiction here on the material earth' Don't be so uptight, crude and primitive'"

[14]Childs, *Book of Exodus,* p 409

thus deceptive Rabbi André Chouraqui says, "Idolatry consists precisely in giving an immanent reality, a substitute for the divine, the worship due to the totality of the Creator Being "[15] At best, an image may capture one or another aspect of God's character—his grandeur, his complexity, his beauty, his simplicity But no image can ever capture the totality of the living God In fact it gets in the way and distracts us For example, while God has appeared in material form, most fully in Jesus Christ, he is also fundamentally invisible and spiritual, and those who worship him must do so "in spirit and truth" (Jn 4 23) Thus Calvin wrote that "every visible shape of Deity which man devises is diametrically opposed to the divine nature "[16]

But it would be a mistake to think that the command is just spiritual versus material The issue here is partial versus whole Hybels writes,

We could never shape, paint, or chisel anything that would be an adequate representation of who God is To attempt to do so would be like asking a scholar to explain the history of the world in one sentence, or a sculptor to make a replica of Mount Rushmore on a single grain of sand, or a musician to play Beethoven's Fifth Symphony with a referee's whistle It just can't be done

Thus, even if Israel's golden calf captured part of God's character, it missed other critical components Their festival soon "degenerated into a sacrilegious orgy Could it be that they focused their attention on God's power, and forgot about his holiness?"[17]

Freedom and vitality or rigor mortis? Idolatry is wrong because it worships what is dead and fixed, whereas God is alive and free Re-

---

[15] André Chouraqui, *Les Dix Commandements Aujourd'hui* (Paris Robert Laffont, 2000), p 113

[16] Calvin *Institutes of the Christian Religion* 2 8 17 I find most artistic representations of "Jesus" appalling A Palestinian Jew could not possibly have looked anything like the Euro-Jesuses often depicted They are deeply alienating and offensive, especially to many people of non-European origin (to say nothing of what the real Jesus must think, looking at this stuff) Jesus could have posed for a sculptor way back when if he thought it was important for us to see him represented this way He chose not to Do you want to disagree with his choice? Do you want people to have to accept your preferred image of Jesus, however historically impossible and culturally alienating it may be to others?

[17] Hybels, *Laws*, pp 23-25

member that freedom is one of the four basic rules of the road for our ethical map The absence of freedom and vitality in idols is a constant theme of the prophetic denunciation

> The idols of the nations are silver and gold,
>> the work of human hands
> They have mouths, but they do not speak,
>> they have eyes, but they do not see,
> they have ears, but they do not hear,
>> and there is no breath in their mouths
> Those who make them
>> and all who trust in them
>> shall become like them (Ps 135 15-18)

Choosing not to imprison God in a fixed image brings us freedom as well Idols and images imprison their makers and worshipers When we eliminate God's freedom, we eliminate our own we tie ourselves to a fixed, predictable, tame substitute for God instead of linking arms with the untamed energy of the living God.

The freedom issue is the key to the whole commandment

Any image eliminates God's freedom to be alive and dynamic in relation to us Jesus died for us once, let's not "kill" him again by confining him to a dead, fixed image Alphonse Maillot argues that the second commandment, "like all the others, is first of all a *deliverance* The Decalogue liberates us now from *representations* of God We no longer have to make an image of God *We no longer have to imagine God* "[18] Choosing not to imprison God in a fixed image brings us freedom as well Idols and images imprison their makers and worshipers When we eliminate God's freedom, we eliminate our own we tie ourselves to a fixed, predictable, tame substitute for God instead of linking arms with the untamed energy of the living God

The living God is vivacious, meeting us day by day, at times angry and jealous, at times compassionate and forgiving God speaks and acts, we listen, watch and respond The very best an idol could do is

---

[18] Alphonse Maillot, *Le Decalogue Une morale pour notre temps* (Geneva Labor & Fides, 1985), p 37 (italics in original)

imitate life [19] Lochman writes,

> God cannot be imprisoned in the forms of this world He is the free and sovereign Lord of his creation, and beyond creation's control No image or mental concept can capture him No cultic practice and no place of worship can guarantee his presence No institution or movement "possesses" him There are no automatic methods of "manipulating" him [20]

"Idolatry substitutes the thing for the person "[21] Bill Hybels puts it this way "Bowing down before any god but the true and living God of Scripture is like hugging a mannequin It can't respond It can't produce It can't offer anything to anyone "[22] Worshiping an image of God is analogous to choosing to relate to *photos* of our children rather than to visit and be with them in person Still worse, it is like adoring someone's drawing or photo of an idealized child while our own living child looks on in sadness and rejection Idolatry is leaving the living God standing there while we play "pretend" with some dead, partial, controllable little representation of God This is ridiculous and insulting

Worshiping an image of God is analogous to choosing to relate to *photos* of our children rather than to visit and be with them in person Still worse, it is like adoring someone's drawing or photo of an idealized child while our own living child looks on in sadness and rejection

Justice and love exclude idolatry. Any idol or image radically contradicts and violates the other three grand rules of the road love for God, love for your neighbor and justice The justice issue is that God deserves—God has a right—to be accepted for who he is, not for what we want to make him out to be He has a right to choose how to repre-

---

[19]Let's be very careful about using high-tech, interactive, virtual reality media to present Jesus to people The more lifelike the medium, the more deceptive, distracting and blinding the effect A more symbolic, caricatured Jesus (like in *Godspell*) is vastly preferable to the "realistic" Jesus of *The Last Temptation* (wholly apart from the historical and theological truths of the former and lies of the latter)

[20]Lochman, *Signposts*, p 48

[21]William Barclay, *The Ten Commandments for Today* (Grand Rapids, Mich Eerdmans, 1973), p 22

[22]Hybels, *Laws*, p 13

sent himself Still more, we have a love issue If the first movement of true love is exclusivity, the second is surely freedom and vitality Love sets the beloved free Love does not impose on the will of the beloved Love does not confine and bind the beloved but instead nurtures growth and vitality

> The justice issue is that God deserves—God has a right—to be accepted for who he is, not for what we want to make him out to be. He has a right to choose how to represent himself.

Think again of human relationships isn't it disastrous to be committed to an image of one's spouse rather than to a living reality? Next only to the pain we feel when we're ignored or treated as dispensable and replaceable is the pain we feel when someone refuses to give us space to become all we can be Love means setting the beloved free, and it begins most fundamentally with our refusal to replace the living God with any images of any kind

The only acceptable images. God has already made the only acceptable image of himself and put it in the world Jesus Christ is "the image of God," "the image of the invisible God" (2 Cor 4 4, Col 1 15) It is to us a paradox that Jesus accepted the natural limitations of human flesh while yet the "whole fullness of deity" dwelled in his body (Col 2 9, Phil 2 7) Jesus was (and is) alive in a way that no humanly made image could ever be The Creator and Redeemer God was present and made visible in his life This is the only image of God we can worship

It is also true, of course, that *every* human being has been made in God's image and likeness—although it may be more accurate to say that *all of us collectively* or *humans in relationships* (especially symbolized in the partnership of man and woman) represent God's image and likeness We are all scarred and broken, but we still carry the recognizable image of our Maker Harrelson argues that "making images stands in the way of seeing   The best possible representation   is the human being "[23]

> Area Principle 2. Never make, serve or worship any humanly made image or representation of God. Rather, honor and pursue the freedom, vitality and reality of the living Lord God.

Let's try now to summarize the basic principle in its positive and negative forms

---

[23]Harrelson, *Ten Commandments*, p 64

Why Is Idolatry Such an Attractive Temptation?

Why would we ever be prone to exchange the glorious freedom of a relationship to the living God for the boring substitute a of static relationship with any idol or image? It seems like such a stupid and costly exchange that few would be tempted by it On the other hand, the temptations of defecting to another god (which we saw in the previous chapter) are at work here as well That is, we might prefer a substitute god that will not expose the painfulness and folly of our sinful habits and choices

But in the case of idols, our temptation is further enflamed by the prospect of a god we can control We think and say that we want the wild and exciting adventure of the living God, but actually we often prefer a more comfortable and mundane security Our idols won't surprise us In fact they won't talk back to us at all All is tame, predictable and safe Our egos may be involved as well "You will be like God," promised the serpent to Adam and Eve (Gen 3 5) Many are somehow tempted to become the Creator Chouraqui says, "The prohibition of idolatry intends to banish all temptation to enclose the supreme being in one's egocentrism, representing it by an image or statue with which one identifies The worship given to the idol becomes worship given to oneself "[24]

Maillot asks,

> Why do we, including we believers, always return to images of God, others, the world, and ourselves? It is because we are at the same time very intelligent and very diminished Reality escapes us to a great extent, others escape us even more, and God still more Therefore we seek to capture them for ourselves by defining them, what they are, what they must be The image is our strangely ambiguous power over the world, over others, over the heavens It is our means of controlling, of creating and recreating It is the means of self-divinization in knowing (or believing

---

[24]Chouraqui, *Les Dix Commandements,* p 76

we know) what others are and, still more, what they must be [25]

Twenty-First-Century Idolatry

Do we have a true idolatry problem today? Is there any evidence that we are creating images of God and substituting them for the real, living God? We should be careful not to overlook the most obvious starting points Is it a positive trend for Christians to be drawn toward the use of religious images, justifying them as (mere?) "icons"? Is bowing, gesturing, praying and burning candles before images and statues—or parading through city streets with huge ornate stuffed Mary dolls and Jesus statues—at all questionable in terms of the second commandment?[26] Overtly religious idolatry is by no means a phenomenon of the past Protestants have no grounds to feel superior here among them the Bible itself is sometimes venerated not just as a vehicle through which God speaks but as a sort of magical object in itself Some jest that the Protestant Trinity is really the "Father, Son and Holy Bible "

But I do not think that this commandment has to do only with self-evidently religious idols and images Idols, like gods in the more inclusive, general sense, do not necessarily come with labels on them saying, "I am an idol " We have to be discerning and self-critical in our analyses Recall again the basic characteristics idols are (1) made by human beings, (2) looked on with holy awe and admiration, (3) passionately defended when attacked or ridiculed, (4) placed at the center of life, meaning, identity and purpose, and (5) looked to in times of need Characteristics (2) through (5) apply to gods as well as to idols It is (1) that makes something specifically an idol in violation of the second commandment Idols are something we make and then treat as our god

Now, with that definition in mind, what might the problem of idolatry in the twenty-first century look like? I suggested at the beginning of this chapter that there are two ways to make an idol either we start

---

[25]Maillot, *Le Decalogue,* p 48

[26]I do not question the motives or piety of those who do these things, nor do I doubt that God is pleased by even our most absurd, bumbling and roundabout efforts to worship him The issue is whether these practices lead us toward or away from the vitality and reality of God

with God and then try to pull downward, squeezing him into some fixed image or form, or we start with something we make and push it upward until we treat it as our god standing over our life In an era of unprecedented wealth and technological wonders, it is not off the mark to suggest that we are prone to push our money or our technology upward and deify them and give them divine status over our lives Remember that Jesus warned that Mammon (money) could be a rival to God So too our "things" can become idols to us—the sources of our life's meaning, the objects of our awe and sacrifice Technology can become our hope and salvation also if we are not careful

Many of today's most serious potential idols come in the form of various ideas As cited earlier, Childs says that in Moses' day the Hebrew term *temunah* (idol) did not stretch to include ideas and thought systems But the functional equivalent of those little icons and statues today is often an idea or a set of ideas Chouraqui reminds us of Henri Bergson's statement that "man is a maker of idols he represents them in their sanctuaries by images and sculptures but more dangerously by ideas, theories, or inventions which transform man into a sorcerer's apprentice "[27]

One of the most serious of these threats comes in the form of the "ism " An "ism" often converts something good into something bad that must be resisted An "ism" is a sort of system, an interpretive and evaluative framework, a worldview or philosophy For example, *technology* can be a great tool in our lives, but when it becomes an all-embracing method applied to all domains at all times, it is *technologism* and must be rejected *Science* helps us understand a lot about our world But when the scientific method is treated as the only method producing reliable or significant knowledge, it is *scientism* and must be resisted *Race* and *nation* can be good things, *racism* and *nationalism* are often idolatrous *Sex* and *gender* have their place and importance, but *sexism* and *genderism* are often idolatrous These "isms" can become powerful control centers in the lives of their devotees, rivaling the place of God Only "Jesus-ism" protects us from the potential idolatry of the "ism "

Getting still closer to home, Alan Redpath writes,

---

[27]Chouraqui, *Les Dix Commandements*, p 89

Another way in which we are in danger of breaking this command is not by the crucifix, or an image, or the priesthood, but in our own mind The images a man makes are not always on the walls of a temple or a house, but on the walls of the mind, graven there secretly worshipped   The graven image of imagination before which we bow down and serve is a very real menace [28]

Redpath has in mind "unholy desires" and "impure thoughts," but he could also include *positively* intended mental constructs Even a dream of a great church could become an obsession and idol

Christians must be extremely careful never to replace the living God with a theological or liturgical system or to put God in a box Hardcore five-point Calvinism, dispensationalism and the name-it-and-claim-it school of modern charismatic televangelism are three examples of systems that can box God in and thus violate the commandment Remember how the devil tried to tempt Jesus with a name-it-and-claim-it approach "throw yourself off this temple, blah blah blah " The living God must not be subordinated to a set of formulas, no matter how well intended they are The paradox and mystery—the "loose ends" of Scripture—must not be denied or papered over to give the illusion that all is perfectly clear This too can become idolatry, replacing the living God with a fixed human system (even if the system is experienced in a noisy tent meeting) God gets jealous of any idols we set up—even Christian ones

Maillot is certain that philosophers and theologians are just as prone as anyone else to fabricate images of God that can only end in a violation of the command We often project on God the human qualities we lack (eternity, omniscience, perfection, etc) In fact, "there is no

[28]Alan Redpath, *Law and Liberty A New Look at the Ten Commandments in the Light of Contemporary Society* (Old Tappan, N J Revell, 1978), p 26

worse slavery than that of ideas and systems which are transformed into ideologies "[29] Ideologies that intend to liberate people end up imprisoning them Ideologies can lead us to disdain the real world or the real church [30]

Iconoclasm and the Freedom of God in Our Life

The good news is that all of these enslaving idols can be toppled and smashed, and we can be set free We need to do a kind of idol inventory once in a while, evaluating our lives using the list of characteristics of idols and images If and when our idol detector goes off, we must desacralize and profane these real—or potential—idols Let's knock all idols off their pedestals Throw them against the wall Tag them with graffiti Be a true "iconoclast " Mock them and smash them Treat them with contempt Use them for ordinary, mundane purposes Deliberately give them away

Woe to us, however, if we get stuck and don't get past the negative, critical iconoclast phase The gospel in this law is the invitation to embrace the living, unpredictable God whose mercies are new every morning, the God who repents and changes in his deep mercy The true God is the God of our second chance, the God who helps us grow, who teaches us, bringing things new and old to us every day

And think about this amazing reality God never replaces *you* with any image of any sort! God doesn't relate to you through some abstraction or system but patiently works with you just as you are To be sure, we are all being sanctified and gradually conformed to the image of God's Son, Jesus Christ But this

> Think about this amazing reality God never replaces *you* with any image of any sort! God doesn't relate to you through some abstraction or system but patiently works with you just as you are

must not be understood in any narrow or restrictive sense Jesus' image is as large and richly diverse as is the image of the body of Christ And at the very same moment that God's Spirit is at work within you,

---

[29] Maillot, *Le Decalogue,* pp 38, 46

[30] Dietrich Bonhoeffer's *Life Together* (1938, New York Harper & Row, 1954) is a powerful little essay about the way well-intended, perfectionist ideas can become instruments of terror and division

God invites you to make choices, to take responsibility, to go this direction or that

Maillot's eloquent and powerful book shows that God never confines
us to any fixed stereotype or image To be created in the image of God
means to be free

Man is the *living* image of a *living* God   We are always new
before him Always ourselves, but always diverse, always new
[God] refuses to "stereotype" us, he believes us capable of invention, of repentance or of conversion, to use the biblical terms, of
a renewal of intelligence God does not believe we are predeter-
mined by our origins, our milieu, our heredity, our education,
our culture, our chromosomes, our good or bad character, and
still less by a divine decree where in advance he would himself
harden us in a posture either to be saved or damned God doesn't
believe in Marx, nor in Freud, nor in Calvin (the Calvin of dou-
ble-predestination) I repeat, God does not believe in images [31]

In the Bible we often see people making choices that are different
(sometimes even opposed) to what God has suggested It was not God's
original intention, for example, that Israel have a king Nevertheless,
God does not reject the people of Israel but rather accepts, redeems
and remolds their lives toward his ultimate purposes God maximizes
our freedom to be and become who we are Love makes no images The
good news—the gospel—is that we are never stuck with a formulaic,
distant, fixed God, rather we are warmly, passionately invited to go
with our living Lord and embark on an indescribable adventure in freedom Idols and images are wrong because they block and prevent that
great adventure

Two Ways the Second Commandment Helps Your Neighbor

The command to make no idols is not just a command to love God
Like the first commandment, it is also a crucial guideline for loving
our neighbor as ourself First, it is good for my neighbor that I maintain a vital, living relation with the living God and that I do not reduce or replace God with a narrow image or idol of my own making
It is good for my neighbor if I am alive and growing in my knowledge

---

[31]Maillot, *Le Decalogue*, pp 40-41, 47-48

of this God of all creation and all humanity

Second, relating to God in this vital fashion also habituates me to the second way of expressing love to any of my neighbors, all of whom are made in God's image Let's return to the example of marriage The worst thing one can do to a spouse is allow a rival to threaten his or her unique, exclusive place (This is the first principle we discussed in the previous chapter) The second worst thing is to create and focus on an image of your spouse, instead of relating to her or him in freedom and living reality We can now state the corollary to the basic principle

> **Corollary 2 1 Never view people through stereotypes and images or as fixed and unchangeable. Rather, do everything possible to guard their freedom and nurture their life and growth**

Lochman is one of few commentators who see this point

> This prohibition of images is also of vital importance for our human relationships with one another We human beings have a notorious and almost incorrigible tendency to "image making" in relation to our neighbors We make our own image of them, seek to "capture" them, take possession of them, to define for ourselves and for them what they "really" are   Caricatures of this sort obstruct our real access to one another and diminish our mutual human freedom, just as God's freedom is endangered when we make a fetish of our theological images and concepts [32]

Lochman quotes Max Frisch, saying,

> The miraculous thing in love is the way it keeps us in a living state of suspense, ready to follow a person through all possible developments   Love releases us from every portrait   The exciting, adventurous, really breathtaking thing about love is that we can never master the loved one, just because, and as long as, we love them   The loved one is rich with every possibility, rich in mysteries, inconceivable [33]

Maillot pushes us in the same direction God "wants also for others

---

[32]Lochman, *Signposts*, pp 49-50
[33]Ibid , p 51

to always be new, never fixed, never assassinated by a definition in an image or in a statue " Stereotypes of people violate the command and undermine our compliance with the other commands

> God has prohibited images   because they freeze one attitude and one definitive personality, that which we imagine In so doing they freeze our relationships with them, and they then freeze ourselves in one definitive attitude The image "murders" the other as much as ourselves It makes of the other, even of God, a statue now silent and stiff that can only repeat itself And by the same action it makes us into a petrified statue The image imprisons the other as much as it imprisons us
>
> [The image] is the death of all freedom, of the freedom of the other as much as our own Let's take an example call someone regularly "an imbecile" and this other, whatever he does or says, will be for you confined, incarcerated in his imbecility, and you too will be fixed in your attitude toward the other by this definitive judgment But for the God of the Bible, life is freedom, not anarchy or craziness but freedom in the sense of newness Life is future and not at all past, open and not at all imprisoned [34]

We can easily see why this is true in loving a child, a patient, a client, a coworker—or an enemy Images get in the way of freedom and love People must be set (or left) free to be alive We will never overcome racial division as long as stereotypes and images rule our thinking about each other Even on the level of international politics, for example, the United States will never be able to relate constructively to Iran or Libya or Korea if it always relates to a fixed image that assumes these people cannot grow or change Any good manager or business leader approaches people with respect for their freedom, vitality and growth, refusing to stereotype any employee as "only a techie" or "only a secretary" or "only a bureaucratic functionary " A good manager is open to each employee's potential for growth, she regularly asks what they want to learn next, or how they would like to grow and improve in the coming year, and then she supports and enables this freedom and growth

We can never forgive a hardened criminal or an enemy (or an erring spouse or a child or a parent) if we cling to a negative image of him and

---

[34]Maillot, *Le Decalogue,* pp 40-42, 47-48

assume he cannot change Woe to the father who creates and commits to an image of his son as a certain kind of athlete or professional and does not accept and love him for what God may wish to make of his life and gifts Shame on spouses who hang on to idealized images of their mates at age thirty and fail to value their mates' freedom, change, growth and discovery through their fifties and sixties

Not only must we avoid substituting images for the living God, we must not create images of our spouses, children or coworkers, of other ethnic and national groups, of the opposite sex, or even of our own selves!

In the same way, we must also be careful not to fashion images of our own selves![35] Stereotypes and images are the foils of personal life and growth Think of how many people go through life miserable because they try to measure up to some ridiculous physical image or to an unattainable intellectual or vocational image How liberating it is to accept ourselves as the unique beings God has made us to be and then just "play the hand we have been dealt" for all it is worth Let us stay free and alive and growing and allow our neighbors to do the same

How Shall We Then Make?

The second commandment does not prohibit all material art or sculpture, nor does it imply a rejection of the physical and material world per se What it prohibits is the sacralization of nature or of what we have made The material world is not bad, but what we do with it can be bad William Barclay says that "idolatry means making means into ends In the beginning an idol was   a means toward making memory and worship easier, in the end it became itself the object of worship The means had become the end "[36] Joy Davidman writes, "An idol is only an inanimate object that can do no harm   So is a gun But a man can do great harm with it Idolatry lies not in the idol but in the worshipper It is a psychological attitude that governs his whole life "[37]

God made the earth (he did not just emanate a few great ideas) and called it "very good " God's future promises include a resurrection, not a

---

[35]See Maillot (again on target!), *Le Decalogue*, pp 50-51
[36]Barclay, *Ten Commandments*, p 21
[37]Joy Davidman, *Smoke on the Mountain An Interpretation of the Ten Commandments* (Philadelphia Westminster Press, 1953), p 39

forsaking, of the body and a new earth as well as a new heaven The Bible shows that there is a valued place for art, architecture, building and making in our relations to the living God Thus the ark, tabernacle and temple in ancient Israel—and water, bread and wine in the church—are all material things richly symbolic of God and his truth and life The second commandment warns us that such material art and artifacts are not to be *identified* with God—*associated*, perhaps, but not identified

> "What the Second Commandment prohibits is not all images and all image-making (the plastic arts) but only the religious or ideological transformation of images and pictures into *cultic* objects 'You shall not *bow down* to them nor *serve* them ' The protest here is against the misuse not the use of the plastic arts "[38]

Corollary 2 2· Never think of, or act toward, anything you make as though it is sacred per se Rather, offer everything you make in service and tribute to God.

We need to state this as another corollary to our basic principle

Consequences: For Better and for Worse

This is serious business The consequences of having other gods (forbidden by the first commandment) and of making images (forbidden by the second commandment) are significant God is angry, jealous and displeased We have trampled on his just rights and treated our covenant with contempt Our loving relationship is broken down We are separated and alienated from the God of life As the Exodus text says, "I the LORD your God am a jealous God, punishing children for the iniquity of parents, to the third and the fourth generation of those who reject me, but showing steadfast love to the thousandth generation of those who love me and keep my commandments" (Ex 20 5-6)

What does it mean to say that our Lord gets *jealous*? God is not some impersonal force or an abstract, detached being, but a living, relational person who admits to being jealous He cares He is offended and jealous because he loves us As Patrick says,

> Far from being a base, primitive motive, jealousy is the logical expression of the mutually exclusive relation existing between God and God's people Like a monogamous marriage, which involves

---

[38]Lochman, *Signposts*, p 47

mutually exclusive sexual access, the relationship between Yahweh and Israel excludes any competing relationship [39]

Another explanation is given by Rabbi J H Hertz

> The Hebrew root for "jealous" *kanna,* designates the just indignation of one injured   He hates cruelty and unrighteousness, and loathes impurity and vice, and, even as a mother is jealous of all evil influences that rule her children, He is jealous when, instead of purity and righteousness, it is idolatry and unholiness that command their heart allegiance It is, of course, evident that terms like "jealousy" or "zeal" are applied to God in an anthropomorphic sense It is also evident that this jealousy of God is of the very essence of His holiness [40]

The second lesson to be drawn from this text is that our actions and choices affect those around us, across the generations Our fundamental choices about the God we worship, as well as about our aim and purpose in life, affect those around us for better or worse If we reduce the living God to a fixed image of any kind, the results are tragic for those under our influence

On the other hand, our good choices have even more extensive positive effects on those around us The third lesson here is that the anger of God and the grace of God are not equally balanced The rabbis looked at the three to four generations who suffer in comparison to thousands of (i e , at least *two* thousand) generations who are blessed and concluded that God's gracious love is at least five hundred times as powerful as his anger' Elsewhere we read that ours is a God of mercy and generosity whose "anger is but for a moment" but whose "favor is for a lifetime" (Ps 30 5) This is not a balanced scale The side bearing the good is far heavier We sometimes think the Old Testament presents an angry, stern God of judgment whereas the New Testament presents a loving Father But the same God of overwhelming grace and mercy is present in both testaments

The fourth lesson is a bit more complex How (and why) does God visit the sins of the fathers on the children to the third and fourth generation?

---

[39]Patrick, *Old Testament,* p 43

[40]J H Hertz, ed , *The Pentateuch and Haftorahs Hebrew Text, English Translation and Commentary,* 2nd ed (London Soncino, 1988), pp 295-96

This troubling statement must be understood in the broader context of Scripture, which makes clear that we are personally responsible before God for our own sins, not for those committed by others "It is only the person who sins that shall die" (Ezek 18 4) "Parents shall not be put to death for their children, nor shall children be put to death for their parents, only for their own crimes may persons be put to death" (Deut 24 16)

Still, we are not isolated, autonomous individuals God created a humanity in relationship, a humanity in varying degrees of solidarity, for better and for worse We both benefit and suffer from what others do

In this sense God *visits* consequences on others not by a direct decision to punish Joe for what Jane has done but by his more general action in creating the world in such solidarity and allowing things to take their course according to our decisions

> **We both benefit and suffer from what others do In this sense God *visits* consequences on others not by a direct decision to punish Joe for what Jane has done but by his more general action in creating the world in such solidarity and allowing things to take their course according to our decisions.**

In particular, with this text, the rabbis explained that almost any ancient household contained three or four generations in close proximity (The isolated, two-generation nuclear family is a more recent invention of industrialized Western societies) From great-grandparents to great-grandchildren, people lived together (and still do in most parts of the world) Thus when a father or grandfather brought strange gods or idols into a household, it corrupted and negatively affected the household to the third and fourth generation until he finally died and his idols could be taken out with him

> The Torah expresses this concept in terms of four generations because it is common for that many generations of a family to be alive at the same time, with the youngest generation observing the bad examples of grandparents and great grandparents The great-grandchild may then be judged as having opted for the ways of his father, grandfather, and great-grandfather   Children share the responsibility—and hence deserve the punishment—only if they adopt the sins as their own [41]

[41]Feuer, *Aseres Hadibros*, pp 35, 34

That the corruption was appropriated by those third and fourth generations is indicated by the phrase *of those who hate me*

Calvin wrote that "the visitation of which we now speak is accomplished when God withdraws from the children of the wicked the light of his truth   [and they are] left to walk in their parents' steps   The miser[ies] which they suffer in time   are thus punishments   for their own iniquity "[42] It is in this way that iniquity is visited on children and grandchildren [43] Our actions have consequences on those around us, this is built into the nature of the world and human relationships Let's opt for vitality and reality not just for ourselves, but also for those affected by our choices

For Reflection and Discussion

1 What, in your view, are the major false images of God today? Have you ever felt trapped by a false image of Jesus or God or the Holy Spirit?

2 Have you ever felt hurt or hindered in some way by an image or stereotype imposed on you by someone else? What did you do about it?

3 What are the most harmful stereotypes and images you notice in our culture today? How about within the church? What can be done to remove these images?

4 How do you respond to the author's explanation of the way God's judgment and blessing affect others in our families and communities? Do you agree that this is how it works, or do you have a different way of explaining these matters?

---

[42]Calvin *Institutes* 2 8 20

[43]In my opinion, *most* of the punishments and judgments of God in the Bible follow this pattern God is excluded and withdraws his presence, allowing nature and society to take their course Only on rare occasions do we see God "pulling the trigger" or directly "pushing a judgment button " The curses of Genesis 3 on Adam and Eve are also of this type in that painful childbearing and childrearing, toilsome, difficult labor, and a more fundamental marital alienation and sexual stereotyping are the natural result of forsaking and excluding God

5

Word Power
Naming and Respect

Traditionally, the third commandment seemed pretty simple and straightforward to follow First, do not curse and swear Second, when you raise your hand and take an oath in court to tell the truth, you had better do so But what is the territory covered by this area principle? What is the itinerary here for life's ethical journey? How does the third commandment relate to the two that precede it and to the four rules of the road (our cover principles)?

The third commandment says, "You shall not make wrongful use of the name of the LORD your God, for the LORD will not acquit anyone who misuses his name" (Ex 20 7 par Deut 5 11) The King James Version put it in the familiar language of not taking the name of the Lord "in vain " The threat on the end of this command helps us understand that, whatever else this commandment is about, misusing God's name is serious business to God "Any prophet who speaks in the name of other gods, or who presumes to speak in my name a word that I have not commanded the prophet to speak—that prophet shall die" (Deut 18 20) On the other hand, great blessing comes with the right use of God's name

The third commandment follows logically from the first two The first two orient our hearts and lives to the living God Luther observed that "the first things that issue and emerge from the heart are words "[1]

---

[1] Martin Luther, *The Large Catechism*, trans Robert H Fischer (1529, Philadelphia Fortress, 1959), p 15

The second commandment forbids making an image as a representation of God, the third guards God's chosen mode of self-revelation through his name That is, the third commandment is about speech and communication "Who gives speech to mortals? Is it not I, the LORD? Now go, and I will be with your mouth and teach you what you are to speak" (Ex 4 11-12) God created the world by speaking his word (e g , "Let there be light," Gen 1 3) God redeemed the world by sending his Word to be made flesh The third commandment launches us on an ethical itinerary in the arena of human communication

The Importance of God's Name

What is it about God's name that is so important? The great Old Testament scholar Brevard Childs wrote that "the use of the name of God played an important role in Israel's faith from the beginning "[2] Rabbi André Chouraqui says, "The Name of Adonai/Yahweh is the key to all biblical revelation This Name is protected in an absolute manner by the divine Legislator when he presents himself it is the most sacred Name of the Bible which conditions the whole Revelation in its most universal components "[3] In Jewish tradition, the name of God is regarded as so holy that it should only rarely be pronounced Rather than saying "Yahweh" many Jews say (or write) "HaShem" (the name) or write "G-d " Something like this reticence to use God's name casually also explains why Matthew's Gospel substituted "heaven" for "God", that is, Matthew writes of the "kingdom of heaven" whereas Mark and Luke write of the "kingdom of God")

In biblical times, names in general meant more than they often do today Adam named the animals at God's request—and then renamed woman Eve after the Fall, *not* at God's request[4] When parents named

---

[2] Brevard Childs, *The Book of Exodus A Critical, Theological Commentary* (Philadelphia Westminster Press, 1974), pp 411-12

[3] André Chouraqui, *Les Dix Commandements Aujourd'hui* (Paris Robert Laffont, 2000), p 203

[4] Before the Fall, Adam says, on seeing the woman, "this one shall be called Woman" (Gen 2 23) Note that, first, he does not personally name her (active voice) but rather describes (passive voice) what she shall be called, and second, that the two similar terms for man and woman, *ish* and *ishah*, emphasize their closeness, common flesh and complementarity After sin enters the Garden, Adam names (active voice) his partner Eve, which means "mother of all living" (Gen 3 20) Let me make

their children, it was a major event Even naming places was full of significance (e g , Bethel means "house of God", Salem means "peace")
Names expressed and designated character Abraham ("father of a multitude"), Sarah ("princess"), Sarai ("Jah is prince"), Jacob ("sup-
planter"), Israel ("striving with God"), Esau ("hairy"), David ("beloved"), Peter ("rock")—all of these names designate something about
that person's character and qualities They were not chosen just because they sounded nice

There are many "gods" but only one true God (Elohim), who reveals
himself through his various names and titles God names himself as well
as what he has made Walter Kaiser says that God's name reveals and
describes to us "(1) his nature, being, and very person,   (2) his
teaching and doctrines,   (3) his ethical directions and morals "[5] Yahweh, the name by which God revealed himself to Moses and Israel, is related to the Hebrew verb "to be" and to phrases such as "I am who I
am," "I will be," "I will be with you" or "He is" (Ex 3 12, 14-15) God
shall be called "Wonderful Counselor, Mighty God, Everlasting Father,
Prince of Peace" (Is 9 6) Later on, the Messiah incarnate would be
named Jesus, for "he will save his people from their sins" (Mt 1 21) He
will be called Immanuel, which means "God with us" (Is 7 14, Mt 1 23)

The major issue here is respect Do we insist on having dominion
and naming God as we wish? Or will we respect God's dominion over
his own name and its use? Speaking a name either affirms or denies
those persons of whom or to whom we speak If we speak their name as
they have taught and asked us, we are respecting who they are and
their freedom If we give them another name (or even another pronun-
ciation), we are asserting our power over them Saying a name is (always symbolically, often practically) the first word we speak in starting
a conversation or establishing a relationship It sets a tone It initiates
the relationship It is a powerful act to say a name *What* we use as a

---

two observations First, by the act of naming, Adam is establishing a hierarchy God
didn't specify Adam was to name the animals, which are under his dominion, not
the woman, his mate and partner Second, Eve, "mother of all living," is a great
name, but it is stereotyped and does not represent fully the job description woman
and man were given together in Genesis 1—2 This limitation is part of the curse of
sin God *describes* it, God never *prescribed* it We must overcome it
[5]Walter C Kaiser Jr , *Toward Old Testament Ethics* (Grand Rapids, Mich Zondervan, 1983), p 88

name often has tremendous impact on the relationship How we say it affects the conversation and relationship that follow

Think about this for a moment How you would feel if after you introduced yourself to someone carefully and clearly, she rarely used your name to speak to you, even when you were in the same room? (What an insult!) And how would you feel if every

> Saying a name is (always symbolically, often practically) the first word we speak in starting a conversation or establishing a relationship It sets a tone. It initiates the relationship It is a powerful act to say a name How we say it affects the conversation and relationship that follow.

time something bad happened to her, she yelled out your name in anger? Well then, how do you think God feels when we treat him this way? How do you think Jesus reacts? Imagine again that you hear someone yelling out your name in panic You come running but find that whoever was yelling didn't really mean it He had no interest in you whatsoever It's just that something terrible happened to him and that was the name he yelled Will you always be standing, eager for a warm relationship with such an ignorant, disrespectful person like this? One of the first ways of demonstrating respect for others is to learn the names (and labels) they have chosen for themselves and to use them in a respectful way

Wrongly Using God's Name

Israel was forbidden to revile God (Ex 22 28), to profane God's name (Lev 20 3), to blaspheme (Lev 24 13-16), to curse (2 Kings 2 24), to defile (Ezek 43 8), to abuse (Prov 30 9) or to swear falsely with God's name (Ex 23 1, Lev 19 12) The phrase translated in the KJV as "in vain" (Heb *shaw*) has the root meaning of "empty" or "groundless." As Childs explains,

> Isaiah 1 13 speaks of "worthless" offerings Psalm 31 7 calls idols *shaw* because they are without substance and vain Psalm 12 3 suggests that flattery is *shaw* because it is without substance False prophecy can be *shaw* not because of the intention to deceive, but because objectively it is without any reality, and therefore false [6]

---

[6]See Childs, *Exodus*, pp 410-11, for these examples and this explanation

The name is not itself empty, of course, it is the user and the justification that can be empty and vain

Alphonse Maillot does not like the translation of *shaw* as "vain" because, he argues, there is no use of God's name that is actually empty, vain or without impact God's name is indissolubly linked with God's presence Our human names represent us, but since we are finite, we cannot and do not always respond when our names are lifted up But God *always* hears, *always* responds

> Its pronunciation is always followed by consequences Besides, the Hebrew mind does not conceive of nothingness or of a neutral act An action is always "for or against " One cannot translate with "in vain" for the simple reason that in the Old Testament it is not possible to take the name of the Lord in vain It is not possible to pronounce the name without anything happening,   without consequences for better or worse, as much for the recipient as the author Because when the name of the Lord is pronounced certain things happen—the Lord is there, present [7]

To take God's name in vain means to abuse it, to use it in an empty, ordinary or profane way, to use it for mischief or harm, to use it lightly or idly, insincerely or falsely, to use it for unreality, or to use it in a frivolous or groundless fashion Rabbi J H Hertz says,

> The third commandment forbids us to dishonor God by invoking his name to attest what is untrue, or by joining His name to anything frivolous or insincere   This verse, according to the rabbis, forbids using the Name of God in false oaths   as well as in vain and flippant oaths   God's Name is, moreover, not to be uttered unnecessarily in common conversation [8]

As Kaiser outlines it,

> the vain or empty purposes to which God's name may be put are (1) to confirm something that is false or untrue, (2) to fill in the gaps in our speech or prayers, (3) to express mild surprise, and

[7] Alphonse Maillot, *Le Decalogue Une morale pour notre temps* (Geneva Labor & Fides, 1985), pp 59-61

[8] J H Hertz, ed , *The Pentateuch and Haftorahs Hebrew Text, English Translation and Commentary,* 2nd ed (London Soncino, 1988), p 296

(4) to use that name when no clear goal, purpose, or reason for its use is in mind, whether it be in prayer, in a religious context, or absent-mindedly invoked as table grace when no real heart, thankfulness, or purpose is involved [9]

Calvin wrote that God's "name is profaned with vain and wicked abuse because it is applied to a purpose foreign to that to which it is consecrated "[10]

Perjury—swearing falsely—is one of the wrongful uses of God's name Perjury is when one makes an oath (or a vow or a promise) that invokes God's name and witness and then breaks that oath "The LORD your God you shall fear, him shall you serve, and by his name alone you shall swear" (Deut 6 13, cf Deut 10 20) When you swear or make an oath, you must perform it (Num 30 2-4, cf Jer 5 2, 7 9, Zech 5 4, Mal 3 5) If one says, "I swear in God's name that I'm telling the truth," and then is not truthful, he has misused and profaned God's name It shows contempt for God to commit such perjury

Jesus tells us to avoid the common practice of binding oneself by sacred oaths "Do not swear at all, either by heaven, for it is the throne of God, or by the earth, for it is his footstool   Let your word be 'Yes, Yes' or 'No, No', anything more comes from the evil one" (Mt 5 34-37) Later, Jesus was put under oath at his trial (Mt 26 63) Paul gave a sworn pledge to the Galatians (Gal 1 20) We can conclude from this that perjury is always wrong and that binding ourselves with oaths should be minimized lest we be guilty of vainly using of God's name

Blasphemy is the worst form of misuse, it is a direct verbal assault on God and his name One who blasphemes curses or reviles God by speaking against the Name (Lev 24 10-23) Jesus was accused of blasphemy for claiming to be the Son of God "[We] are going to stone you   for blasphemy, because you, though only a human being, are making yourself God   Jesus answered,   "Can you say that the one whom the Father has sanctified and sent into the world is blaspheming because I said 'I am God's Son'? If I am not doing the works of my Father, then do not believe me" (Jn 10 33-37, see also Mt 26 63-65)

---

[9] Kaiser, *Toward Old Testament Ethics*, p 88
[10] Calvin *Institutes of the Christian Religion* 2 8 22

Profanity is to use the sacred Name for ordinary purposes, thereby
making it common It profanes the Name to use it in an empty, vain,
idle, trivial or groundless fashion When God's name is used in cursing
someone (or something), this is almost certainly profaning his name
because either we do not even think about God when we say his name
or we may actually intend that God damn or punish someone as we
speak the curse even though this wish totally contradicts God's will
and character

Hypocrisy, professing and adopting God's name but acting in a way
that contradicts the claim, is another violation of God's name In fact
this may be one of the most common and worst of the violations of the
third commandment [11] Chouraqui says, "To *lift up the Name* necessarily implies taking responsibility for the orders which are promulgated
and authenticated by this name   *Lifting up the Name* implies an alliance, a marriage with him, an obedience to his orders, an adhesion to
his wishes, an adherence to his presence, a constancy "[12]

Being called by God's name and then not acting like it brings shame
on the Name Isaiah says, "Hear this, O house of Jacob, who are called
by the name of Israel,   who swear by the name of the LORD and invoke the God of Israel, but not in truth and righteousness" (Is 48 1)
Ezekiel, too, recounts such hypocrisy

> When the house of Israel lived on their own soil, they defiled it
> with their ways and their deeds   They had shed [blood]
> upon the land and   defiled it [with their idols]   I scattered
> them among the nations,   [and] wherever they came, they
> profaned my holy name, in that it was said of them, "These are
> the people of the LORD, and yet they had to go out of his land "
> (Ezek 36 17-20)

The rabbis taught "do not wear holy articles to look like a man of God

---

[11]Laura Schlessinger and Stewart Vogel write that "the true translation of this commandment from the Hebrew points to 'carrying the Lord's Name in vain ' That
means that actions, behaviors, and positions we take in God's name must not de-
fame Him History is pockmarked with episodes of torture, murder, rape, and plun-
dering all in 'God's name ' This, of course, is a deeper profanity" *The Ten
Commandments The Significance of God's Laws in Everyday Life* (New York HarperCollins, 1988), pp 68-69

[12]Chouraqui, *Les Dix Commandements,* p 91

and then, disregarding his Name, go forth and commit transgressions "[13]
In the New Testament, Jesus gives a similar warning

> Not everyone who says to me, "Lord, Lord," will enter the kingdom of heaven, but only the one who does the will of my Father in heaven On that day many will say to me, "Lord, Lord, did we not prophesy in your name, and cast out demons in your name, and do many deeds of power in your name?" Then I will declare to them, "I never knew you, go away from me, you evildoers " (Mt 7 21-23)

Many were profaning the Lord's name in this way (cf 1 Jn 1 6-7, 10, 2 4-5)

Magic is another wrongful use of God's name Maillot says that magic is "very simply, the attempt, through various rites and spoken formulas, to put in motion the divinity or the divine powers and to order them to carry out what, by ourselves, we have neither the opportunity or power to do "[14] In the ancient Near Eastern context of the Old Testament, this was a common view of how the names of gods work

> **Perjury, blasphemy, profanity, hypocrisy and magic are five forms of the misuse of God's name.**

Word Power: Naming God with Respect

The positive, gospel side of the third commandment is extraordinary As Luther says,

> With the words, "You shall not take the name of God in vain," God at the same time gives us to understand that we are to use his name properly   in service of truth and all that is good when we swear properly   when we teach properly   when we call on his name in time of need, or praise and thank him in time of prosperity   God is well pleased with the right use of his name and will as richly reward it, even as he will terribly punish its misuse [15]

---

[13] Avroham Chaim Feuer, *Aseres Hadibros The Ten Commandments, A New Translation with a Commentary Anthologized from Talmudic, Midrashic and Rabbinic Source* (Brooklyn, N Y Mesorah, 1981), p 38

[14] Maillot, *Le Decalogue*, p 62

[15] Luther, *Large Catechism*, pp 17-19

In Israel, one praised, called on, prophesied in, blessed in, trusted in and sought refuge in the Name of the Lord God (Gen 4 26, Deut 18 19, Jer 11 21, Ps 69 30, Ps 72 19, Is 50 10, Zeph 3 12) The good news at the heart of the third commandment is that we *can* know the true God by name We can call out his name in prayer We are adopted into God's family, and that brings with it a new family name and identity Israel

---

Area Principle 3. Never use any of God's names in a trivial, negative or disrespectful way. Rather, speak to him by name daily, share his name with joy, and live up to his name as you bear it

---

and the church are called by his name Individual men and women are the sons and daughters of God We are God's own children, with family—true brothers and sisters, parents and children—all over the world We can approach our heavenly Father in the name of Jesus and be heard and cared for in an amazing way "Ask anything in my name," Jesus tells us (Jn 14 13-14)

This privilege of knowing and rightly lifting up God's name is good news Jesus taught us to pray, "Our Father in heaven, hallowed be your name" (Mt 6 9) This means "let your name be holy" (sacred, different), not lost among other names or treated as an ordinary name Let it be (and let it be seen as) different and holy, not as profane and ordinary Jesus also glorified God and his name by "completing the work" God gave him to do—making God known in the world, speaking God's words, doing God's acts, fulfilling God's will We too can glorify God's name in all the earth by our lives As Paul put it, "Do everything in the name of Lord Jesus" (Col 3 17)

As we have seen in the first two commandments, so with the third God not only commands this practice concerning his name, he demonstrates it perfectly in his relationship to his people and their names God knows my name My name is written down in his book of life (Rev 21 27) He calls my name, and he accepts and respects me for who I am He also gives me a new name of promise and challenge He speaks to me with total respect The Good Shepherd "calls his own sheep by name" (Jn 10 3) God never misuses or belittles our name He speaks to us whenever we are ready, through Jesus and Scripture, with and through the Holy Spirit and the church

Today's Misuses of God's Names

We are surrounded today by a culture of disrespect, loud profanity, cursing and vulgarity I want to join in the protest—with three additional comments First, I think it important to be clear about *what* is wrong and *why*, and not lump all offensive speech together Second, I want to move beyond the common focus on vulgar and profane speech to consider some other, perhaps less obvious, misuses of God's name today Third, I want to comment on the debate about male terms for God (e g , Father)

Profanity and vulgarity. *Casual profanity* is very common today How often do people casually say, "O my God," "O Lord Almighty" or, worst of all, "Jesus Christ"? The name of God is being said without the speaker's meaning it, without her actually thinking of, or calling out to, the reality of the one named It is a totally empty summons In particular, the phrase "Jesus Christ" grates on our ears so intensely because it is the personal name of God's Son, our Savior The casual uses of "God" and "Lord" offend a little less because they are more like titles than proper names And yet since we only know one God and one Lord, the connection is impossible to miss

Cursing is a popular form of profanity "God damn it" is pronouncing a curse, expressing a wish to consign a person or situation to punishment in hell I suppose we could say that the curses "God damn cancer," "God damn incest" or "God damn war" have more going for them! Nevertheless, we need to be very careful about casually, or angrily, throwing out such curses in the name of our God To say to a person, "Go to hell" or "God damn you" trivializes a rather serious issue

Let's go a step further Many old-timers (not so many of our contemporaries) got very upset about what they called "minced oaths " These are words that intentionally come close to the sound and impact of banned cuss words, such as "darn," "dang," "heck," "gosh darn it," "golly," "gee," "gee whiz" and so on The list is long Should we worry about this? Ask yourself these three questions First, *How does this affect me? (Am I really thinking and meaning "damn" when I say "darn" or "Jesus" when I say "gee whiz"?)* Second, *How does this language affect those who hear me? (Are they startled by its similarity to "damn," "Jesus," etc ?)* Third, *How does God feel when I play such word games with his names?* The minimum criticism we must

make is that people who rely on language like this lack imagination and
a decent vocabulary'

Alongside but distinct from profanity is *vulgarity* Vulgar means
"common, coarse or unrefined " Vulgarity is often offensive and insulting even though it is not really a violation of the third commandment
We would do better to get our
categories straight and concern
ourselves with the big stuff, such
as profanity Vulgar talk usually
refers to sexual acts, to our excretory functions or to the body
parts involved in these [16] Sometimes the holy and the vulgar are
combined to further maximize
the auditory impact

> **Vulgar means "common, coarse or
> unrefined " Vulgarity is often offensive
> and insulting even though it is not really
> a violation of the third commandment
> We would do better to get our categories
> straight and concern ourselves with
> the big stuff, such as profanity**

In my opinion, sexual vulgari-
ties are the ones that should trouble us most Sex should be a joyful,
mutual and creative part of our marriages Using sexual euphemisms as
insults or as expletives when terrible things happen or as threats of violence is a *terrible* message to communicate Combining sexual refer-
ences with thoughts of violence and anger and disaster is a mistake We
should not participate in such talk under any circumstances, and we
should do whatever we can to limit such talk in our family and society

On the other hand, when something terrible happens (e g , you
hit your thumb with a hammer or you fail to get your proposal done
because your computer crashes), it is not wholly inappropriate to
think of such disasters in metaphors and language representing useless and foul-smelling waste products This insults and degrades no
one The only issue here is that we should not unnecessarily give offense to others

Christian misuse of the Name? Is it profanity to casually put
bumper stickers with the name "Jesus" on your car or to say, "God
bless you" or "God bless America" unthinkingly? Laura Schlessinger
brings up another issue

---

[16]I have sanitized my text and deleted examples of these vulgar terms, but frankly, I
would urge parents and teachers to say the words out loud in discussions with kids
Discuss the words, explain them and demystify them

Did you ever wonder about the prayers offered by football teams huddled together before the beginning of the game? Will God help the team with the best prayer? If their prayer is asking God to help them win, it is a vain prayer When we turn God into a coach who can have an impact on the outcome of a game, we belittle his essence and take His name in vain If football players gather together and pray that they play to the best of their abilities and exhibit the highest standards of sportsmanship, they acknowledge the true role of God in their game [17]

To this list Alan Redpath adds

using the name of the Lord in jokes, the frivolous use of the name of Jesus in songs, the superficial lighthearted program that so often we put over, the exaggerated account of God's blessing on his work in order to produce funds for future operations The hypocrisy of the Church is far worse than the profanity of the street The blasphemy of the pew is a more insidious form of evil than the blasphemy of the slum To pray and not to practice, to believe and not to obey, to praise and yet at heart to rebel, is to take the name of the Lord in vain [18]

Too often we hear preachers claiming to speak for God Too often we hear enthusiastic Christians claiming that "God told" them to do this or that This may sound great, but it is unacceptable and profane if these words express just a wish or way of speaking Walter Harrelson is especially concerned about religious leaders who misuse the name by trying to threaten, intimidate and frighten others, and who are "maintaining their financial empires by threats against sinners in the name of God Equally appalling is the issuing of palliatives in the name of religion, offering a soothing syrup in place of a demand for justice "[19]

Maillot thinks the worst form of misuse is when magic invades the church

---

[17] Schlessinger and Vogel, *Ten Commandments,* p 79

[18] Alan Redpath, *Law and Liberty A New Look at the Ten Commandments in the Light of Contemporary Society* (Old Tappan, N J Revell, 1978), pp 37-38

[19] Walter Harrelson, *The Ten Commandments and Human Rights* (Philadelphia Fortress, 1980), p 75

Do not think simply of our Catholic brothers and what we call their superstitions   There are many Protestants for whom the essential work of Jesus Christ is still to help them escape their sicknesses   or to promise them a win in the national lottery or to have a successful grade on the final examination Jesus Christ is for them a sort of "all risk insurance" in a difficult existence He is no longer the Word who saves, who pardons, who renews He is a passbook for a savings bank account[20]

It gets even worse At least since the conversion of Constantine, Christians have invoked the name of God in crusades, holy wars and holocausts Maillot says we have the dreadful contradiction that "you do not have the right to say 'Oh God'—but you have the right if not the duty to say 'In the Name of God, I exterminate you' "[21] It is a terrible thing to think—and say—that God is on our side, or with our nation or armed forces, or with the executioner as a criminal is put to death

Is God our Father? Finally, there has been a heated debate about whether we could or should call God by names other than the masculine terms *Father, Lord, King* and so on I am strongly in favor of using inclusive language in the Bible, in ordinary speech, in hymns and so on (more about this below) But I reject today's efforts to *prohibit* reference to God as Father or King My philosophy is simple and consistent I believe in calling others what they ask to be called I believe Jesus was the Son of God So when Jesus says, "Pray then in this way Our Father   " (Mt 6 9), I'm going to do it If I thought that God was only a pro-

---

My philosophy is simple and consistent. I believe in calling others what they ask to be called I believe Jesus was the Son of God. So when Jesus says "Pray like this Our Father," I'm going to do it. If I thought that "God" was only a projection of our human desire or spirituality, then of course I would want inclusive terms since God would actually be us But I don't believe that we are God God exists outside of us and deserves the same respect we give to women (no longer "girls"), African-Americans (no longer "Negroes"), or "the artist-formerly-known-as-Prince."

---

[20]Maillot, *Le Decalogue*, p 65
[21]Ibid , p 67

jection of our human desire or spirituality, then of course I would want inclusive terms since *God* would actually be *us* But I don't believe that we are God God exists outside of us and deserves the same respect we give to women (no longer "girls"), African Americans (no longer "Negroes") or "the artist-formerly-known-as-Prince " Let God choose his own names, and let us respect him by using them [22]

Why We Misuse God's Name

Why do we do use God's name in an empty way? One explanation is that we want to add force or emphasis to our weak and pathetic communication Adding God's name intensifies and reinforces the emotional impact of our communication Names carry the power of their rightful owners The reason why "Jesus" works as a curse (or as a prayer) is that reality and power stand behind that name [23] You gain clout when you drop some names ("Yes, when Wayne Gretzsky and I played hockey back in junior high school ", "Yeah, Bill and Melinda

---

[22]Does this mean that God is male? Absolutely not Man and woman, male and female, equally and (more importantly) together bear the image of God Femaleness originates in God's being as much as maleness does That is not the issue My name, David, does not exhaust who I am Nor does "he" or anything else you can call me "Father" does not exhaust who God is either He is also our Mother in some important ways But he wants to be called "Father," so I'm going to call him that One of our problems is that we do need a mother! The church has failed abysmally by not teaching that Israel and the church are our "Mother" that is, the spiritual reality of the church and Israel is our Mother and has given us birth, nurture, etc (The earth is not our mother) Finally, though, is God great enough and big enough and understanding enough to "handle it" if some well-meaning (if mistaken!) souls pray without saying "Father," or by saying "Our Father and Mother," or by calling God "she"? I think he is Don't get me wrong I don't want to minimize God's holiness, power, dignity or general right to swat us down like impudent flies Nonetheless, I personally cannot imagine that God fails to understand and graciously accept our prayers in this confused generation, even when we address the Father as "Mother "

[23]It's interesting that we live in a time of disrespect for God's names ("name deflation") and "name inflation" almost everywhere else (possibly as a compensation for our perceived lack of power) Why do so many people want to be called "Doctor" today? (The bachelor of laws degree was renamed the juris doctor degree a few years ago The doctor of ministry degree now gives pastors a better shot at being called "Doctor ") So with our institutions Colleges, especially the lower-quality ones, now want to be called "universities " When a nearby rival college changed its name from "college" to "international university" (with still only six hundred undergraduate students at the time, I think), I urged (tongue-in-cheek of course) the public relations department at my own to discuss changing our name to "intergalactic university "

Gates stopped by last night   ") These names get people's attention
They can open doors (or sometimes close them) We pray in Jesus'
name because it has influence and power in heaven We might curse in
Jesus' name because it still has some power on earth But it should embarrass the profane (and vulgar) among us to be so weak and unimaginative that they must add curses
and vulgarities to prop up every
wimpy sentence they utter

Of course, such weakness in
vocabulary and personality
wouldn't be enough to bring on
such profanity if it were not for a
second factor our lack of respect for God Jan Milič Lochman says, "To misuse the name
of God means   that instead of
placing ourselves at God's disposal we place him at ours, do-
mesticating his holy name for our unholy or pseudo-holy purposes
The God of liberation is turned into a domestic deity, a household
god "[24] Many of us are blind to God in front of and next to us If we saw
him there, we wouldn't be so cavalier with his name Ignorance of God
leads to disrespect of his name

Observing or Breaking the Rules of the Road

This command brings up a justice issue. God *deserves,* he has a right,
to be spoken to with respect It is a violation of Jesus' rights for anyone
to use his name in any of the profane, empty, angry or blasphemous
ways we have reviewed above If we hear a loved one spoken ill of, do
we have an obligation to speak up and defend that person's interests
and rights? If a loved one's name is "spoken in vain" or improperly,
wouldn't we act? What about God's name? It is a basic justice issue

We must also consider the issue of freedom Speaking God's name, as
it is intended, opens the conversation and intensifies the relationship

---

[24]Jan Milič Lochman, *Signposts to Freedom The Ten Commandments and Christian
Ethics* (Minneapolis Augsburg, 1982), p 54

we have with our Liberator Naming God sets us *free for* the adventure with God Obeying the third commandment also sets us *free from* our enslavement to profanity and superficiality Some people are so addicted to profane and vulgar speech that it litters their every sentence Far from "free speech," this is "bondage speech " Get over it! The same mouth cannot be a fountain of blessing and cursing (Jas 3 10-11) Get free from the trash talking so the good stuff can flow freely

This is, third, an issue of love Spouses in our culture often share a common surname, increasingly, couples are combining their names into a new (hyphenated) surname Parents' and family names are also perpetuated in children's names Taking your beloved's name as your own or naming a child after someone is a sign that you respect and value that person [25] In an act of love for us, God gives us his name It is our act of love to wear it with pride and speak it with respect and warmth Speaking God's name is the third act of love for God

Naming Our Neighbors

The third commandment benefits my neighbor, first, in that it is always good for my neighbor when I treat God respectfully This God is *for* my neighbor If I get closer to this God, it is always good for my neighbor If I pray for my neighbor "in Jesus' name," that also is good for my neighbor

The third commandment also teaches us the third basic movement in loving someone By practicing the third commandment with God, we are habituated to a pattern for relating to people—all of whom are made in God's image and likeness This is the first commandment dealing directly (though not solely) with our speech and communication To speak a name is the first step in communication Saying someone's name establishes a relationship and initiates a conversation The *way* the name is said affects the character of the relationship think about a stern teacher spitting out a student's name, about a lover calling the beloved's name alluringly, about an old friend calling out your name as he spots you on a crowded street

Names are important Speaking a name initiates communication

---

[25] An interesting side phenomenon that is worth thinking about is that good friends often grant to each other (but only to each other, not to strangers or oppressors) the right to give them nicknames

and relationship An important practice of this great principle is to
work hard at getting to know the names of people around us in our
church, workplace and neighborhood If we don't know the names of
those around us, we cannot very well begin a conversation Conversation is what builds relationships, and relationships build lives' Ask
someone what her or his name is (It's okay to start a conversation by
saying, "I'm sorry I have a terrible memory Could you tell me your
name again?") If you need to, write the name down and review your
list of names to help you remember them better Use a person's name
to help you remember it Call out his name when you see him Reach
out with the name'

Thus, the way we speak the names of our friends, spouses, children
and coworkers matters The way we speak *to* them and the way we
speak *about* them, both in and out of their hearing, establishes our relation to them and affects others' relations to them, for better or worse If
we speak their names contemptuously or sar-
castically, it shows disrespect and undermines
our relationships If we speak their names
fondly and appreciatively, it shows honor and
respect and builds human relationships

So too with strangers and even enemies
Respecting their names, pronouncing and
spelling them accurately, remembering and
honoring them—these are crucial to the
kinds of relationships that we establish Using
stereotypes, epithets, slurs and sometimes even innocent-sounding
nicknames are ways of pronouncing value judgments that distance
"us" from "them " The prohibition, the boundary condition, is not to
use the names of other people in a vain, disrespectful way The positive
strategy is to seek good, mutually edifying conversation

Corollary 3.1 Never use or impose a demeaning, trivializing or derogatory name on others. Rather, learn the name they have chosen, use it respectfully, and initiate conversation.

How we say *anybody's* name is important [26] For example, I respond
differently to each name I'm called "Professor Gill" (this person respects me), "David" (this is a friend'), "Dave" (this is a wannabe friend
who doesn't know me yet) or "hey, idiot" (this is an impatient, insult-

[26]Comedian Stan Freburg had a hilarious, often copied, routine in which he simply
said "John" and "Marsha" back and forth many times with different intonations to
convey different messages

ing stranger, honking and yelling at me because I was napping when the light turned green)

To understand how important this principle is in human relationships, think about how grown children sometimes *rename* themselves as a way of building an independent identity and separating from their youth or past And think about how "liberated" groups usually rename themselves (or their countries, e g , Congo to Zaire to Congo) to express their new freedom and identity It is an important assertion of strength and power So the "girls" and "ladies" asked to be called "women " (Some of them even prefer "womyn ") African slaves achieved some progress and respect when insulting epithets were replaced by "colored people" (as in the NAACP) and "Negroes " They really came out in power in the sixties when they insisted on being called "Blacks" and "Afro-Americans " (The appropriate terms are now "African Americans" and "people of color ") If a black person says to me, "Now I want to be called an 'African American,' not an 'Afro-American,'" or "Call me a 'person of color,' not a 'colored person,' " I am going to comply without hesitation because doing so is a critical sign of my respect of a people who have been humiliated beyond all measure over the past four centuries—often in the form of names and labels imposed on them If Malcolm Little says, "Call me Malcolm X," if Lew Alcindor says, "Call me Kareem Abdul-Jabbar," or if Betty X decides to change her name to "Betty Shabazz," I'm going to do it Respect the name

Language, including naming, is fluid Words, including names and labels, can receive denotations (in dictionaries as well as in community practices and standards) But these denotations always interact with varying connotations over time *Bad* can even come to mean *good* (as it has in some street parlance) And it does no good to try to deny language this fluidity

If some women (it doesn't need to be *all* women) say that they don't feel included in traditional English male terms for humanity (e g , "Blessed is the man") and that they prefer more inclusive language (e g , "Blessed is the one," "Blessed are those," "Blessed is the person"), then I am on board with them right now Language changes—sometimes irresistibly and irreversibly It is respect for women that requires today's change toward more completely inclusive language Where the Bible intends *all humanity,* we must translate the Greek or

Hebrew terms with our language's or our culture's terms for *all human-ity* To fight against this is to make older English an idol and to refuse to love and respect people made in God's image It is both ludicrous and outrageous for men to dig their heels in on this issue

Word Power: Learning Languages

Chouraqui points out that "the modern world has lost awareness of the value of words One forgets that the word has an impact on the being itself and that words can 'denature' the being that it supposedly desig-nates From the ontological point of view, words become approxima-tions of the truth "[27] Jacques Ellul has written about the "humiliation of the word," of its degradation in our world of images and the visual [28] The third commandment affirms to us the importance of the word If the first commandment orients us to the true, unique God, the Creator in whose image we have been fashioned (Gen 1—2), the second re-minds us that there is an improper work of our hands (idols) and the third that there is an improper word of our mouths

One great step along this path is to begin (or continue) learning an-other language Languages are ways of "naming" the world We cannot enter much at all into another culture unless we learn its language, its ways of naming things and activities One reason many of today's Americans find it hard to understand and relate to other cultures and nations is that we insist everyone speak English and we fail to learn other languages It is extremely difficult to learn another language— and it is incredibly rewarding as our eyes are opened to other people and cultures with their distinctive sensibilities and sensitivities Learn-ing to speak someone's name with respect is the beginning of commu-nication and relationship Learning languages is a fruition of this same attitude, a practice of this essential principle

For Reflection and Discussion

1 What do you think of the author's distinctions between profanity

---

[27] Chouraqui, *Les Dix Commandements*, p 98 Chouraqui translated the Hebrew Bi-ble, the Greek NT and the Arabic Koran "Reestablish the meaning of words—this is what I have attempted to do for readers of the Bible," he says (p 106)

[28] Jacques Ellul, *The Humiliation of the Word* (Grand Rapids, Mich Eerdmans, 1985)

(taking God's name in vain) and vulgarity (which is not good but which is a less serious speech problem than profanity itself)? Do you agree that sexual vulgarity is a worse problem than excretory vulgarity?

2 What can we do in our families, churches, schools and popular culture to fight back against our epidemic of profanity and vulgarity?

3 Which of God's names do you like best and why? What are the positive, good ways that you use God's names in your personal life?

4 What is your viewpoint on male, female and inclusive language when referring to *people*? when referring to *God*?

5 What does your own name mean to you? Has either your name—or the meaning of your name—changed at all over the years?

6

Rhythm Time
Being With and Working For

The fourth commandment is really a double commandment, both to rest and to work It is also the commandment with the greatest and most significant differences between the Exodus and Deuteronomy versions As we shall see, these differences are intensely illuminating (contra some critics who can only understand such dialectic as a mindless and meaningless patchwork) Here is the basic text from Exodus (Ex 20 8-11), with the Deuteronomic text (Deut 5 12-15) given in italics

Remember the sabbath day, and keep it holy
Observe the sabbath day and keep it holy, as the LORD your God commanded you

Six days you shall labor and do all your work
Six days you shall labor and do all your work

But the seventh day is a sabbath to the LORD your God, you shall not do any work—you, your son or your daughter, your male or female slave, your livestock, or the alien resident in your towns
But the seventh day is a sabbath to the LORD your God, you shall not do any work—you, or your son or your daughter, or your male or female slave, or your ox or your donkey, or any of your livestock, or the resident alien in your towns, so that your male and female slave may rest as well as you

For in six days the LORD made heaven and earth, the sea, and all that is in them, but rested the seventh day, therefore the LORD blessed the sabbath day and consecrated it

Remember that you were a slave in the land of Egypt, and the LORD your God brought you out from there with a mighty hand and an outstretched arm, therefore the LORD your God commanded you to keep the sabbath day

The sabbath day is significant already in the Genesis creation story "And on the seventh day God finished all the work that he had done, and he rested on the seventh day from all the work that he had done So God blessed the seventh day and hallowed it, because on it God rested from all the work that he had done in creation" (Gen 2 2-3) On the "seventh day," after "all the work that he had done" (both phrases repeated three times), God finished, God rested, and God blessed and hallowed the day This is the foundation of work and rest for men and women made in God's image and likeness

Thus the sabbath tradition precedes the giving of the Ten Commandments (just as idolatry, profanity, murder, theft and so on were also recognizably wrong before the Ten Commandments were given) For example, the Israelite pilgrims were provided manna six days a week, but none came on the seventh day "Tomorrow is a day of solemn rest, a holy sabbath to the LORD Six days you shall gather [manna], but on the seventh day, which is a sabbath, there will be none" (Ex 16 23, 26)

Israel's Book Of The Covenant (Ex 21—23) and Holiness Code (Lev 17—26) elaborated particular sabbath regulations Sabbath must be observed even during the plowing season and the harvest, the busiest times of year (Ex 34 21) No fires were to be built in one's house on the sabbath (Ex 35 3) Sabbath distinctives were drawn carefully and must be observed completely To break the sabbath was a capital offense, the law breaker must die (Ex 31 12-17, Num 15 32-36)

Inevitably, Israel's actual practice of the sabbath was irregular The law was repeated, the prophets warned, the poets celebrated, and the priests officiated—but the law kept getting broken or ignored The Lord declared through the prophet Ezekiel, for example,

I led them out of the land of Egypt and brought them into the wilderness I gave them my statutes and showed them my ordinances, by whose observance everyone shall live Moreover I gave them my sabbaths, as a sign between me and them, so that they might know that I the LORD sanctify them But the house of Israel rebelled against me   and my sabbaths they greatly profaned (Ezek 20 10-13)

And again, through the prophet Isaiah, God reminded the people

If you refrain from trampling the sabbath, from pursuing your own interests on my holy day, if you call the sabbath a delight and the holy day of the LORD honorable, if you honor it, not going your own ways, serving your own interests, or pursuing your own affairs, then you shall take delight in the LORD, and I will make you ride upon the heights of the earth, I will feed you with the heritage of your ancestor Jacob, for the mouth of the LORD has spoken (Is 58 13-14)

Jesus was accused by the Pharisees of being a sabbath breaker when his hungry disciples plucked some grain to eat and when he healed a man with a withered hand on the sabbath day Jesus explained that, first, the Son of Man is Lord of the Sabbath and, second, it is always lawful to save life, do good and heal on the Sabbath The sabbath was made for man, not man for the sabbath (Mt 12 1-14 par Mk 2 23—3 6 par Lk 6 1-11) Jesus was not trying to disregard or disrespect the sabbath He had already stressed that not even one dot or stroke of the pen could be removed from the law, it must all be fulfilled and our righteousness must exceed that of the Pharisees (Mt 5) Jesus taught that the sabbath serves God and it serves the people If the sabbath (or any other command) becomes more important and authoritative than the Commander, then we are observing it wrongly, if the sabbath (or any other command) is not a means of bringing love and freedom to our neighbor, then we have misunder-

> Jesus taught that the sabbath serves God and it serves the people.
> If the sabbath (or any other command) becomes more important and authoritative than the Commander, then we are observing it wrongly; if the sabbath (or any other command) is not a means of bringing love and freedom to our neighbor, then we have misunderstood its interpretation and application

stood its interpretation and application [1]

The attitude of the early church followed that of Jesus Sabbath practices must not, Paul wrote, be a means of judging others or preempting their freedom before God (Rom 14 5-8, Col 2 16-19) Some people observe a special day to the Lord, others regard every day as equally belonging the Lord The sabbath day is a symbol and a shadow of something bigger than itself Furthermore, our accountability is to our living Lord, not to an abstract code or to a judgmental observer

Does this mean the sabbath day is unimportant or that it disappears from the Christian horizon? Absolutely not Luke reports that, after the crucifixion, "on the sabbath they rested according to the commandment" (Lk 23 56) In the longer Christian eschatological perspective, "a sabbath rest still remains for the people of God Let us therefore make every effort to enter that rest" (Heb 4 9-11) Of course, after the resurrection of Jesus, the first day of the week began to be thought of more and more as the Lord's Day, and much of the significance of sabbath was transferred

> **Area Principle 4: Set aside and guard regular sabbath time focused on being with God. Give six days of creative and faithful work each week in service for God**

to Sunday The first day of the week seems especially noteworthy in John's Gospel (Jn 20 1, 19, 26), and John's Apocalypse seems to refer to the first day of the week as the Lord's Day (Rev 1 10)

Being with God on the Sabbath

When is the sabbath? Let's now try to understand the fourth commandment a little better [2] "Most probably in Hebrew the noun *sabbat* is derived from a verbal form meaning 'to rest, cease from work ' "[3] The sabbath is a sign of the covenant, "a reminder both to God and Israel of the eternal covenantal relationship which was the ultimate purpose of creation "[4] The sabbath was, of course, the seventh day of each week,

---

[1]Isaiah's prophetic denunciation of religious formalism makes this same point (Is 58 1-12)

[2]Abraham J Heschel's *The Sabbath Its Meaning for Modern Man* (New York Farrar, Straus & Giroux, 1951) is a modern classic by a great Jewish teacher

[3]Brevard Childs, *The Book of Exodus A Critical, Theological Commentary* (Philadelphia Westminster Press, 1974), p 413

[4]Ibid , p 416

but can the sabbath *only* be the seventh day of the week, or might we observe its reality on the first day? William Barclay argues strenuously, but unpersuasively, that it is wrong to merge the Jewish sabbath with the Christian Lord's Day

> For the Christian the Sabbath has ceased to exist The Sabbath is simply a day which he does not observe   Again, to put it very plainly and very definitely, this fourth commandment is not binding on the Christian at all, for there is no evidence in Scripture that the rules and regulations which govern the sabbath were ever transferred by divine authority to the Lord's Day [5]

Barclay argues that both the early church and the Reformers made this clear distinction and left the sabbath behind as a part of the ceremonial law Part of where Barclay's argument goes wrong is in viewing the sabbath only from the perspective of the rest from creation motif (Ex 20 11) Barclay believes the Jewish sabbath celebrates creation whereas the Christian Lord's day celebrates resurrection But this ignores the Deuteronomic sabbath tradition, which celebrates exodus and redemption While the Exodus version recalls creation, Deuteronomy recalls the Israelite's passing through the Red Sea and being redeemed and liberated from slavery in Egypt Everything Barclay proposes as appropriate celebration of the Lord's Day could just as well be said of the sabbath

Remember and observe. Two different verbs are used in the Exodus and Deuteronomy versions to describe how to relate to the sabbath The rabbis explained that to *remember* the sabbath (Ex 20 8) is to perform positive "acts that enhance the sanctity of the Sabbath," such as studying Scripture [6] To *observe* the sabbath (Deut 5 12) is to refrain from negative acts that would desecrate the day, including not only work itself but too much conversation about work! One observes the sabbath also by leaving aside worries, cares and sad thoughts Per Calvin, "We must rest entirely, in order that God may work in us "[7]

---

[5]William Barclay, *The Ten Commandments for Today* (Grand Rapids, Mich Eerdmans, 1973), p 4

[6]J H Hertz, ed , *The Pentateuch and Haftorahs Hebrew Text, English Translation and Commentary*, 2nd ed (London Soncino Press, 1988), p 297

[7]John Calvin *Institutes of the Christian Religion* 2 8 29 (All quotations are taken from the edition translated by Henry Beveridge and published by Eerdmans in 1975)

Marva Dawn explains that "to cease working on the Sabbath means to quit laboring at anything that is work Activity that is enjoyable and freeing and not undertaken for the purpose of accomplishment qualifies as acceptable for Sabbath time "[8]

We are to *remember* the sabbath day at all times It should be

the focal point of all our activities   Do not count days as others count them   Count every weekday in relation to the Sabbath   Other nations consider the weekdays to be unrelated to each other Thus, they give each day a separate name after one of the heavenly forces (i e , Sunday means "sun's day," Monday means "moon's day," etc) Israel, however, counts all days in reference to the Sabbath "One day toward the Sabbath, two days toward the Sabbath " Thus we fulfill the command *Remember the Sabbath,* every day of the week [9]

Holy and delightful. The sabbath is to be remembered and observed by keeping it *holy* To be holy means "to be sanctified" or, more literally, "different" or "separate " This distinctiveness is achieved by "resting"—doing no regular work—but also by reciting benedictions, dressing differently, eating and drinking differently

The command to hallow is not identified simply with not working or resting, but over and above both of these is the positive action of making holy It presupposes the cessation of the normal activity of work in order to set aside the sabbath for something special The nature of the special quality is not spelled out, but briefly characterized in the phrase "the sabbath belongs to Yahweh your God "[10]

The sabbath is the Lord's Day in a special sense (though of course the other six days are his as well)

Although some silence and receptivity must be part of sabbath holiness (more Mary, less Martha), the prohibition is against ordinary

---

[8]Marva Dawn, *Keeping the Sabbath Wholly Ceasing, Resting, Embracing, Feasting* (Grand Rapids, Mich Eerdmans, 1989), p 5 This is a superb study, historically well-informed, solid in biblical exposition and theology, creative and practical in application

[9]Avroham Chaim Feuer, *Aseres Hadibros The Ten Commandments, A New Translation with a Commentary Anthologized from Talmudic, Midrashic and Rabbinic Sources* (Brooklyn, N Y Mesorah, 1981), pp 39-40

[10]Childs, *Book of Exodus,* pp 415-16

work, not against the exertions of sabbath celebration To sanctify the
sabbath is to go beyond a minimal *remember* or *observe* One is to *hallow* the day, to "make it the very essence of his being, the soul of his
time,   [to] immerse himself in its powerful spirit and thrill to its sensation The Jew should use every precious moment of the Sabbath to
lift himself closer and closer to God "[11] The same applies to Christians
What does this look like in practice?

It is the absence of religious duties to be performed on the Sabbath that makes the day so striking One grim story from the
Book of Numbers relates how a person was stoned to death for
daring to gather sticks on the Sabbath (Num 15 32-36) But
nowhere do we find specifications of what ought positively to be
done on the Sabbath [12]

Laura Schlessinger suggests not just resting from our work, but
avoiding even discussing people's jobs, networking and preparing for
the week's work ahead She says also that "the Sabbath is a good day to
stay away from the technological marvels that bring things to us in an
instant In breaking free from our reliance on machines, we elevate the
importance of the *human* factor in life "[13]

Sabbath observance has often been a rather negative, grim and sober affair, as legalistic as any Pharisee or Puritan could conceive
Though he certainly has a point, Alan Redpath veers a little in this direction as he scolds us

When the Sabbath day of rest becomes the day of recreation
instead of the day of worship, it never achieves its purpose The
problem in the church today is that the Lord's day has become
the Lord's *half* day People attend the morning worship or education hour and then spend the rest of the day in various recreational activities [14]

---

[11]Feuer, *Aseres Hadibros*, pp 40-42
[12]Walter Harrelson, *The Ten Commandments and Human Rights* (Philadelphia Fortress, 1980), p 84
[13]Laura Schlessinger and Stewart Vogel, *The Ten Commandments* (New York HarperCollins, 1998), pp 109, 116
[14]Alan Redpath, *Law and Liberty A New Look at the Ten Commandments in the Light of Contemporary Society* (Old Tappan, N J Revell, 1978), p 45

But I think Joy Davidman captures something important when she asks, "How does one keep a day holy? By making it unpleasant, and restrictive, and boring—or by making it joyous? By making it as much as possible like hell, or as much as possible like heaven?"[15] We should remember that even Calvin, the rather severe Genevan Reformer, "allowed certain games on Sunday, and occasionally played bowls himself" and that the English King James I "took a moderate line on the matter in his *Book of Sports* (1618), allowing archery and dancing, and disallowing more brutish sports"[16] The Jewish sabbath was supposed to be a delight—happy and cheerful "The Sabbath planted a heaven in every Jewish home, filling it with long-expected and blissfully greeted peace   The Sabbath banishes care and toil, grief and sorrow All fasting (except on the Day of Atonement   ) is forbidden, and all mourning is suspended "[17] Good food, table songs and joy are part of the authentic sabbath experience

Dawn suggests four themes for our sabbath observance [18]

- We *cease* our work, productivity and accomplishment, our anxiety and worry, our control, possessiveness and enculturation, and even our humdrum and meaninglessness

- We *rest*—spiritually, emotionally, physically and intellectually

- We *embrace* "intentionality" (rather than thoughtless conformity), Christian values, time (instead of space), giving (instead of requiring), our calling in life, shalom/wholeness and the world

- We *feast* on the Eternal, with music, beauty, food and affection

Sabbath inclusiveness. The sabbath command has direct implications for both sexes, for all family members, for those who work for us, for our animals, and for any strangers and unbelievers within our influence All of these are to be granted sabbath rest If anyone

[15]Joy Davidman, *Smoke on the Mountain An Interpretation of the Ten Commandments* (Philadelphia Westminster Press, 1953), p 52

[16]Rupert Davies, *Making Sense of the Commandments* (London Epworth, 1990), p 57, see also Barclay, *Ten Commandments,* pp 41-42 King James did forbid the baiting of bulls and bears I would also affirm this restriction

[17]Hertz, *Pentateuch and Haftorahs,* p 298

[18]Dawn, *Keeping the Sabbath,* passim

Sabbath observance is intended to be *holy*— different, distinctive from our ordinary weekday lives It is intended to be delightful, not grim, to be a day of freedom and joy, not of obligation and guilt

thinks that biblical ethics has no concern for those outside the faith or for the nonhuman creation, surely this command is good evidence to the contrary Biblical ethical principles are intended to bless all the nations and peoples of the earth as well as the rest of God's good creation A faithful Jew or Christian will not be found piously observing sabbath among friends and family while his or her employees (pagan or otherwise) are carrying on a day of frantic business

Rabbi André Chouraqui describes this eloquently

The seventh day introduced, with the notion of a weekly rest, a revolutionary innovation in the history of humanity For the first time, the worker, including the slave and the foreigner residing in the country, but also the beasts of burden, must rest at least once per week, the seventh day, from one sundown to the next   The Sabbath erased the discriminatory barriers between males and females, young and old, servants and their masters, parents and children, resident foreigners and native born, people and animals each and all are obligated to cease from all work before the setting of the sun on the sixth day and only recommence their activities the next evening on the seventh day [19]

Chouraqui points out that the sabbath celebrates the end of God's creation of *everything* that exists and is, thus, the most universal celebration conceivable

The priority of sabbath. One major lesson here is the priority of sabbath over work, of the one day over the six others We do not rest in order to work (at least that is not the primary motive) As we shall see, work is not to be despised, it is a critical part of our humanity, freedom and love Nevertheless, both the point of departure and the *telos* of human history is sabbath, not work Walter Harrelson reminds us that the first man and woman "were created before the garden was created,

[19]André Chouraqui, *Les Dix Commandements Aujourd'hui* (Paris Robert Laffont, 2000), p 116

they were not made first and foremost for work "[20] Too often our culture teaches us to view things in a utilitarian fashion Something has value as a means, an instrument, to something else Thus, vacation is valued because it gets us ready for more work The sabbath, however, has an *intrinsic* value it is good in itself, whether it prepares us for work or not

The significance of work. Unfortunately, many abbreviated versions of the Ten Commandments fail to make clear that this is a double command There are two imperatives, not one remember (or observe) the sabbath day, and work six days The priority is on the sabbath, but the command to work is equally binding and important The fourth commandment teaches us not only how to rest and have sabbath, but how to approach our work "Work during the six days of the week is as essential to man's welfare as is the rest on the seventh No man or woman, howsoever rich, is freed from the obligation of doing some work, say the Rabbis, as idleness invariably leads to evil thoughts and evil deeds "[21] "If a person has no work, let him find work' If he has an abandoned property, let him build on it, if he has a desolate field, let him revitalize it "[22]

> Biblical ethical principles are intended to bless all the nations and peoples of the earth as well as the rest of God's good creation A faithful Jew or Christian will not be found piously observing sabbath among friends and family while his or her employees (pagan or otherwise) are carrying on a day of frantic business.

So work is as essential to our humanity as is rest Redpath finds even the reference to *six* days significant "Now please notice that the Bible does not suggest a five-day week 'Six days you shall labor' "[23] Work was as much a part of God's goodness as was his rest on the sev-

---

[20]Harrelson, *Ten Commandments,* p 85 Notice the sequence "Then the LORD God formed man from the dust of the ground   And the LORD God planted a garden   The LORD God took the man and put him in the garden of Eden to till it and keep it" (Gen 2 7-8, 15)

[21]Hertz, *Pentateuch and Haftorahs,* p 297

[22]Feuer, *Aseres Hadibros,* p 42

[23]Redpath, *Law and Liberty,* p 45 Most of us do work on the sixth day, perhaps doing chores around the house Work is not defined by our being paid money but by our exerting effort on the necessary tasks of life

enth day "In the six week-days the children of Israel are God's partners in Creation by working to improve and enhance everything that
God fashioned "[24] Luther wrote,

> All our life and work must be guided by God's Word if they are to
> be God-pleasing or holy Where that happens the commandment
> is in force and is fulfilled   Conversely, any conduct or work
> done apart from God's Word is unholy in the sight of God, no
> matter how splendid or brilliant it may appear, or even if it be
> altogether covered with holy relics [25]

Whatever the differences between the Exodus and Deuteronomy accounts, it is clear that human work is as essential as human rest Certainly work can be enslaving, dangerous, depressing and dehumanizing
(note the Deuteronomy passage's "slavery in Egypt" theme) But it is
also deeply dehumanizing *not* to work It is stamped into our nature to
do things and make things (note the Exodus passage's "creation"
theme) If we are denied opportunities to express our personality and
our basic humanity through some form of work, we are not able to be
fully human [26] As Alphonse Maillot argues,

> We must denounce unemployment as one of the worst curses on
> humanity Man-in-the-image-of-God has an inalienable right to
> work, to a true work that helps him to flourish On the other
> hand, it is necessary to stop looking at retirement as becoming
> someone without value or as a time of cessation of activity
> Everyone must have the possibility of preparing for a true retire-
> ment, that is, a new activity, chosen and relaxed [27]

---

[24] Feuer, *Aseres Hadibros*, p 42
[25] Martin Luther, *The Large Catechism*, trans Robert H Fischer (1529, Philadelphia
Fortress, 1959), p 21
[26] It is significant that Jesus was resurrected not on the sabbath, the religious day (Saturday), but on the first working day of the regular week (Sunday) Jesus was crucified and buried on Friday, the last day of the Jewish workweek He was in the grave
through Saturday (the sabbath) and came back to life on the first day of the week
Christians now observe Sunday as the Lord's Day and think of it as the new "sabbath" day But we must remember that Jesus did not rise on a religious holy day but
in ordinary time Lesson the resurrected Jesus shows up in our work week—not
just in our religious times and places
[27] Alphonse Maillot, *Le Decalogue Une morale pour notre temps* (Geneva Labor &
Fides, 1985), pp 82-83

Sabbath, Work and the Rules of the Road

Observing this principle is, first of all, a matter of justice God has a right to our full sabbath attention To snub God, to refuse to cease from our work and busyness and give him this holy time is an insult and an outrageous denial of what God deserves from us And in exactly the same way, God deserves to have us work for him six days of the week We rest *with* him and work *for* him

And note well this is exactly what God himself practices toward each one of us The God of billions of people can be counted on to spend special time with each of us—and not just care for us en masse through the operation of providence, common grace or natural law¹ God shows his love by spending focused time with us, by meeting us in prayer and worship, in quiet and in celebration And God is at work for us, sustaining and caring for us at all times If God does this for us, he deserves our reciprocating in the same pattern

It is also a matter of love How can we possibly say we love God with all

> **Human work is as essential as human rest** Certainly work can be enslaving, dangerous, depressing and dehumanizing (note the Deuteronomy passage's "slavery in Egypt" theme) But it is also deeply dehumanizing *not* to work. It is stamped into our nature to do things and make things (note the Exodus passage's "creation" theme)

our heart and then neglect or refuse to spend weekly time together with him? It is plainly false to say "I love God" and then fail to schedule sabbath time with him Sabbath is like our modern phrase *quality time* Giving God quality time—time free of work and distraction, time that focuses on God—is the fourth movement of genuine love But we also love God by working for him This is not an either-or pattern We love God both by working for him and by being with him Lying around all the time, doing nothing, being lazy and so on cannot be excused by saying it is quality time for God Sabbath has meaning as the culmination of a week of work It does not stand by itself

Observing sabbath also brings freedom It is a liberation from any slavery to our work and to the mundane preoccupations of our lives Sabbath practice sets us free in our time It frees our body from toil It frees our mind by carving out time to think, to listen, to meditate before God More broadly, Chouraqui argues that if slavery is defined as the obligation to work against one's will, with little or no remuneration and with no chance of escaping such subjection, then millions of men, women and children are in such virtual slavery today around the world, and the number is growing By not refusing to benefit from such slavery, the Western world reinforces it We must hear once again the biblical duty to grant sabbath as liberation from slavery to everyone everywhere [28]

> God shows his love by spending focused time with us, by meeting us in prayer and worship, in quiet and in celebration. And God is at work for us, sustaining and caring for us at all times If God does this for us, he deserves our reciprocating in the same pattern

Good and Bad Work

As Maillot says, "There is not one sabbath command but two, profoundly different in their form and in their basis "[29] The first (Exodus) stresses the day of celebration and one's rediscovery of the rest of the Lord, just as one has participated in the creative work of our Lord during the week The second (Deuteronomy) stresses the idea of observing or safeguarding the sabbath in light of the slavery in Egypt, with a reminder that this is God's command Maillot warns that we should not try to harmonize these two versions or to choose one over the other

> Israel accepted this message in two voices, rarely harmonious and, instead, continually dissonant They listened to this word of God in counterpoint, this contradictory word of God, even enriched by its contradiction They did not practice theological terrorism   in which the prophet silenced the priest and vice versa, this terrorism where even in our Churches, there is only one voice which has the right to express itself [30]

In the Exodus version of the Ten Commandments, the sabbath is

---

[28]Chouraqui, *Les Dix Commandements,* pp 126-27 Further still, Chouraqui argues that the land, the earth itself, needs to repose Our technology and science bring wonderful things, he says, but we must orient them toward good instead of allowing them to lead to pollution or the threat of war or the destruction of species (pp 128-29)

[29]Maillot, *Le Decalogue,* p 73

[30]Ibid , p 74

grounded in creation We observe sabbath because "in six days the LORD made heaven and earth, the sea, and all that is in them, but rested the seventh day, therefore the LORD blessed the sabbath day and consecrated it" (Ex 20 11) In Deuteronomy, however, the sabbath is grounded in the exodus from Egyptian slavery "Remember that you were a slave in the land of Egypt, and the LORD your God brought you out from there with a mighty hand and an outstretched arm, therefore the LORD your God commanded you to keep the sabbath day" (Deut 5 15) Sabbath rest is a celebrative ceasing from the good work of creation *and* a grateful release from the toilsome work of Egyptian bondage

Good work. Man and woman were created in the image and likeness of God God (the pattern, the model) is the creator and maker of good things God created the heavens and the earth God saw that "the earth was a formless void and darkness covered the face of the deep" (Gen 1 2) God gave form and order to what was formless, filled what was void and empty, and illuminated what was in darkness Man and woman are set free to express what they are in God's likeness Furthermore, they are commissioned to "be fruitful and multiply, and fill the earth and subdue it, and have dominion," to till and keep God's garden, and to name the creation (Gen 1 28, 2 15, 19)

> Our drive to make things, to organize, to entrepreneur, to create and invent, to understand and explain—this is rooted in our nature in the image of God At its best then, our work is creative and good It is *for life*—good for humanity, good for the animals and the earth, good for our coworkers

This is the fundamental root of *homo faber,* "man the maker " Our drive to make things, to organize, to entrepreneur, to create and invent, to understand and explain—this is rooted in our nature in the image of God At its best then, our work is creative and good It is *for* life—good for humanity, good for the animals and the earth, good for our coworkers These are the themes, the ethical guidelines and the criteria for good work

But even at its best, work must not be allowed to dominate us We must cease from our good work for sabbath We must not become workaholics who cannot stop, who know no boundaries around their work Good work becomes bad (for us, for others, for the earth) when it no longer has any boundaries The fourth commandment (in Exodus) directs our attention back to the creation, where good work was bounded in time There was a day when work *could* be done but was not God did not stop on the seventh day because he was tired or because he had to, but because it was good to stop The time outside of work could be a blessed and good time

> There was a day when work *could* be done but was not. God did not stop on the seventh day because he was tired or because he had to, but because it was good to stop The time outside of work could be a blessed and good time. There was also a tree that could be harvested but should not be
>
> Work cannot be good if it fails to set and observe boundaries of both time and space

Good work was also bounded in space There was a place, a tree, that could be harvested but should not be We could also say that good work was work that was bounded by the word and example of God Good work is not just any work, it is work that extends the mission, purposes, values and themes of God's work If human work is in dissonance with the themes of God's creative work, it cannot be good work

Commenting on the Exodus passage, Maillot reflects,

> The seven days of each week given to man are the perpetual actualization of the seven days of Creation There are thus *six* days where man by his work actualizes the creative work of God and *one* day where he actualizes, rediscovers, and shares in the rest of God In the text of Exodus, work is viewed in a very positive manner Human work there is the resumption of the fundamental, primordial work of God Human work is thus the continuation, the actualization of the divine creation Finally, it is the great liturgy in which during six days man is affirmed as the heir of God, as the prince of Creation which he must, precisely through his work, steward and lead [31]

All human work does not automatically have this character One critical requirement is that the six days be accompanied by the seventh

---

[31]Ibid , pp 75-76

Humanity with its work and culture is still not the ultimate goal of God's creation   The sabbath brings out the truth that the creation, far from being an end in itself and left to its own devices, finds its meaning only in fellowship with God The goal of creation is the praise of God offered by the whole creation with humanity at its head [32]

Bad work. But all of our work is not the good work of creation Some work is more like slavery in Egypt This is fallen work It is work that respects no limits It could be slavery—work that fills seven days a week, respecting no boundary of time It could ruthlessly require that we try to make bricks from straw, respecting no limits of space or nature It could squelch all human creativity and leave only mindless grunt work, hauling bricks to pyramid building sites It could honor the gods of Egyptian wealth, power and empire rather than the God of all creation Some of our work today is like this drudgery Sabbath is grateful relief from such toil Sabbath is not just to celebrate good creative work, but also to celebrate the cessation of bad work "The Sabbath is *the day on which freedom is commemorated*   It may not be kept to oneself, reduced to a personal privilege, clutched to oneself On the contrary, it is meant to bring relief to those especially who are most heavily burdened   This is why this day is obligatory on all and liberating for all "[33]

Maillot points out that in Deuteronomy, God *commands* the sabbath, whereas in the Exodus version, God *blesses* the sabbath In the Deuteronomy version the sabbath is constantly menaced and threatened by the nature of work as slavery and toil The slave masters may threaten it, our forgetfulness may threaten it So it must be commanded, safeguarded and protected Even if one owns beasts and servants (as in the Deuteronomy version), work remains slavery and toil This passage stands in relationship to Genesis 3 and Ecclesiastes, not to Genesis 1—2 and God's creative work Here the sabbath is the radical counterpoint to the workweek, it is not in harmony with it, as in Exodus In this sense the sabbath is like the Independence Day in

---

[32] Jan Milič Lochman, *Signposts to Freedom The Ten Commandments and Christian Ethics* (Minneapolis Augsburg, 1982), p 62, citing Ernst Jenni
[33] Lochman, *Signposts*, p 61

America or Bastille Day in France a day of liberation, a reminder of the slavery from which we have been delivered

In our contemporary experience, work shares both realities Hopefully, the creative, good side is dominant and the toilsome, bad side is not Rarely does our work offer absolutely no opportunities to be creative, and rarely will we entirely escape the toilsome burden of work The two forms of the fourth commandment thus express precisely the paradox and the dialectic of our actual work "Israel had the audacity and the genius to make these two irreducible versions coexist Consider also the fact that all work (even pastoral work) seems on certain days like the accomplishment and joy described by Exodus—and on other days like the painful toil of Deuteronomy "[34]

The fourth commandment thus provides us with a way of bringing ethical judgments into the arena of our work Good work, the kind of work we should seek and promote, is work that carries on the themes of God's creation It allows men and women to work together in partnership, in creative stewardship of God's good earth, in pursuit not only of utility but beauty It is work that exercises our imaginations and challenges our powers to the limit, but retains a fundamental human balance and perspective We want to avoid or eliminate meaningless, dehumanizing, unimaginative, toilsome drudgery and slavery We want to reintroduce healthy boundaries of time and space, respect for species and creational order, and opportunities to work in teams We want to set people free from the curse of bad work and give them opportunities to start anew

Getting Control of Our Time and Work

Unfortunately, we live in a world of workaholics, on the one hand, and thank-God-it's-Friday types on the other The pace and pressure of life in our world have intensified The boundaries of both nature (e g , the need to stop working when it gets dark) and culture (e g , laws or traditions against doing business on the sabbath) have been eradicated almost entirely The peasants of the past may have had a grinding existence, but weather, seasonal changes and periods of darkness bounded their work Cultural traditions further limited work throughout most of human history Even the ancient Romans had large numbers of official

---

[34]Maillot, *Le Decalogue*, pp 80-81

holidays By contrast, in today's world we are urged to shop, study, trade stocks, work or amuse ourselves twenty-four hours a day, seven days a week Naturally, we don't do it quite to that extent, but we are nevertheless lost without boundaries or guidelines

The sabbath command provides us with some good advice We can begin to regain control of our time by reforming our *week* Our daily schedule is too narrow a window, and the month or year is too broad The week is the place to start [35] Harrelson believes the one-day-in-seven sabbath is a tradition "flying in the face of any of the regular rhythms of the season or of the heavenly bodies This is what is so remarkable about the appearance of the Sabbath—the fact that it ignores all normal rhythms "[36] Dawn, a much wiser voice, urges, "The key to experiencing the Sabbath in the richness of its design is to recognize the importance of its rhythm Which day is used to observe the Sabbath is not as important as ensuring that the day occurs every seven days without fail "[37]

> We can begin to regain control of our time by reforming our *week* Our daily schedule is too narrow a window, and the month or year is too broad. The week is the place to start

Once we establish a weekly rhythm, we can work on our daily schedule and on our months, seasons, years and lifetimes The Israelites were told to mark their *days* by reciting all of the commands "when you lie down and when you rise" (Deut 6 7) Their *years* were marked out by various festivals at seedtime, harvest and so on Every seventh year was to be observed as a special sabbatical year and, after seven-times-seven years, the fiftieth year was to be a special Jubilee

---

[35] See Earl F Palmer, *Old Law, New Life The Ten Commandments and New Testament Faith* (Nashville Abingdon, 1984), pp 67ff , for this great insight

[36] Harrelson, *Ten Commandments,* p 81 Israel did have harvest festivals and seasonal rhythms in their annual calendar As for the sabbath day and Harrelson's "normal rhythms," long historical experience seems to show that it *does* in fact conform to our bodily and spiritual needs Efforts to change to one in ten days (in the French Revolution) have failed Could it be that this witnesses to our being made in the image of God, who created for six days and rested on the seventh? I think there is a natural basis for this weekly rhythm Elsewhere, Harrelson suggests that we work only four days and have a three-day weekend for an Islamic Friday, Jewish sabbath and Christian Sunday (p 90)

[37] Dawn, *Keeping the Sabbath,* p 7

year (Ex 23 10-17, Lev 23, 25) The sabbath rhythm is to characterize our lives to the very end of our days Our work may change but it will not cease, nor will our need for weekly sabbath

Jesus' teachings and the other New Testament writings remind us not to be legalistic and treat the form as more important than the substance Nevertheless, we must find concrete ways of putting a healthy, biblical rhythm back into our life Some may need to make their sabbath a half day on Saturday and a half day on Monday Others will want to make the traditional Jewish sabbath their own (Friday sundown to Saturday sundown) Those who have frantic, intense work lives may need to concentrate on tranquil, peaceful sabbath Those whose work is sedentary may need to have more active sabbath celebrations We must remember that the commands are for a community, not lone individualists Try to invent and celebrate your sabbath patterns with others [38]

Keeping the sabbath is always based on a double promise First, we believe that God will, in fact, meet us as promised whenever we devote our sabbath to being with him Second, our taking a sabbath demonstrates faith that God will take care of our work (or study) for one day while we turn our attention away from it to him It is no wonder that our Jewish forebears emphasized this command so much It is a law full of gospel

How the Fourth Commandment Helps My Neighbor

How does this express love for our neighbor? First, as with the first three commands, we can say that it is always good for our neighbor that we develop our relationship with this God If we get close to God, we will be better neighbors to anyone If we disobey sabbath and give our time and effort to work and money alone, or to the service of some other god, our neighbor needs to be on the alert

Second, this command even more directly affects our neighbor in that we are commanded to grant sabbath not just to ourselves but to everyone around us, to all under our influence The neighbor's benefit is thus very clear in this command The third way this helps our neighbor is that it habituates us both to spend quality time *with* others and to work *for* others, whether that work is enjoyable and creative or toil-

---

[38]In my view, we have a lot of freedom here in how we live out the principle of the sabbath However, there is a lot to be gained by maintaining conscious continuity with our historical community—our spiritual mothers, Israel and the church

some drudgery What is true for interpersonal relationships also goes for our businesses and even our international politics All good human relationships require that we work on behalf of others and also carve out time to be focused on the other Sitting in the United Nations General Assembly, for example, while essential, is insufficient for building good relationships with other nations We must also send envoys, hold summits, have educational and cultural exchanges, and actively work for those nations This is a basic principle of life and relationships that Christians can and should support in all domains

> **Corollary 4 1· To care for any person (relative, friend, colleague, neighbor), we must invest focused, attentive time *with* them and work creatively and redemptively *for* them**

Practicing Our Principles

If we apply the fourth commandment across the range of our experience, what other practices might be illuminated? We have already seen how this commandment informs our ethic of work and rest Let's take a brief look at two other arenas

Welfare and workfare. The public policy debate over welfare and workfare should be clear in a Christian value system It is heartless and cruel to remove all safety nets from under the poor and unemployable But it is also demeaning for men and women made in the image of the Creator and Redeemer to be made a permanent underclass, dependent on welfare handouts People need jobs and work to be fully dignified and healthy human beings It is insulting to treat people as irresponsible and incapable of productive work (even if they have been brainwashed into believing this of themselves)

The movement toward workfare, then, is a good and positive one But we must not rest content until such work is as much as possible like creation and redemption and as little as possible like slavery in Egypt Job-training programs are great—give someone a fish and you feed her for a day, teach her how to fish and you feed her for a lifetime—but let's try to make these programs as creative as possible Microlending programs (loaning small amounts of money, with little or no security, to people who want to buy a few tools or rent some space to start a small business) are also a proven strategy for alleviating poverty

Such programs usually work because we are made in God's image as creative workers

The God of good technology. Technology is a form of work—in terms of both tools and methods It is a dominant force in our world Today's work is inseparable from technology, but so too, it seems, are our play, entertainment, interpersonal relationships, communication, health and perhaps even our spirituality No matter how awesome it is, technology must not become an idol or rival god in our lives Technology can *assist* our Lord and Savior, but it must not *become* our lord and savior

Technology has the potential to help us communicate with our loved ones more fully, frequently and faithfully, but it also amplifies our human potential for perversity Using information technology we can more easily bear false witness, spread disinformation, profane and degrade God and others, and hide behind anonymity Technology can bring great creativity into our work lives, in effect helping redeem and set people free from drudgery But technology also introduces the dullness of data entry and the proliferation of computer addictions of various sorts Technology can help liberate us for better, fuller sabbath celebration and rest, but it can also invade and corrupt our sabbath since work is no longer confined to the office

The critical issue in the technological domain is to decide who will be the god (the center, the purpose, the telos) of our technology If technology serves money, power, selfishness or nationalism, look out But if it serves the God of Israel and Jesus Christ, we will know the God of good technology in both our work and our sabbath

For Reflection and Discussion

1 How have you and those around you (your family, your community, your church) approached sabbath rest or Sunday practices? How do you currently celebrate or observe the sabbath?

2 Is your work more like creation or like slavery right now? How does that affect what you do on your time off?

3 Do your key relationships exhibit a balance of focused time *with* and good work *for* the other person?

4 In your view, are workaholism and busy-ness serious ethical issues in today's world? If so, how should we respond to these challenges?

7

Extended Love
Agency and Honor

The fifth commandment is "Honor your father and your mother, as the LORD your God commanded you, so that your days may be long and that it may go well with you in the land that the LORD your God is giving you" (Deut 5 16 par Ex 20 12) This command (to adult children, not to infants) is elaborated in Scripture in many places (e g , Ex 21 15, 17, Lev 20 9, Deut 21 18-21, 27 16, Prov 1 8, 15 5, 19 26) The stories of the patriarchs in Genesis offer many examples of honor and dishonor Ham dishonored his drunken father Noah, whereas his brothers Shem and Japheth threw "the mantle of chastity of their father's shame, only an unnatural child gloats over a parent's disgrace or dishonor "[1] Lot's daughters dishonored themselves and their father Jacob deceived his father with the help of his mother Jacob's son Joseph, however, cared for and honored his father when he had the chance The examples in Israel's later history also abound with dysfunctional family relationships Among the most famous was Absalom's dishonor and revolt against his father David

In the Old Testament children are told to "revere your mother and father" (Lev 19 3, note reversal of order) In fact, those who curse, attack or strike a parent are eligible for the death penalty (Ex 21 15, 17) A stubborn, profligate, drunken, rebellious son can be stoned Per Deu-

---

[1] J H Hertz, ed , *The Pentateuch and Haftorahs Hebrew Text, English Translation and Commentary,* 2nd ed (London Soncino, 1988), p 299

teronomy 21 18-21, a child is to honor parents in word (no cursing), in deed (no striking or drunkenness) and in attitude (no rebellion) Anyone who dishonors father or mother is cursed (Deut 27 16) Many of the Proverbs warn against rebellious, dishonorable children and commend wise, honorable sons and daughters The prophets maintain the same emphases for example, Ezekiel complains, "they have treated mother and father with contempt" (Ezek 22 7 NIV)

Jesus' teaching and practice regarding parents and children has three themes First, he reinforces the fifth commandment when he asks the Pharisees,

> Why do you break the commandment of God for the sake of your tradition? For God said, "Honor your father and mother," and, "Whoever speaks evil of father or mother must surely die " But you say that whoever tells father or mother, "Whatever support you might have had from me is given to God," then that person need not honor the father So, for the sake of your tradition, you make void the word of God You hypocrites' (Mt 15 3-7 par Mk 7 9-13)

Jesus obviously cares about parents and their children He accompanied Peter to the home of his sick mother-in-law and healed her (Lk 4 38-39) He responded to Jairus's plea to heal his sick daughter (Mk 5 22-24, 35-43, Lk 8 41-42, 49-56)

Second, however, Jesus shocks his hearers by saying he has come to divide families "I have come to set a man against his father," and "Whoever loves father and mother more than me is not worthy of me" (Mt 10 35, 37) Worse yet, Jesus says, "Whoever comes to me and does not hate father and mother, wife and children, brothers and sisters, yes, and even life itself, cannot be my disciple" (Lk 14 26) In the broader context of his teaching, Jesus was not intending to reverse the teaching of the fifth commandment but rather, in effect, to subordinate it to the first commandment That is, one's family relationships must be radically subordinated to one's relationship with God

Third, Jesus calls for the creation of a new family Jesus calls God his father and teaches his disciples to do the same (Lk 2 49, Mt 6 9) He boldly says that his true mother and brothers are those who obey God's word (Lk 8 20-21) No wonder his "family of origin" and others

sometimes thought he was crazy (Mk 3 21) These first and third
themes come together at the cross (Jn 19 25-27), when Jesus shows
concern for his mother Mary (honoring one's parents) by saying to her,
"Woman, here is your son," and to the disciple, "Here is your mother"
(belonging to the new family)

In Ephesians, Paul teaches, "Children, obey your parents in the
Lord, for this is right 'Honor your father and mother'—this is the first
commandment with a promise 'so that it may be well with you and
you may live long on the earth ' And fathers, do not provoke your children to anger, but bring them up in the discipline and instruction of
the Lord" (Eph 6 1-4) Paul seems to
have younger, dependent children in
mind when he urges obedience in
this context Even so, his counsel is
qualified by the phrase *in the Lord*
And it is typical of Paul to challenge
parents, as well as children, to responsibility before the Lord [2]

What Is Honor?

The Hebrew word for honor, *kabad*,
is related to terms meaning "heavy "
To honor is to not take someone
lightly but to treat them with seriousness Honor does not imply unilateral
obedience but rather treating someone with care and respect in deed

> Jesus' teaching about parents and
> children has three themes First,
> he reinforces the importance of
> genuinely honoring father and
> mother Second, he shocks his
> listeners by demanding that their
> love for parent or child seem as hate
> by comparison to their love for God
> Third, he inaugurates new, spiritually
> grounded family relationships
> among previously unrelated
> people who now will treat one
> another as brothers, sisters, parents
> and children

and word To honor someone is to treat that person as valuable, to
grant influence, dignity, importance and authority

The choice of the term "honor" carries with it a range of connotations far broader than some such term as "obey " To honor is to
"prize highly" (Prov 4 8), to "show respect," "to glorify and exalt "
Moreover, it has nuances of caring for and showing affection (Ps

---

[2] In *The Politics of Jesus* (Grand Rapids, Mich Eerdmans, 1972), John Howard Yoder
discusses the NT haustafeln, the tables of household duties, which lay down ethical
challenges to both the dominant and subordinate parties in families, society and
business

91 15) It is a term frequently used to describe the proper response to God and is akin to worship (Ps 86 9) Moreover, the parallel command in Lev 19 3 actually uses the term "fear, give reverence to" (*tirau*) which is otherwise reserved for God [3]

Alphonse Maillot puts it this way "It is not 'be stupid and obedient' but rather 'grant importance' or 'reflect with favor '"[4]

William Barclay writes that the fifth commandment requires "gratitude, obedience, and support It means concrete acts of care and not just lip service or respectful attitude "[5] For Luther,

> It is a much greater thing to honor than to love Honor includes not only love but deference, humility, and modesty, directed (so to speak) toward a majesty hidden within them It requires us not only to address them affectionately and reverently, but above all to show by our actions, both of heart and body, that we respect them very highly and that next to God we give them the very highest place

Honor does not imply unilateral obedience but rather treating someone with care and respect in deed and word To honor someone is to treat that person as valuable, to grant influence, dignity, importance and authority.

Luther goes on to say that we show honor not only with our words—how we communicate to our parents—but also by our actions and possessions, serving them cheerfully and generously, not allowing them to be hungry or in need [6] For Calvin, honor means "reverence, obedience, and gratitude "[7]

The Promise of Long Life

Paul noted to the Ephesians that this commandment has a promise attached to it How is it that long life can come to those who

---

[3]Brevard Childs, *The Book of Exodus A Critical, Theological Commentary* (Philadelphia Westminster Press, 1974), pp 418-19
[4]Alphonse Maillot, *Le Decalogue Une morale pour notre temps* (Geneva Labor & Fides, 1985), p 93
[5]William Barclay, *The Ten Commandments for Today* (Grand Rapids, Mich Eerdmans, 1974), pp 60-61
[6]Martin Luther, *The Large Catechism*, trans Robert H Fischer (1529, Philadelphia Fortress, 1959), pp 23-24
[7]Calvin *Institutes of the Christian Religion* 2 8 36

honor their parents? The answer is probably rooted in the dynamics of the extended family It is well known that elderly people who are honored, loved and cared for live longer and better lives Those in retirement facilities who live without seeing children, grandchildren, visitors and good friends tend to get sicker more often, more seriously, and to heal more slowly Neglected parents often die at earlier ages

Guess what? Our kids are watching us and how we treat their grandparents In the ordinary course of events, they will then treat us as they saw us treat our parents Joy Davidman says, "The naked and crude point of the Fifth Commandment [is] honor your parents lest your children dishonor you "[8] Thus, if we establish patterns of honoring father and mother, we will eventually benefit from it by living longer and better ourselves Laura Schlessinger notes that "if we take care of our parents, our children will take care of us, helping us to live longer "[9] And Rabbi André Chouraqui writes,

> The *weight* given to parents conditions the prolongation of days given by Elohim to man on earth This relationship is explained by the principle of reciprocity *Do not do to your parents what you would not want your children to do to you* A son who neglects to maintain his elderly parents gives a bad example to his own children He will risk suffering, in his turn, when he arrives at his old age [10]

Why Should We Honor Father and Mother?

Martin Buber sees a special connection between the fourth and fifth commandments Both are stated in positive terms ("Remember the sabbath" and "Honor your parents") and thus stand out from the eight other commandments, which begin with the phrase *You shall not* But, he says,

> There is a connection other than the purely formal one The two of them, and only these two among all of the Ten Command-

---

[8]Joy Davidman, *Smoke on the Mountain An Interpretation of the Ten Commandments* (Philadelphia Westminster Press, 1953), p 61

[9]Laura Schlessinger and Stewart Vogel, *The Ten Commandments The Significance of God's Laws in Everyday Life* (New York HarperCollins, 1998), p 147

[10]André Chouraqui, *Les Dix Commandements Aujourd'hui* (Paris Robert Laffont, 2000), p 138

ments, deal with *time,* articulated time, the first with the closed
succession of weeks in the year, the second with the open succession of generations in national duration   the lesser rhythm of
the weeks, and   the greater rhythm of the generations [11]

Our *remembering* the sabbath maintains a never-to-be-interrupted
"consecution of consecration", our *honoring* parents maintains a
never-to-be-broken "consecution of tradition " This is a brilliant insight from Buber

Walter Harrelson also sees a relationship between the fourth and
fifth commandments The sabbath command teaches us that our worth
as human beings does not lie only in our six-day work productivity, the
command to honor parents teaches us that the elderly "have worth
and significance when the time for their productive working years has
run its course "[12] So remembering sabbath and honoring parents lead
us to recognize the rhythms of both the week and the generations as
well as the intrinsic worth of people both at rest and in retirement

Still, why should we grant parents this honor? It is not necessarily
because we enjoy our parents "Enjoying our parents makes honor easier to give, but enjoyment is something quite other than honor   Our
parents do not have to be our favorite companions, they need to be
honored as those who once were called to be God-with-us "[13]

Lew Smedes sees the importance of parental authority and honor in
shaping a healthy identity

> Parents cannot give up authority   without robbing their chil-
> dren—and eventually society—of strengths neither can do with-
> out The first thing a child loses in a home without authority is a
> strong sense of his own identity We become strong individuals
> when we spend our childhood in a strong family The child with a
> clear sense of place in a family is likely to develop a clear sense of
> who and what he is outside of it [14]

[11]Martin Buber, *On the Bible Eighteen Studies* (New York Schocken, 1968), p 108

[12]Walter Harrelson, *The Ten Commandments and Human Rights* (Philadelphia Fortress, 1980), p 93

[13]Lewis B Smedes, *Mere Morality What God Expects from Ordinary People* (Grand
Rapids, Mich Eerdmans, 1983), p 92

[14]Ibid , p 75

Often, our mothers and fathers *deserve* to be honored because of what they have given us "None of us starts life from zero," writes Jan Milič Lochman "We always stand within some historical context, in community with parents and even grandparents Without this tradition life would be impossible The wise thing is to accept this critically and deliberately   wrestling with the past rather than choosing an uncritical flight from it "[15] Many of our fathers and mothers have not just given us a minimal existence, but have protected us, nursed us through sickness and injury, put up with us and forgiven us for the very trying times we have put them through They have taught us the truth, made us laugh, cried with us, shared and encouraged our dreams, protected our secrets, and launched us out into free adulthood Parents like these deserve the highest honor To selfishly, forgetfully deny honor to them is a travesty of justice They deserve better They have a right to be honored by us

Nevertheless, the foundation of this commandment is not in enjoyment, in desert, in parental rights or in psychological identity The foundation of the fifth commandment lies in *our* relationship to God The phrases "as the LORD your God commanded" (which is found in Deuteronomy) and "the LORD your God is giving you" (which is found in both Exodus and Deuteronomy) stress the fifth commandment's connection of the first four It is not uncommon for commentators to divide the Ten Commandments into "two tables" in which the first four are duties to God and the last six (including honoring parents) are duties to *neighbors* As I have said earlier, I think that the Bible teaches that all ten are equally duties to God and that all ten concern duties to neighbors In the case of the fifth commandment, the connection to God as well as neighbor is very explicit

The basic grounding of the fifth commandment is in the fact that parents are *God's primary agents and representatives to us* We honor them, first of all, not because we feel love toward them, or because they deserve it, or because there is something in it for us personally, but because we love God Just as we reach out and care for the children or the friends of someone we love or care about, so we care for our parents be-

---

[15] Jan Milič Lochman, *Signposts to Freedom The Ten Commandments and Christian Ethics* (Minneapolis Augsburg, 1982), p 82

cause we love God Just as God accepts us in the name of Jesus our Advocate, so we accept our parents in the name of God This is a command about *agency* and *representation* Rabbi J H Hertz writes that this commandment "is among the Commandments engraved on the First Tablet, the laws of piety towards God, because parents stand in the place of God, so far as their children are concerned Elsewhere in Scripture, the duty to one's parents stands likewise next to the duties towards God (Lev 19 3) "[16] Alan Redpath has the same view

> The parent is regarded as being in the place of God to the child
> The supreme facts concerning God will be impressed upon the child as he sees them in his parents, and what God is to the adult, the parent is to the child—lawgiver, lover, provider, guide, and so on What the Lord is to us, we are to the child [17]

> **The basic grounding of the fifth commandment is in the fact that parents are *God's primary agents and representatives to us* We honor them, first of all, not because we feel love toward them, or because they deserve it, or because there is something in it for us personally, but because we love God**

Luther writes, "God has exalted this estate of parents above all others, indeed he has appointed it to be his representative on earth This will and pleasure of God ought to provide us sufficient reason and incentive to do cheerfully and gladly whatever we can "[18] Laura Schlessinger also makes this connection "Just as we must honor God, the creator of all life, we must honor our parents, who gave us life In truth, parents are like gods to their children, especially younger children Parents are an important connection to God   By honoring our parents we learn to honor God "[19] In Smedes's wise opinion,

> The parent is always the person who once stood for God in the child's life and therefore had an authority that no one ever can have ever again No matter how fully free the child may be, he is

---

[16]Hertz, *Pentateuch and Haftorahs*, p 298
[17]Alan Redpath, *Law and Liberty A New Look at the Ten Commandments in the Light of Contemporary Society* (Old Tappan, N J Revell, 1978), p 57
[18]Luther, *Large Catechism*, p 26
[19]Schlessinger and Vogel, *Ten Commandments*, p 139

never free from the moral obligation of honor to that person In fact, it is only when we are free from their authority that we can freely honor parents as those who once had that authority [20]

Rabbi André Chouraqui elaborates further

On the earth, created *in the image and likeness* of the Creator, the male-female couple has as its primary vocation to become father and mother, having received the fabulous power of giving life, of procreation To honor father and mother is equivalent to celebrating the gift of life, the transmission of which belongs to every living creature The symmetry is thus perfectly equal between the honor of father and mother, the praise of the Creator, and the celebration of life [21]

This is the ideal, the intended pattern our father and mother are God's agents and representatives to give us physical life God does not create us out of a new pile of dirt or a new rib but with a mother and father Then our parents raise us and provide for us as we grow up Paul says, with respect to this basic parental care, "whoever does not provide for relatives, and especially for family members, has denied the faith and is worse than an unbeliever" (1 Tim 5 8)

Parents are also God's agents in bringing us spiritual life and truth Our faith (normally, at least) doesn't come in response to a special mystical revelation but through our parents Our image of God comes from our parents' teaching and example If men and women think of God as a kindly, wise, forgiving being, it is usually because their parents told them about God and were themselves kindly, wise and forgiving Again, Paul instructs us "Fathers, do not provoke your children to anger, but bring them up in the discipline and instruction of the Lord" (Eph 6 4)

God's intention in giving us the Ten Commandments is "that you and your children and your children's children may fear the Lord all the days of your life so that your days may be long [and] so that it may go well with you" (Deut 6 2-3) "Recite them to your children and talk about them when you are at home and when you are away,

[20]Smedes, *Mere Morality,* pp 85-86

[21]Chouraqui, *Les Dix Commandements,* p 134

when you lie down and when you rise" (Deut 6 7) "When your children ask you in time to come, 'What is the meaning of the decrees and
the statutes and the ordinances that the Lord our God has commanded
you?' then you shall say to your children, 'We were Pharaoh's slaves in
Egypt, but the LORD brought us out of Egypt with a mighty hand'"
(Deut 6 20-21)

Parents are the agents of God and we honor them because of our
love and respect for the God who has sent them They are not perfect,
of course Our homes are not always places of warm, satisfying remi-
niscence and conversation about the meaning of history and ethics and
life, as Deuteronomy prescribes Still, even with their weaknesses and
mistakes, parents are God's representatives and people through whom
God blesses us

**Area Principle 5· Honor and care for
those who are God's agents and
representatives in your life Never
treat God as though he relates directly
to you without using any agents.**

The implication for parents,
clearly, is to strive to become good
agents and representatives of
God—to be *worthy* of honor
Luther writes that "it would be well
to preach to parents on the nature
of their office, how they should
treat those committed to their authority "[22] Parents, he says, are ac-
countable to God for this office Many do not take it seriously enough
"The greatest achievement open to parents is to be ever fully worthy of
their children's reverence and trust and love "[23] What is honorable
parenting? William Barclay outlines six essentials basic nourishment,
care and support, training and discipline, encouragement, sympathetic
understanding, respect for the child as a person, and love [24] Good, honorable, worthy parenting provides unconditional love, sacrificial care,
and wise counsel, discipline and mentoring God is the model father
here, and the "supermom" described in Proverbs 31 is an ideal model
mother in many respects

---

[22]Luther, *Large Catechism*, p 32
[23]Hertz, *Pentateuch and Haftorahs*, p 299
[24]Barclay, *Ten Commandments*, pp 62-68 Barclay spends as many pages discussing
honorable parenting as he does honoring parents

What Father and Mother Do I Honor?

The audience addressed by this command is composed of adults, responsible men and women. This command is not just for young children or for a Sunday school lesson. Maillot reminds us that God's commandments are never to be used as weapons *against* others, including our children. That is, God's word here is addressed to me. Its challenge is to my relation to my parents wherever and whoever they are. It is not something for me to quote to my children as I demand their honor.

It is also important to observe that both father and mother are to be honored. There is no patriarchal prejudice here. Chouraqui notes that "the fifth commandment is formulated in terms that establish an equality between father and mother, the two equally and on the same plane."[25]

But does this command really mean that we must honor an absent, neglectful, abusive or even dangerous parent? "Only in cases of extreme rarity (e g , where godless parents would guide children towards crime) can disobedience be justified," writes Hertz. "Proper respect to parents may at times involve immeasurable hardship, yet the duty remains."[26] The command guides us toward honoring whatever mother and father we have, irrespective of their performance.

Lochman points out that at different life stages, the application of *honor* will differ. The commandment needs to be especially carefully interpreted and applied in cases "where children's lives, far from being enriched and encouraged by parents, are on the contrary disturbed and even ruined by them." In any case,

> the Fifth Commandment is controlled by the First. The Acts of the Apostles draws the correct conclusion, "We must obey God rather than men" (Acts 5 29) This stimulates a critical questioning of every proudly and arrogantly self-assertive authority in human affairs. Moreover, the history of Jesus himself points us in the same direction   "Who are my mother and my brothers?
> Whoever does the will of God is my brother and sister and mother" (Mrk 3 31ff)[27]

---

[25]Chouraqui, *Les Dix Commandements,* p 140
[26]Hertz, *Pentateuch and Haftorahs,* p 299
[27]Lochman, *Signposts,* pp 75, 80

Calvin makes these distinctions

It ought to be observed, by the way, that we are ordered to obey
parents only in the Lord   Hence, if they instigate us to transgress the law, they deserve not to be regarded as parents, but as
strangers attempting to seduce us from our obedience to our true
Father The same holds in the case of rulers, masters, and superi-
ors of every description [28]

We must always remember that all of these commands and ethical
principles are given by God to a *community* to interpret and apply, not
to isolated individuals Both in interpreting hard cases and in carrying
out difficult tasks, we must never try to go it alone We must have the
help and participation of others We must also recall what Jesus said
about the sabbath it was made for us, not us for the sabbath So too, the
fifth commandment is to guide peo-
ple to long and good life, not to misery and abuse Finally, all of these
commands remain subordinate to
their commander The fifth commandment must not be interpreted
in a wooden way that deprives God
of his freedom in our life

> We must always remember that all of
> these commands and ethical principles
> are given by God to a *community* to
> interpret and apply, not to isolated
> individuals Both in interpreting hard
> cases and in carrying out difficult
> tasks, we must never try to go it
> alone We must have the help and
> participation of others

So, with these advance qualifica-
tions, we must ask again who are
the mother and father I must
honor? My biological parents are
certainly my father and mother in some fundamental sense They were
God's agents to give me the DNA that has a lot (but not everything!) to
do with what and who I am They are my biological link back to God's
creation of Adam and Eve My "birth" mother probably "labored" and
endured some considerable pain as she brought me into the world after
carrying me in her womb for nine months This is where we start the
discussion

But being a sperm donor alone doesn't qualify you for honor as a father! Nor does the greater contribution of providing an egg and a
womb qualify you for honor as a mother Providing a sperm, egg or

---

[28]Calvin *Institutes* 2 8 38

womb does bring responsibility Those who create new children have a responsibility before God—and the rest of us—to take care of what they have produced Abdicating that responsibility makes you guilty of a great sin against God, against other people who must step in and care for the child you have created, and against the child you now abandon But the simple biological contribution alone doesn't make you a father or mother This is the case of the irresponsible, disappeared biological "parent "

What do we do about the embarrassing parent? The mentally or emotionally ill parent? The addicted or alcoholic parent? The thieving parent? The crude and rude parent? The divorced parent who ruined our family? Worst of all, what do we do about the parent who beat me or sexually abused me?

We could say that even our enemies—including a parent who has become an enemy—deserve some minimal respect, if not honor, as humans made in God's image, however degraded and repulsive they may have become If our parent is just an absent, irresponsible bum, maybe we can do something to establish a minimal but honorable relationship We can try to recognize the parent's uniqueness before God, to destroy our images and stereotypes of him or her, to call out his or her name with respect, to ask for some time to develop a healthy (though careful) relationship, and to begin to express some honor and care

I am not recommending that those with a dangerous or abusive parent approach that person It may be that the best thing—the thing that honors that parent as a responsible person—would be to blow the whistle and get the parent some help Such an action honors his or her reality far more than our papering over or denying evil deeds In all such cases, it is crucial that we proceed in the company of wise and supportive friends

When people say, "I want to meet my *real* father," they often mean the biological father they have not met or spent much time with But this is a misuse of language *Real* parenting can only be experienced with those who fulfill the basic responsibilities of parenting we have listed above My *real* parents are the people who *serve* as my parents, the people who do the things that parents do Luther extended the fifth commandment to all those who have "parental authority" over us "All who are called masters stand in the place of parents and derive from them their power and authority to govern "[29] For Luther this included the civil government as well as faithful pastors

My view is that the fifth commandment should be applied to all who have parental function or parental impact, rather than defining parents formally and structurally as Luther did Nobody parents perfectly, of course But adoptive parents who raise children are the *real* parents (not the biological parents) There is no possible comparison between the two Sperm donation and genetics are not what decides who a real father is Any parents (biological, adoptive, stepparents, etc) who abandon, neglect or abuse children under their care are *abandoning their status as real parents,* though they are still accountable before God[1]

In the biggest family picture, God is my real father (Deut 32 6, Is 9 6, Mt 6 9) In fact, God is called *Abba,* "dad" (Rom 8 15, Gal 4 6) Israel and the church are, in this big picture, my mother The church is also the bride of Christ, and we are born again into God's family through the faithfulness of this bride and mother to the Word

When people say, "I want to meet my *real* father," they often mean the biological father they have not met or spent much time with. But this is a misuse of language. My *real* parents are the people who *serve* as my parents, the people who do the things that parents do

Even more concretely, the Christian church provides us with a new family to support us in all the dimensions of our lives—helping us with our material needs, health, education, and emotional and spiritual growth Paul, for example, said to the Corinthians that he "became their father through the gospel" (1 Cor 4 15) Paul also mentions Timothy's faithful mother and grandmother, Lois and Eunice, but says nothing about Timothy's Greek father beyond a brief mention (Acts 16 1) Where was he? In any case, Paul often referred to this younger co-worker as "my beloved and faithful child" or "my loyal child"(1 Cor 4 17, 1 Tim 1 2, 2 Tim 1 2) Thus, Timothy had three "fathers"—God, his biological father (about whose role in his life we just don't know) and Paul, his mentor and spiritual-intellectual father Paul (a single man) and Peter (a married man) are spiritual fathers to several others

---

[29]Luther, *Large Catechism,* p 28ff

The first letter to Timothy urges all Christians to treat older men in the church as fathers, older women as mothers, and younger men and women as brothers and sisters (1 Tim 5 1-2)

This language of *fathers, mothers, sisters, brothers, sons* and *daughters* is very common in the Christian community It is not just that God is my father in the big sense, but some older guys in the church can be my fathers in important ways Some older women can be my mothers (and aunts) Even when we have great "natural" parents, we do well to adopt some special family members in the church One father may not give me all the kinds of fathering I need If you do not have adequate fathering or mothering in your life, adopt the parents you need! Get to know some prospective parent mentors by spending intentional time with them "The true 'fathers' in the Church," says Maillot, "are those who help their 'sons' to become adult, that is to think, to live, to act on their own "[30]

> **If you do not have adequate fathering or mothering in your life, adopt the people you need Even when we have great "natural" parents, we do well to adopt some special family members in the church**

How the Fifth Commandment Helps My Neighbor

While the fifth commandment is first of all a guideline on how to love God (by honoring those he sends to us as his representatives), it is also the case that our parents are the first actual "neighbors" we meet in life If we can't love and honor our parents, then we probably can't love and honor our other neighbors, to say nothing of our enemies They are the first "others" of whom we become conscious Our learning to live with other egos, needs, tastes, convictions, strengths and weaknesses begins with our parents and then our siblings All of the principles of the Ten Commandments need to be practiced in relation to God and then in relation to our first neighbors, our parents So this command helps my neighbor in that I practice ethical living on my closest neighbors, my parents

---

[30]Maillot, *Le Decalogue*, p 95 I am not worried if my son or daughter has some other fathers and mothers That's good as far as I am concerned I have adopted several more sons and daughters in the Lord also

It is also very good for all of our neighbors that we take care of our parents, rather than leaving them to the general care of society If I honor my father and mother, maybe they won't end up as a burden on my neighbors (e g, my parents won't depend on tax-supported services) It also helps my neighbor and relieves societal burdens if my family and I are healthy instead of dysfunctional Close, extended families produce less divorce, truancy and crime than do broken, dispersed families Not wanting to shame, dishonor or pain a parent (or grandparent) is an important check against temptations to violate or bail out on our commitments Wanting to please and honor our parents and grandparents is strong motivation to be responsible citizens and neighbors

Finally, the fifth commandment helps our neighbor by habituating us to the practice of honoring the agents of another Honoring our parents is fundamentally honoring God's representatives, but all people have such representatives and agents in their lives We don't live autonomous existences We have friends and family One important way to love a spouse is to honor the spouse's friends and relatives One important way we love our kids is by accepting and honoring their close friends

---
Corollary 5 1. Show love to others by giving care and honor to their significant others, their agents

---

As we have seen in the previous four commandments, so with this one God not only teaches this principle, he practices it God honors *our* representatives, the people who matter to us In one famous Old Testament example, God honors Abraham's faith and his relationship to Lot, who would otherwise have been destroyed with Sodom, his hometown (Gen 18—19) In the New Testament a believing spouse "sanctifies" an unbelieving spouse (1 Cor 7 13-16 NIV), this shows that God honors our representatives, our agents

Practicing Our Principles: Rebuilding Our Households and Families

We live in a world of messed up family relations Parents are often so wrapped up in their careers and personal quests, so exhausted by the frantic pace of life, that kids are neglected Absent fathers, working mothers, latchkey kids and day-care-raised children are all members of our community Many parents fall into one of two extreme camps the walk-all-over-me wimps or the crushing tyrants Family life has lots of distractions and lots of television, but it is harder to find a family hearth—family dinners are rare, family conversation is in decline And all of that is to say nothing of the special challenges various families face broken homes, stepparents, foster parents, live-in lovers, drunken uncles and so on Worst of all is child abuse—sexual, physical and psychological The family is for many children a place of fear, a place from which to escape, instead of a place where shelter and protection can be found

Many of the problems we face could be ameliorated if grandparents and other relatives were more involved We have basically forgotten how to live as extended families Our elderly are often stored, institutionally warehoused, in retirement homes They are often neglected, ignored, scorned, rejected, even robbed On the other hand, difficult grandparents could carry out their roles in a better fashion Rather than being critical, meddlesome, nagging and demanding, grandparents should be wise, kind, generous and positive They should pray for and build up their children and grandchildren

> Many of the problems we face could be ameliorated if grandparents and other relatives were more involved. We have basically forgotten how to live as extended families On the other hand, difficult grandparents could carry out their roles in a better fashion.

Is our treatment of the elderly, in both the church and the broader society, an ethical issue? How does the practice of this ethical principle—honoring one's parents—change in a highly mobile, modern welfare state with its social security and retirement programs, with its senior-citizen housing and elder hostel programs? Does the command need to be updated? According to Maillot,

> We are entering a world where there will be more and more elderly but where less and less will they be given a place, a friendship, a hearing, a world where there will be less and less honor, not only of their age but of their humanity Increasingly one puts them in "pre-cemeteries"—in the antechambers of hell where they no longer serve any purpose and where they are no more than dead-in-waiting [31]

---

[31]Ibid , p 94

An older pattern, with a lot to recommend it, would involve extended families trying hard to live together in the same neighborhoods (if not the same houses), even if this requires some professional and personal sacrifices It does not mean that we have to co-own our houses or work together in a family business Nor does it mean that we must all go to the same church or eat together every evening Perhaps we still draw our social security checks and maintain separate finances All individuals need some personal as well as shared time and space, of course We need to be creative here and explore the alternatives We need to address the needs of children growing up, the stresses on working parents and the neglect of the elderly I don't think we should simply yield to popular trends in society The fifth commandment should prod us to think creatively here

For Reflection and Discussion

1 How have you tried to honor your parents? What are your specific ideas of how we should honor our parents today? How is it different for children in different age groups (e g , preteens, teenagers, twentysomethings, middle-aged adults)?

2 Do you agree with the author's point that we should try hard to keep our extended families close enough geographically to have significant ongoing, even weekly, contact?

3 What should we (or can we) do to reduce the negative effects of television, movies and popular music on our families? How can we use these media to positive ends?

4 Can you describe any of your *agents* (your special friends or relatives)? Is it right to say that anyone who cares for you will need to show at least some honor and respect to the people whom you value?

8

Life Guarding

You shall not murder," the sixth commandment, begins the second half of the Decalogue (Ex 20 13) It has been traditional to speak of commandments six through ten as the "second table" of the law and to say that these commandments turn to our ethical duties to our neighbors [1] Now it is true that each of the first five commandments makes explicit reference to "the Lord your God" and the second series refers explicitly to "your neighbor" in nine and ten But we must be careful to notice that the first five also make reference to people, not just to God And commandments six through ten provide further guidance on how to love God and defer to his rights over his creation Remember, all ten are about how to love God, and all ten are about how to love our neighbor

Nevertheless, the design in this second half of the Decalogue is clearly distinctive from that in the first half Commandments six through ten comprise five basic guidelines for a healthy and good human life Furthermore, these are given not in a random order but in a fivefold progression from the most immediate and concrete to the most detached and spiritual aspects of life It is not quite right to say they are in descending order of importance, either to God or to our neigh-

---

[1] Strictly speaking, remember, this would be the second side, the "back side," of each of the two, duplicate copies of the covenant Also remember that the numbering of the commands varies somewhat among Jewish and Christian traditions Some have argued that "honor father and mother" (or even "remember the sabbath day") begins the second series rather than concluding the first series See the preceding chapters for further discussion

bor The best way to describe the progression is that these commands
are in descending order of immediacy and concreteness

The first principle in this series, then, concerns our basic, physical
existence as individuals Protecting your neighbor's physical life and
health is the ethical point of departure for the second table How immediate and concrete is this? If you are dead, nothing else on the list has any importance Murdering one's neighbor is the most immediate and concrete assault one can make on him or her His or her life (and health) is the first aspect of existence to address

**Commandments six through ten comprise
five basic guidelines for a healthy
and good human life. Furthermore, these
are given not in a random order but
in a fivefold progression from the most
immediate and concrete to the most
detached and spiritual aspects of life.**

First, we must be alive As Alan Redpath has written, "The giving of life
creates the possibility of every other relationship, and the cessation of
life ends them all "[2]

Jan Milič Lochman says,

> From both a human and a theological standpoint, *murder* is in
> every sense the last thing, the worst thing a human being can do
> to another human being In murder we cross the ultimate boundary in relation to the fellow human being, i e , by the irrevocable
> breach of this relationship, a breach which the perpetrator can
> never repair Murder is the "final solution" to the human conflict [3]

Lochman uses the terms *last, ultimate* and *final,* but his point is the
same as mine murder tops the list

Rather than "you shall not kill," the text should be translated "you
shall not murder" (Ex 20 13 par Deut 5 17) The Hebrew word here
(rasah) almost always refers to the intentional killing of one's personal
enemy or to the accidental killing of one's neighbor (manslaughter) Intentional *rasah* (premeditated murder) was punishable by death, for
unintentional *rasah* (manslaughter) one could flee to the cities of ref-

---

[2]Alan Redpath, *Law and Liberty A New Look at the Ten Commandments* (Old Tappan, N J Revell, 1978), p 69

[3]Jan Milič Lochman, *Signposts to Freedom The Ten Commandments and Christian
Ethics* (Minneapolis Augsburg, 1982), p 89

uge (Deut 19 1-13) We are commanded never to personally cause another human being's death As Brevard Childs explains,

The verb *rasah* at first had an objective meaning and described a type of slaying that called forth blood vengeance In order to protect innocent blood, an escape was provided in cities of refuge for the unintentional slayer, but this exception did not alter the objective context of the verb itself However, at a somewhat later date—at least before the eighth century—a change in meaning can be observed The verb came to designate those acts of violence against a person which arose from personal feelings of hatred and malice The command in its present form forbids such an act of violence and rejects the right of a person to take the law into his own hands out of a feeling of personal injury [4]

The Bible has plenty of instruction about this topic In the very first family Cain murdered his brother Abel (Gen 4) The Pentateuch is full of warnings and laws against killing and violence Israel's prophets thundered against murder and violence among God's chosen people (e g , Jer 7 9, Hos 4 1-2) The Wisdom writers remind us that God hates "hands that shed innocent blood" (Prov 6 16-17) The New Testament Gospels and letters repeat the sixth commandment (e g , Mt 5 21, Rom 13 9, Jas 2 11) and make it plain that bloodshed and murder cannot be part of God's kingdom (Mt 15 19, Rom 1 29, 1 Tim 1 9, Rev 21 8, 22 15) In fact, Jesus says that the ultimate enemy, Satan, "was a murderer from the beginning" (Jn 8 44)

Jesus' Fulfillment of the Laws of Violence

Jesus was, of course, brutally and unfairly put to death, as were most of his early band of followers In a decision that was intensely symbolic, the crowds at Jesus' public trial, according to all four Gospels, chose Barabbas, a murderer (Lk 23 18-19), over Jesus, the healer and life-giver, and screamed "Away with him! Crucify him!" at Jesus (Jn

---

[4]Brevard Childs, *The Book of Exodus A Critical, Theological Commentary* (Philadelphia Westminster Press, 1974), p 421 Num 35 30 uses *rasah* for the execution of a murderer who has been tried in court, so we do not have a rigid, exceptionless definition for the term *Haroq* (165 occurrences) and *hemit* (201 occurrences) are the more common OT Hebrew words for killing They could refer to killing personal enemies but also to war, capital punishment or death by God's judgment

19 15) Jesus saw his death coming, prayed to avoid it but then accepted it Then he defeated it by coming back to life on Easter morning Thus, Jesus knows violence not just because he had special insight as God's Son, but because as a human being he suffered it

Jesus frequently addressed issues of violence during his life In the Sermon on the Mount, Jesus explained the fulfillment of the law and the "righteousness [that] exceeds that of the scribes and Pharisees" in relation to murder and violence (Mt 5 17, 20) The Beatitudes culminate with "Blessed are the peacemakers, for they will be called children of God" (Mt 5 9) In three of his six "antitheses" ("You have heard it said, but I say   ") that follow the Beatitudes in his Sermon on the Mount, Jesus dealt with issues of violence The fifth and sixth antitheses deal more generally with violence, hatred and vengeance, so we will begin with their broader picture Then we will look at Jesus' first antithesis, in which he explains the meaning of the sixth commandment

In the fifth antithesis Jesus cites the famous law of retaliation, the *lex talionis* of the Old Testament "You have heard that it was said 'An eye for an eye and a tooth for a tooth ' But I say to you, Do not resist an evildoer" (Mt 5 38-39) This law of retaliation, in its original Old Testament context, should not be understood as a barbaric perpetuation of violence but as a *limitation* we are to take *only* one eye for an eye, and not yield to our vengeful instinct to take two of yours if you take one of mine' But now, Jesus says, don't seek any payback Instead, turn the other cheek, give to those who demand from you, and go the second mile beyond people's demands (Mt 5 38-42)

In the sixth antithesis, Jesus says, "You have heard that it was said, 'You shall love your neighbor and hate your enemy ' But I say to you, Love your enemies and pray for those who persecute you" (Mt 5 43-44) The command to love your neighbor as yourself was already made explicitly clear in the Holiness Code (Lev 19 18) This love for one's neighbor had a broad reach for example, "love the alien as yourself" (Lev 19 34) But now Jesus pushes it a step further—to love your *enemy* No text in Scripture actually says to "hate your enemy " But Jesus makes the call to love as wide as possible and repudiates hatred, even where an enemy is concerned (Mt 5 43-48)

Lochman argues that even in the Old Testament a clear limitation on revenge is drawn The "mark on Cain," the cities of refuge, the strict laws of evidence and even the *lex talionis* show that Old Testament faith has no place for indulging a vengeful, murderous attitude In the New Testament, Lochman adds, the "line is continued and *radicalized* to a quite unexampled degree For Christians the law of revenge is not simply limited but handed over to God "[5] Redpath reminds us that Jesus rebuked his disciples when they wanted to call down fire from heaven on those who refused their message (Lk 9 54-55) Jesus rebuked Peter for using his sword (Mt 26 51-52) He said his kingdom was not of this world, otherwise his disciples would fight (Jn 18 36) "In other words, Jesus denounced war and killing—notice this—at the very point where it was suggested for his own defense against the most unholy alliance the world has ever known "[6]

The whole logic of vengeance has been overturned by Jesus Christ Jesus has taken the place of our enemy on the cross "Right at the heart of the revelation of the Bible is a record of a murder for which the whole world is guilty "[7] We are the murderer who must be forgiven Jesus has taken on himself all the penalties due as a result of our sins (and our enemy's sins) We must read all vengeance and justice texts in Scripture in light of their fulfillment on the cross [8] Paul strongly reinforces this message

> Bless those who persecute you, bless and do not curse them
> Do not repay anyone evil for evil, but take thought for what is noble in the sight of all If it is possible, so far as it depends on you, live peaceably with all Beloved, never avenge yourselves, but leave room for the wrath of God, for it is written, "Vengeance is mine, I will repay, says the Lord " No, "if your enemies are hungry, feed them, if they are thirsty, give them something to drink, for by doing this you will heap burning coals on their heads " Do not be overcome by evil, but overcome evil with good (Rom 12 14-21)

Peter argues the same way

---

[5] Lochman, *Signposts*, pp 90-91
[6] Redpath, *Law and Liberty*, p 72
[7] Ibid , p 73
[8] See Earl F Palmer, *Old Law, New Life The Ten Commandments and New Testament Faith* (Nashville Abingdon, 1984), p 101, for an eloquent statement of this point

If you endure when you do right and suffer for it, you have God's
approval   Christ also suffered for you, leaving you an example, so that you should follow in his steps "He committed no sin,
and no deceit was found in his mouth " When he was abused, he
did not return abuse, when he suffered, he did not threaten, but
he entrusted himself to the one who judges justly (1 Pet 2 20-23)

So the law of retaliation is reversed because of Jesus' death and resurrection Jesus died for the sins of the world After Calvary there is
no longer any basis for trying to make sure that anyone pays for his or
her sins [9]

Jesus' first antithesis considers directly the sixth commandment

You have heard that it was said to those of ancient times, "You
shall not murder", and "whoever murders shall be liable to judgment " But I say to you that if you are angry with a brother or sister, you will be liable to judgment, and if you insult a brother or
sister, you will be liable to the council, and if you say, "You fool,"
you will be liable to the hell of fire So when you are offering your
gift at the altar, if you remember that your brother or sister has
something against you, leave your gift there before the altar and
go, first be reconciled to your brother or sister, and then come
and offer your gift Come to terms quickly with your accuser
when you are on the way to court with him, or your accuser may
hand you over to the judge, and the judge to the guard, and you
will be thrown into prison Truly I tell you, you will never get out
until you have paid the last penny (Mt 5 21-26)

It is misleading to call this an *antithesis* because Jesus does not propose an antithesis at all (as he does for the law of retaliation or for the
tradition of hating your enemy) Rather, Jesus "fills full" the sixth commandment in two basic ways First, he deepens and broadens its meaning Narrowly, the command says not to murder the body, but Jesus
broadens and deepens it to include murderous language ("you fool!")

---

[9] Discipline and consequences are often important as a pedagogical device, i e , to
teach someone, especially someone very young or ignorant, to think clearly But for
everyone who believes in what Jesus did at Calvary, there is no place for any efforts
to make someone pay as a kind of cosmic balancing of the scales of justice, Jesus
balanced those scales already

and the murderous attitude (anger) Luther says about this command that "we must not kill, either by hand, heart, or word, by signs or gestures, or by aiding or abetting "[10]

The rabbis believed the sixth commandment had broad implications for example, we should not publicly embarrass a fellow human being, fail to provide for and protect guests leaving our homes, or cause someone to lose his livelihood [11] "The Saviour is interested not only in knocking the gun out of a man's hand," Redpath says, "but in taking the devil out of his heart "[12]

> Jesus, the Lord of our ethics, repudiates the law of retaliation and calls on his followers to love, forgive and bless not just their friends, but also their enemies and attackers

Second, Jesus "fills full" the command by pointing to the positive gospel contained or implied by the law It is not merely a *negative* "don't take a life," but a *positive* "go" to the offended one and "protect life " It is not just a *negative* "watch your attitude (anger, hatred) and speech (insults)," but a *positive* "go and talk about terms of reconciliation " Luther says, "This commandment is violated not only when a person actually does evil but also when he fails to do good to his neighbor, or, though he has the opportunity, fails to prevent, protect, or save him from bodily harm   Not only is murder forbidden, but also everything that may lead to murder "[13] Luther reminds us of Christ's teaching about the judgment of those who ignore the poor and hungry "I was hungry and thirsty and you gave me no food, I was thirsty and you gave me nothing to drink" (Mt 25 42-43) We are, in effect, murderers whenever we can do good and do not, whenever we can prevent harm and do not, and whenever we contribute in any way, no matter how small or indirect, to death in the world

According to Calvin,

We are required faithfully to do what in us lies to defend the life

---

[10]Martin Luther, *The Large Catechism,* trans Robert H Fischer (1529, Philadelphia Fortress, 1959), p 33

[11]Avroham Chaim Feuer, *Aseres Hadibros The Ten Commandments, A New Translation with a Commentary Anthologized from Talmudic, Midrashic and Rabbinic Sources* (Brooklyn, N Y Mesorah, 1981), p 55

[12]Redpath, *Law and Liberty,* p 76

[13]Luther, *Large Catechism,* pp 34-35

of our neighbor, to promote whatever tends to his tranquility, to
be vigilant in warding off harm, and when danger comes, to assist
in removing it   To be clear of the crime of murder it is not
enough to refrain from shedding man's blood   If you do not
according to your means and opportunity study to defend his
safety, by that inhumanity you violate the law [14]

Jesus broadens the prohibition of the
sixth commandment to include not only
murderous acts but insulting,
"murderous" speech and hateful,
"murderous" attitudes. He insists that
the command is fulfilled only when the
negative *prohibitions* are accompanied
by positive *actions* that seek peace
and reconciliation

Jesus' explanation of the sixth
commandment's full meaning
provides boundaries that we
should not cross murderous
acts, insulting speech and hateful attitudes The whole, entire
complex of violence must be rejected But equally important is
the positive agenda protecting
and nurturing life In considering any form of violence (capital
punishment, warfare, suicide,
abortion, euthanasia, lethal self-defense, etc) we have not understood
the sixth commandment fully until we discover the good to pursue in
overcoming the evil we recognize We must ask, what are the redemptive, gospel alternatives to capital punishment, war, suicide, abortion,
euthanasia and lethal violence?

Three Reasons Why Murder Is Wrong

Why is murder so clearly and fundamentally "of the devil"? How do we
know it is wrong? Certainly our feelings are not a very reliable foundation Almost all of us, including the most peaceful and gentle, have a
deep-seated instinct toward vengeance The outrage we feel when we
are personally trampled is one thing Perhaps even more difficult to
contain are the vengeful feelings that arise when we see some remorse-
less, grinning predator who has inflicted abominable cruelties on others for absolutely no reason But, we remember, "Vengeance is mine, I
will repay, says the Lord" (Rom 12 19) Good thing it is his

Nor does the sixth commandment rest on a sort of "let's all just be

---

[14]Calvin *Institutes of the Christian Religion* 2 8 39-40

friends" optimistic humanism like that found in some parts of the pacifist community Rather, the sixth commandment is based on God's will and choice We must not murder because all life belongs to God God's culminating work in creation is making man and woman in his own image and likeness Murder is a direct attack on the pinnacle of God's creation

When capital punishment was instituted after the great flood of Genesis 6—8 God said,

> For your own lifeblood I will surely require a reckoning   from human beings, each one for the blood of another, I will require a reckoning for human life Whoever sheds the blood of a human, by a human shall that person's blood be shed, for in his own image God made humankind And you, be fruitful and multiply, abound on the earth and multiply in it (Gen 9 5-7)

As Rabbi Avroham Chaim Feuer writes, "The murderer defies God by attacking the man who represents God's image "[15]

Murder is so serious an offense against *God* that the murderer does not deserve to live any longer Murder crosses the ultimate line God is the creator and preserver of life Life belongs to him To cause someone else's death is to interfere with something precious that belongs to God When King David arranged the murder of Uriah (after seducing Uriah's wife, Bathsheba), "the thing that David did displeased the Lord" (2 Sam 11 27) Even for Uriah, this non-Jewish Hittite, only God is to be the master of life and death It is for God alone to decide when a life is finished We must have confidence in God's judgment and power over lives and not take matters into our own hands As Lochman explains,

> Consciously or unconsciously, the murderer assumes the sovereignty over life and death and thereby claims the role which, from the biblical standpoint, belongs to the Creator alone He (or she) "plays God," in a flagrant breach of the First Commandment, and in so doing usurps the right which has been bestowed by God on that fellow human being and which can therefore only be withdrawn by God himself, namely, the right to life [16]

---

[15]Feuer, *Aseres Hadibros*, p 54
[16]Lochman, *Signposts*, p 89

Alphonse Maillot points out that the very first commandment makes clear that there is but one God—and you and I are not this God The sixth commandment derives its force from the first "You may not pose as God of your brother—in particular by presuming to take his life from him   This phrase is thus a promise, a protection for these 'others,' because it shows that no one may pretend to be God, to be the master and judge of others No man has the right of life or of death "[17]

Of course, murder is not just an offense against God, not simply a betrayal of our love and a violation of God's rights It is also the ultimate attack on a *neighbor* It is the opposite of love (no matter how twisted our logic, especially in prenatal and end-of-life situations), and it is the ultimate violation of justice and of our neighbor's right to life Death deprives our neighbor of all freedom It almost certainly causes extreme, prolonged pain and grief to relatives and friends of the one murdered

---

Killing another human being is wrong because it violates God's prerogative over life It is also the most serious, irreversible wrong you can do to another human being But it is also a terrible wrong against yourself, a subhuman act of personal degradation and slavery.

Murder also degrades the *murderer* Murder puts one in the subhuman fellowship of Satan Murder deeply wounds—if not destroys—the murderer's own soul and humanity It either wracks us with unending guilt or renders us callously subhuman Murder represents the ultimate form of slavery to one's passions, emotions and folly Even if not physically imprisoned for the crime, the murderer is imprisoned and bound in other ways, always looking over her shoulder in fear of discovery and punishment, imprisoned also by the need to rationalize and justify her horrible, irreversible deed

Why Human Beings Are So Violent

To the question, why is it wrong? we must now add, why does it happen? Part of our response must be to understand and address the un-

---

[17] Alphonse Maillot, *Le Decalogue Une morale pour notre temps* (Geneva Labor & Fides, 1985), pp 98-99

derlying causes of murder and violence We do not fulfill our ethical obligation by only condemning the final, dreadful act [18] Why are people prone to violence against others, even to the point of murder? There is probably no emotion that flares up so quickly as anger Anger and rage have a quicker trigger than even lust, and they are more immediately threatening and injurious to others than any other emotion

Anger, in turn, comes out of hurt When we are frustrated and in pain, we lash out in anger Anger is an act of power by someone feeling threatened or powerless Of course, all humans get hurt and frustrated and sometimes feel cornered and threatened But when anger is combined with a contempt for life and for others, it might be expressed in violent attack It would be wrong, of course, to assume all murders are the result of momentary, uncontrolled rage Murder often is planned obsessively by people seething with resentment for months or even years

Rabbi André Chouraqui points out that humans, from birth to death, are vulnerable to a defensive instinct that can turn us into aggressors—no less today than when our primitive ancestors lived The difference today is not in our nature but in the fact that the same violent reaction can extend its ravages far beyond earlier times

> To build respect for the sixth commandment, it is above all important to understand the essential motives of murder Aside from cases of sickness or purely sadistic killing, most killing is provoked by the desire for revenge, jealousy or fear   The best means for one to overcome these fundamental motives would be to re-center oneself in order to make or rebuild the covenant with the only Being who is greater the Supreme Being, source of life This covenant with the divine transcends all particular covenants among people It is the lynchpin of all covenants entered into here below, which nourishes respect for the Other [19]

---

[18]Christians must not be afraid of this sort of questioning Asking why an evil act happened and whether we might have contributed to it in some way is precisely the sort of humble, realistic thinking the Bible counsels Labeling such self-critical questioning as disloyalty (as happened after the September 11, 2001, terrorist attacks) is shortsighted, foolish and unbiblical Holding yourself responsible doesn't provide a free pass to others

[19]André Chouraqui, *Les Dix Commandements Aujourd'hui* (Paris Robert Laffont, 2000), p 173

Overcoming Violence

Unquestionably, circumstances can encourage or discourage violence
We must avoid situations that we know are likely to send us into a rage
In the same way, we need to try to mitigate or eliminate circumstances
that are likely to contribute to violent reactions by others Whether it
is in the way we (or others) talk and behave around a next-door neighbor, fellow student or coworker—or the way our political representatives, media figures or corporations talk and behave around the
world—the point is the same Do not contribute to conditions that are
likely to add to people's hurt and anger and then to incite violence
Consider the causes and contributing factors of murder and violence

At another level, we must be wise about the availability of instruments of violence Those who express their rage with their fists usually
cause fewer deaths than do those with guns (or airplanes or anthrax)
It rings rather hollow when weapon manufacturers and merchants
deny any responsibility for the irresponsible use of their products (e g ,
"Guns don't kill people, people kill people")

Part of what it takes to overcome violence is self-control People
must learn how to defuse their negative feelings, rather than act them
out This is not so easily done when a hurting person is isolated from
others and surrounded by messages encouraging violence and vengeance Friends and community can help to defuse people's anger and
frustration and to restrain them from acting and speaking violently
And, in turn, self-control is best founded on hope, rather than on stoic
resignation If I have hope for a better tomorrow, that things will get
better, I may not give in to my worst impulses today

The sixth commandment is inextricably linked—more precisely,
"built on"—the five commandments that precede it That is, the best
preventive to violence against others is a clear and robust relationship
with God, as this is described in the first five commandments But remember also that those first five principles of how to relate to God
have clear corollaries guiding our relations with people made in the image of God For example,

- The first commandment teaches me that the enemy whom I may
  wish dead is not a contemptible nothing but rather a unique, irreplaceable creation of God

- Following the second commandment, I cannot reduce my enemy to a fixed image or stereotype, instead, I need to imagine how my enemy could conceivably grow and change into someone different, someone better

- I learn from the third commandment that I need to respect my enemy by knowing my enemy's name and by speaking to him or her
- If I take the fourth commandment to heart, I will attempt to spend some quality time with my enemy and to work for her or him
- The fifth commandment reminds me to honor and love my enemy as a possible agent of God in my life (or someone else's)

Thus, if I live out these first five commandments, I will arrive at a place where it is inconceivable to murder my enemy, where I observe the sixth commandment because I cannot do otherwise Without the foundation provided by the preceding commandments, I can justify pushing away, stereotyping, objectifying, discarding, *even killing* If the sixth commandment is to be effective, the first five must be at work first

The Picture Gets More Complex
What we have done, so far, is to look at the heart of the matter The sixth commandment prohibits murder and manslaughter and, by Jesus' extension, insults and anger, and it requires that we work toward reconciliation and overcoming of evil with good But the picture is still more complex—in both the Bible and our world The Bible seems to allow (or even encourage) killing in certain categories other than murder (e g , capital punishment and war) Moreover, the Bible does not speak directly or at length to some other difficult life-and-death issues such as suicide, abortion, euthanasia and the use of lethal force by police and private citizens How should we practice our Christian principles in these areas?

As we proceed to consider different forms of killing, let us heed Lochman's reminder

> Overcoming violence and killing requires an improvement in the conditions and circumstances that create hurt, anger, despair and a disposition to lash out violently, a reduction of the means (weapons) used to inflict violence on others, and greater self-control based on renewed hope and on a deeper understanding of our enemies as people made in God's image

There are distinctions in killing which are of great ethical importance It would be wrong to relativize these distinctions as if they
were "degrees" of murder At the same time, however, a Christian
ethic has to elaborate and stress the real connections which exist
between them, in order to keep awake the conscience of church
and society [20]

Redpath points out that although more people have been killed in
traffic accidents than in the two world wars,

> that fact does not seem to disturb us We just take it for granted,
> and the fact that we are overshadowed by the imminent danger
> of a final catastrophic war is viewed purely from the angle of poli-
> tics and expediency, without regard for these flaming words from
> heaven I would that these four words could appear like fire in
> the sky so that all may recognize the sovereignty of God over
> human life   This Commandment, in a very simple way and
> yet in most definite language, flings a wall of fire around every
> human being and reserves to God, who first gave life, the right to
> end it [21]

We now examine six specific challenges to our principle of protecting
life and health capital punishment, warfare, suicide, abortion, euthanasia and lethal force (police, self-defense, etc) The discussions below are
not comprehensive analyses but rather "outlines" of ways to think about
and respond to these troublesome issues [22] My approaches to each of
these areas may not be greeted with enthusiasm by everyone, but my
objective is to prod my readers to think carefully and deeply about how
they should respond in faithfulness Finally, we will look at several addi-

---

[20]Lochman, *Signposts*, p 93

[21]Redpath, *Law and Liberty*, pp 68-69 How wonderful and refreshing it is to read an
old-time conservative evangelical with these sentiments So often "Bible-believing,"
evangelical and fundamentalist theologians and pastors are best known for their
passionate enthusiasm for capital punishment and just warfare What a tragic reversal of biblical priorities

[22]Two excellent resources for articles on specific topics in Christian ethics are
David J Atkinson, David F Field, Arthur Holmes and Oliver O'Donovan, eds , *New
Dictionary of Christian Ethics and Pastoral Theology* (Downers Grove, Ill Inter-
Varsity Press, 1995), and James F Childress and John Macquarrie, eds , *The West-
minster Dictionary of Christian Ethics*, 2nd ed (Philadelphia Westminster Press,
1986)

tional ways of practicing this principle in today's world

The Criminal: Can Capital Punishment Be a Christian Ethical Practice?

Capital punishment would appear to be the most likely candidate for an acceptable form of killing It is (ideally) determined and administered by the state in a careful, fair manner It is a re-

> **Area Principle 6 Never do anything that threatens or harms the life and health of another person. Rather, regarding it as God's own creation, do whatever you can to protect that person's life and health and to promote peace and reconciliation**

sponse to the ultimate crime, rarely rising to the level of cruelty and brutality of the criminal's own behavior Laura Schlessinger points out that "capital punishment for murder of an innocent is mandated in each of the (Torah) Five Books of Moses (Genesis 9 6, Exodus 21 21, Leviticus 24 17, Numbers 35 31, Deuteronomy 19 20) In fact, it's the only law in the Torah repeated in each and every one of the Five Books¹ Obviously, this was an important divine consideration "[23]

What Dr Laura glosses over, however, is that capital punishment was prescribed for a long list of offenses in Israel's law—not only for taking another's life by murder (Ex 21 12, Lev 24 17, cf Gen 4 10) but also for child sacrifice (Lev 20 2), negligent manslaughter, if the killer did not flee to a city of refuge (Num 35 9-28), irresponsible ownership of a killer ox (Ex 21 29) and false witness on a capital charge (Deut 19 18-21) Each of these offenses, and their penalties, is related to Israel's basic *lex talionis* (law of retaliation) an eye for an eye, a tooth for a tooth, a life for a life

Capital punishment was also enforceable for the following (1) kidnapping, (2) insulting or injuring parents, (3) sexual misconduct, such as incest, unchastity, rape, adultery, fornication and bestiality, and (4) religious and ritual offenses such as witchcraft, magic, idolatry, blasphemy, falsely claiming to be a prophet, trespassing in the holy place and breaking the sabbath [24] That these were potentially capital of-

---

[23]Laura Schlessinger and Stewart Vogel, *The Ten Commandments The Significance of God's Laws in Everyday Life* (New York HarperCollins, 1998), p 182

[24]For these various capital offenses see the regulations in Ex 21—22, 31, Lev 18, 20, 24, Num 1, 3, 18, Deut 13, 22—23, 27

fenses in Israel shows at the very least that we should take these matters seriously, in our era no less than in the past Our texts do not show clearly whether or how this supreme punishment was carried out, nor do these texts prove that Israel's ancient tribal laws are binding on today's Christians Remember also that Israel's rules for evidence were strict Only in the mouths of two or three witnesses could someone be condemned If someone was found to be a false witness, he would suffer the fate he had intended for the innocent person he accused

Still, Christians have often believed that they should support capital punishment Walter Kaiser expresses a widely held viewpoint

> Capital punishment is not an optional feature in a truly moral and ethically obedient society As Rushdoony succinctly states it, "To oppose capital punishment as prescribed by God's law is thus to oppose the cross of Christ and to deny the validity of the altar " In the case of first-degree murder, Numbers 35 31 specifically requires that there be no remission from the penalty of death If we are to prevent the very ground itself from vomiting forth its inhabitants in order to cleanse its defilement with innocent blood (Lev 18 25), then there had better be a godly exercise of capital punishment against all murderers To extend love or mercy in exchange for justice at this level is to despise both the image of God in the one who has been suddenly felled (Gen 9 6) and, more importantly, to despise the very basis by which we received new life in Christ by the death of the Lamb of God

Kaiser goes on to argue that "the person who destroys another person, who bears the image of God, does violence to God himself—as if he had killed God in effigy   Since all persons continue to bear the image of God, it is fair to say that this ordinance has permanent relevance and validity "[25]

The boldness of Kaiser and Rushdoony's position is startling By contrast, Redpath, former pastor of Moody Memorial Church and dean

---

[25]Walter C Kaiser Jr , *Toward Old Testament Ethics* (Grand Rapids, Mich Zondervan, 1983), pp 148, 167 The reference is to Rousas J Rushdoony's *The Institutes of Biblical Law* (Nutley, N J Craig, 1973), p 77 Rushdoony is a Christian Reconstructionist who argues that the whole law except for ceremonial aspects that are clearly declared fulfilled in the New Testament, remains binding on the Christian Kaiser is considered a conservative evangelical

of Capernwray Bible School, agonizes over this issue "I cannot escape the fact that to end the life of anybody puts that person beyond all possible hope of the saving grace of God, and surely this is a matter which demands very careful thought and prayer " Furthermore, the cross of Christ demands that we forgive others as Christ has forgiven us "You cannot refuse to forgive somebody else if you claim to be a child of God My friend, when you receive God's mercy in forgiveness it is not given in a cup, but you receive it through a pipeline from an inexhaustible supply It is not given to be held for oneself, but we receive it in overflowing abundance to pass on to others "[26] How incredibly different is Redpath's tone and conviction from those of Kaiser and Rushdoony who have not a word of gospel or grace for the situation [27]

Although Israel's laws (against cursing parents, breaking the sabbath, etc) were often broken, it is remarkable how *rarely* we read of these penalties being applied Israel often fell into idolatry, but the gallows were not swinging all day long with violators, as you might expect after reading Kaiser and Rushdoony Moses committed murder but was not executed Aaron the high priest committed idolatry but lived David committed adultery and then arranged a murder but was not executed Was this because of some political and religious lack of rigor at the time? There is nothing in Scripture to suggest that interpretation God was very much awake and involved in these episodes, according to the Bible

What is made clear is that God's mercy and grace in these cases is overwhelming God does not seem to be in any hurry to kill those who offend—even those who offend greatly Remember the woman caught in adultery who was brought to Jesus for stoning by some first-century Rushdoonys (Jn 8 3-11)? Jesus told her accusers, "Let anyone among you who is without sin be the first to throw a stone at her " His words to her were, "Go your way, and from now on do not sin again " This is how Jesus applied that Old Testament law about capital punishment for adultery We might well ask why today's Christian capital punish-

---

[26] Redpath, *Law and Liberty,* pp 73, 77
[27] See Lewis B Smedes, *Mere Morality What God Expects from Ordinary People* (Grand Rapids, Mich Eerdmans, 1983), p 119 Like Redpath, Smedes is deeply moved by God's redemptive grace and forgiveness even as he considers capital punishment

ment advocates don't share just a smidgeon of the graciousness and pa-
tience that characterized the one they call Lord

We also need to be careful about selectively picking our favorite
crimes for capital punishment The Ten Commandments stand out
clearly from all other laws, but there is not a similar list of "ten punishable crimes" that apply in all ages' How do we pick and choose from
among Israel's capital crime list? I am not saying that no case can be
made for capital punishment, especially for premeditated murder But
remember that Paul did not invoke capital punishment for the guy bed-
ding his stepmother in Corinth (1 Cor 5 1-2) Nor, in the most important case of all, did Jesus bring death to those who murdered him He
could have, but he didn't

The bottom line in Christian ethics is something like this a human
being who deliberately murders another human being, or whose gross
irresponsibility leads to another's death, *deserves* to die or at least to
give his or her life for the one killed (say, by a lifetime sentence of hard
labor with all the financial proceeds going to the victim's family) But
are Christians called to make sure that people get the punishment they
deserve? Or to make sure that nobody gets away with anything? Is that
what our ethics and discipleship are all about? If that is so, then let's at
least be consistent and start with ourselves and our family and loved
ones and make sure we all pay in full measure for all of our sins and offenses "Ah," you now say, "but I've been forgiven by God in Jesus
Christ " Rather convenient and self-serving, doesn't it seem?

Perhaps you want to say that murder is a public justice issue and
your sins are merely a private moral issue I'm sorry to have to say that
you won't find that distinction in your Bible Cursing your parents,
idolatry (which, by Jesus' own clear teaching, would include worshiping money, the besetting sin of American business and popular culture), breaking the sabbath—these are all capital crimes in Israel's law
Jesus said that if you even lust after another, you have committed adultery Do you remember the penalty for adultery? Have you ever in your
life done any of these things? Then be consistent go turn yourself in
and take your just punishment

I am not trying to muddy the waters more than they already are I
am merely asking that we be consistent I loathe and grieve over violence and murder today I have little respect for those who demon-

strate against capital punishment outside prison walls but lack the courage to demonstrate against murder in the places where it is actually occurring If they want to stop killing, they need to be present in neighborhoods drenched in violence, not in a safe demonstration outside a prison gate [28]

There is ample evidence that, first, the innocent are sometimes convicted and executed (esp the poor offenders who are often confused, mentally incapacitated and lack adequate counsel and representation) and, second, the guilty often escape punishment (esp the wealthy offenders who can hire a hotshot defense attorney) Thus, if we want to see more justice done, it seems better that we advocate a "life for a life" punishment in the form of life in prison without parole in which the proceeds of the prisoner's hard labor, however minimal, go to the victim's family or to a murder-prevention program of some sort

But isn't the primary thrust of the biblical ethic that Christians should concentrate their energy on addressing the conditions that lead to murderous violence and on bringing good news and hope to those in despair? I do not think we are truly and faithfully practicing the principle of "You shall not murder" until we bring

It is clear that first-degree murderers deserve to lose their life for the one they have taken The problem we face, then, is determining how we can justify this severity while excusing ourselves from the harsh penalties prescribed for idolatry, adultery and so on—of which we are all guilty, given Jesus' new application of the law. Our calling as Christians in the world is not to make sure people get the punishment they deserve but to bring good news, hope and healing in the name of Jesus Let's direct our energy at ameliorating the conditions and attitudes that lead to capital crimes

---

[28]I agree with both points made here by Schlessinger "I am often stunned and saddened at the crowds who hold vigils at the prisons in support of a cold-blooded murderer of a child On my radio program, I have often challenged those same people to carry candles in front of the homes of the victims—and, more importantly, to volunteer to help and support the surviving relative and friends in their grief and loss That they don't is a clear example of how their compassion is misdirected and distorted in a knee-jerk, easy way to feel holy   [But] public executions should not be accompanied by applause, jubilation, cheers, and jeers, which demean the integrity of life This is inhumane and barbaric " *Ten Commandments*, pp 182-83

hope to the hopeless, remove conditions that frustrate and enrage people, reduce the availability of weapons in general, and provide friendship and counsel to those prone to violence Merely to add our vote and voice in favor of hanging, shooting, injecting, gassing or electrocuting those found guilty of murder is a pitiful failure to fulfill the law Let's not get caught up in this issue in any simplistic, narrow or negative way As Christians let's try to be a positive, alternative, gospel-inspired presence in our violent world

The Enemy Nation: Can Warfare Be a Christian Ethical Practice?

War is another form of killing permitted, sometimes even commanded, to Israel These were not especially sanitized "just wars " Israel even heard God tell them at times to brutally exterminate foes who occupied the Promised Land they wished to seize (Deut 20) [29] At the very least, our Old Testament texts teach us that for warfare to be justified, it must both be at the command of God and concern the territorial integrity of God's chosen people and their Promised Land Understand this clearly no other motivation for warfare is acceptable (e g , war to acquire slaves, material wealth or access to oil, wars to fight communism, monarchy or taxation without representation, and so on) [30]

There is a lot of biblical evidence that even the holy warfare of the Old Testament was not God's "plan A " God vowed to make a way for Israel to occupy the Promised Land Couldn't he have cleared the land of other peoples by sending insects rather than weapons? In Israel's wars it was typically little David slaying the giant Goliath, or Gideon's troops fighting with trumpets, candles and jars, or the leaders sending home all but a faithful band to do the fighting It is the presence of the Lord that gives Israel strength

In my opinion, God stooped to participate in Israel's ancient Near Eastern tribal religious wars (his plan B, or even plan J) because he is a

---

[29] We should not hold that every sentiment, word and action recorded in the Bible represents God's personal viewpoint The occasional violence of the imprecatory Psalms indicates not God's feelings but the psalmist's Only in Jesus is God's revelation full, clear and exact Elsewhere, notably in these accounts of tribal warfare, God's revelation is sometimes unclear, inexact and partial

[30] On this ground, only fighting for Israel (not America or other countries) would seem even thinkable And if the church is a "new Israel," where is the promised land that this international diaspora should defend?

God of incarnation he shows up where we are God sometimes appears to be involved in a context we find mysterious and contradictory to his just and loving nature It is very clear that this is so with kingship, polygamy, the city and divorce God shows up because of the hardness of human hearts

Participating in warfare becomes even more questionable when we turn to Jesus and the New Testament On the positive side (i e , evidence that Christians might serve in the military), a centurion at the crucifixion bore witness to Jesus, saying, "Truly this man was God's Son!", that is, he bore witness without being rebuked by the Gospel writers for his military job (Mt 27 54, Mk 15 39, Lk 23 47) The conversion of Cornelius, a Roman military leader, was not accompanied by any condemnation of his professional role in a dreadful occupying force (Acts 10) Paul writes in the famous Romans 13 passage that God works for good and against evil *through* the "sword" of the civil authority (Rom 13 4) Finally, the Revelation of John is full of grand-scale holy war conflict in which blood flows in the streets until Satan and his hosts are finally defeated by the Lord Almighty Thus we cannot rush to a facile condemnation of military participation If Christian discipleship entails rejecting the military, why didn't the apostles make that clear to Cornelius?

On the other hand, the warfare of the Apocalypse is described in passages of fantastic symbolism and imagery, and we must be wary of interpreting them literally [31] Paul's comments on the civil authority *(exousia)* as servants of God must be balanced with his emphasis on the Christian's combat against principalities and powers *(exousia* again, see Rom 13, Eph 6, Col 1—2) There is clearly a call to "spiritual warfare," but when it comes to earthly conflict and violence, Paul writes, "so far as it depends on you, live peaceably with all" (Rom 12 18) Acknowledging that God is at work among secular governmental forces is not equivalent to inviting (still less, mandating) Christians to join them! There is also a huge shift in perspective from Israel as a physical nation occupying a discrete patch of ground as God's holy nation and witness to the world, to the transnational body of Christ as the

---

[31] If, based on Revelation, you expect real blood flowing in the streets, will you also accept the idea of a Jesus who looks like a sheep with eyes all over his body?

new nation and people of God (1 Pet 2) Still less can any earthly nation, like the United States, be considered God's nation and its warfare God's warfare We stole our land from the Native Americans, it was not promised to us by God [32]

Jesus' own refusal to join the Zealot revolutionaries, or to arm his disciples in time of crisis, or to call down the legions of angels at his command is good evidence that he preferred a way other than war and guerilla violence [33] As Jesus said, "If my kingdom were from this world, my followers would be fighting" (Jn 18 36) It is just not part of God's plan for Christians (qua Christians) to be involved in warfare, even though God got involved in Israel's wars in the past There is no more geographic nation to defend The *new Israel* exists on earth as the collective territories rented, owned or otherwise occupied by God's people in every nation, all over the earth

Many Christians would agree with Kaiser, who says that war "is God's ultimate, but reluctant, method of treating gross evil that resists every other patient and loving rebuke of God Christians may only be involved in a 'just war,' but often these become notoriously difficult to define "[34] Redpath, on the other hand, says, "I find no justification for warfare, and though it is a most controversial issue,   I find capital punishment hard to accept " He believes that the mission of Jesus and his followers is to bring redemption and eternal life to others To kill people is to cut short that possibility [35]

Should we participate in wartime killing of our nation's enemies? For example, should we fight against a foe as demonic as Adolf Hitler and Nazi Germany? As a last resort, would we try to stop the Holocaust? The old just-war criteria are helpful

• Is the war undertaken for a just cause (i e , defensive) and as a last resort?

• Does it have a just purpose (i e , peace, not destruction of enemy)?

---

[32] If any people were ever justified in going to war, it would be the Native Americans against the United States

[33] The "two swords are enough" episode is surely a weary jest at someone who still didn't get it (Lk 22 38)

[34] Kaiser, *Toward Old Testament Ethics*, p 178

[35] Redpath, *Law and Liberty*, p 72 Of course, the logic of this could imply that it is acceptable to execute convicts who have confessed the faith

- Is it carried out with just means (e g , not attacking civilians)?
- Is it conducted by a just authority (i e , a legitimate government)?
- Do its benefits outweigh its costs? Is it winnable?[36]

I tend to think that fighting against Hitler's Germany was justified and that I would have taken part in the war Even so, rather than calling it a "Christian" activity, I would prefer to say that such warfare or insurrection is a last resort, a necessity, a terrible choice, but the best action I could take[37] I would also ask myself, *Where were my friends and I as Hitler was coming to power? Are we going to war now because we failed to act earlier against the growth of this cancer?* I'm afraid so

Maillot argues that, in our era, Christians can no longer consider warfare an option

What purpose will be served to finally establish justice if no one is left to enjoy it? It is not a matter of denying certain profound causes of war, such as social injustice But I think, simply, that it is too late for combat by wars and guerillas The hour has finally arrived for a truly universal counsel of all churches where Christians at the same moment refuse to participate in all war and accept responsibility to attack the causes of war in a peaceful way This is a dream, one says Perhaps' But this dream is the only escape by which we can avoid the eternal nightmare which could suddenly surprise us[38]

Is the commandment "You shall not murder" truly a prohibition against all warfare? The biggest challenge to the Christian desire to abstain from warfare is the suffering of innocent people The desire to liberate a suffering people from a violent, rapacious tyrant is a Christian sentiment But holy and good ends are affected, tainted, sometimes

---

[36]Lochman, *Signposts*, p 102

[37]This is essentially the position of Jacques Ellul, see his *Violence Reflections from a Christian Perspective* (New York Seabury, 1969) It is a position that rejects the crusades and Holy Wars and is fundamentally committed to nonviolence But it recognizes that in some extreme case one might do violent, warlike acts, but urges that these not be justified or claimed as Christian acts

[38]Maillot, *Le Decalogue*, p 105 Maillot goes on to say that he does not deny the eternal felicity promised in a new heaven and new earth, but that he believes we shall nevertheless give an account for how we treat this earth

even corrupted or undermined, by unholy means This is why prayer and diplomacy are the best means available to Christians wishing to promote peace and justice in the world If we do resort to force and violence, we must test our motives (to eliminate egoism, nationalism and hatred) before proceeding, we must rigorously confine our activities to the minimum necessary, and we must refuse to drag the name of Jesus into the fray Again, as in the case of capital punishment, let's try to get away from the polarized, politicized stances of our surrounding culture and instead be the representatives of a third way—the way of the gospel of the kingdom and the ministry of reconciliation

> The greatest contributions Christians can make to a warring world are to teach and demonstrate Jesus' way of peacemaking and reconciliation based on righteousness, justice and mercy, and to address the causes and conditions of conflict, hatred and war before violence erupts.

The Despairing Self: Can Suicide Be a Christian Ethical Practice?

Could it ever be ethically permissible to commit *suicide*? In the Old Testament, five cases stand out Abimelech (Judg 9 54), Samson (Judg 16 30), Saul and his swordbearer (1 Sam 31 4-5), Ahithophel (2 Sam 17 23) and Zimri (1 Kings 16 18) In the New Testament, there is the case of Judas Iscariot hanging himself after realizing the horror of his betrayal of Jesus (Mt 27 5) In all of these cases, suicide is an act of despair that follows defeat and disgrace Only Samson seems to have been motivated also by an element of sacrifice

Jesus himself, of course, gave up his life, but suicide was not his preference "If it is possible," he prayed, "let this cup pass from me" (Mt 26 39) He did not want to die, but he accepted death on behalf of others In an analogous way, soldiers have leaped on grenades to save their fellow soldiers, bodyguards have taken bullets for their leaders, and parents have courted death to save their children In none of these cases is death an act of renouncing one's own life per se It is always a renunciation on behalf of others, usually to save them from the same fate This is the ultimate sacrifice—to die for another (Jn 15 13) To give up one's life for another, or even to die for "principle" (e g , dying out of faithfulness to God, like the martyrs), is not in the same category as suicide

Suicide is one's murder of oneself When people realize the heinousness of their crimes (as did Judas), they sometimes desire death partly to escape and partly because they feel they deserve it But is this right? I don't think so The first reason why we are not to murder people (including ourselves) is that we *belong* to God It is a lack of respect for God's rights to your life to kill yourself Furthermore it is an insult to our Lord—who died precisely so that you could live—for you to give up in despair Suicide shows no faith, no hope, no love It cannot be the right thing to do And finally, although one may think that she is freeing the world from having to endure such a loathsome person as herself, suicide almost always deeply wounds (rather than relieves) those around us They feel guilty, lonely and bitter about what happened In fact, sometimes this is the intention of a suicide to hurt those who have let one down in life Lashing back at others is not an acceptable motivation for a Christian act

Having said all that, we must have the greatest possible sympathy and empathy for those who feel suicidal There are many contributing factors to such despair Our society promotes selfishness, autonomy, unrealistic expectations, isolation, ephemeral relationships and frantic consumerism, among other things It does not promote deep self-worth or a meaningful philosophy of life that helps us account for life's tragedies, sorrows and injustices It does not make it easy to find or sustain meaningful friendships and community through hard times There is every reason to expect more suicides among all age groups in coming years Rather than spending a lot of time condemning suicide as wrong (though it is), the Christian ethical response should be to address the conditions that give rise to suicidal thoughts and to reach out to those around us who are especially vulnerable to such despair[39]

Before leaving the subject, however, we must also note that the slow suicide of an unhealthy lifestyle is, ethically, just as bad as quicker acts of violence against oneself Self-destructive behaviors (e g , excessive drinking, smoking and eating, reckless driving, and inflammatory social conduct) can be instances of a sinful "death wish" that is morally equivalent to suicide

---

[39]Lochman, *Signposts,* pp 94-97

The Unwanted Baby: Can Abortion Be a Christian Ethical Practice?

A fourth type of killing to address is *abortion* As many as one-third of all pregnancies are terminated by abortion today One loud group in society today, the prolife movement, is crying out that abortion is nothing but murder and that we are watching a veritable holocaust take place, killing millions of children, mostly because they are inconvenient Another loud group, the abortion-rights movement, is arguing that whatever one may say about fetal life (this group avoids terms like "human life" and "personal life"), the pregnant woman must always retain her right of freedom of choice concerning her own bodily functions and thus her pregnancy No one should be able to force her to carry a baby against her will

A Christian ethical discussion of abortion must begin by acknowledging that the intentional taking of human life is wrong Our sixth principle is that we must protect and nurture life and health The Bible does not directly address the taking of fetal or prenatal life, but it does indicate that God is at work in the womb "You formed my inward parts in my mother's womb   I praise you, for I am fearfully and wonderfully made" (Ps 139 13-14, cf Ps 127 3) God does not wait to begin his work *until the moment a woman chooses* to have her baby Of course we must say also that God is at work well before conception, making sperm, making ova and so on The whole life process deserves our wonder and respect From the moment of fertilization, a complete human genome exists—all that it takes *genetically* for a child to develop

While the Psalms celebrate the work of God in the womb, the laws of Israel did not consider it murder or manslaughter to irresponsibly cause a miscarriage, as we might otherwise have inferred [40] To cause a miscarriage was serious, and there was a fine to be paid, but it was not *rasah* Though we may forget this in the heat of today's debates, Jews and Christians have long made distinctions on these matters Thus, it has not been common to have funerals for miscarriages If we are consistent in believing that every fertilized egg is a full human being, why don't we observe these deaths? The idea that all conceptuses (fertilized eggs) are human beings has some serious difficulties It is almost uni-

---

[40]Kaiser argues at length against the interpretation of this text as miscarriage, see *Toward Old Testament Ethics,* pp 168-72

versally accepted that half to two-thirds of all fertilized ova do not successfully implant in the mother's womb and are naturally (and unknowingly) discarded by the woman's body during her regular menstrual cycle The position that human life begins at fertilization requires us to believe that half to two-thirds of the human race (created in the image of God with an eternal destiny) never see the light of day and never experience even a day of nurture in their mothers' wombs Are we ready for that?

The abortion debate is currently posed in terms of a clash of absolutes prolife versus prochoice If we are ever to get beyond this polarized conflict, we must find ways of carefully affirming both choice and life We certainly need a robust affirmation of the sanctity and value of human life The life of a pregnant woman, for example, is sacred and valuable and, because of that, the tragedy of sacrificing the life of the unborn baby to save that of the mother has been viewed as justifiable in Christian mainstream thinking over the centuries

But the life of an unborn child is also sacred and valuable Our culture has devalued fetal human life at the same time that higher ethical standing (rights) and even spiritual or divinized status have been granted to those of nonhuman nature Surely the life of a six-month old fetus is more valuable than that of a household pet (and this is not to belittle the latter) Prolife activists, for their part, would gain a lot of credibility if they not only spoke out for fetal life, but also spoke against the threats to life posed by uncontrolled gun access, saber rattling and warfare, and capital punishment The protection and care of infants and children (in an era of epidemic child abuse and neglect) also need aggressive advocacy

On the other hand, we need a robust affirmation of freedom of choice, a core value in human life Choice is a feature of freedom, one of the four great cover principles, or ground rules, of Christian ethics Free choice must be protected for all human beings, including those who by reason of social position or other conditions are likely to find their freedom constricted or abrogated Infants need to be nurtured toward lives of freedom of choice Women, as well as men, need to be given a radical freedom of choice, including the freedom to make mistakes and wrong choices

But choice cannot be divorced from the correlative notion of responsibility To the extent that our choices are free, responsibility for those choices follows No prochoice position has any credibility if it is not at the same time a proresponsibility position Furthermore, to demand that at every moment in time one be free of responsibility for free choices one has made earlier is an untenable position It is not inconsistent to be both prolife and prochoice If a man and a woman freely choose to have sexual relations, they have exercised their freedom of choice and must accept responsibility for the consequences, including the protection of a baby they may have created

It also must be said that it is unfair to make women carry the whole burden of unwanted pregnancies A good part of the sympathy vote for a woman's so-called right to choose originates in the fact that impregnating males have been able to evade responsibility My response is that since the mother bears the physical burden of the pregnancy, the father should bear the financial responsibility for both the woman's and baby's health care during and immediately after the pregnancy and should reimburse the mother for salary lost during the time she is unable to work (six months, perhaps) This is certainly not the ideal solution, but it moves us toward more fairness

Advances in DNA research have made it possible to identify a child's paternity A woman who declines to help identify the father, of course, would bear the financial responsibility of the pregnancy by herself If the father is identified and cannot or will not provide the appropriate financial support, he could be sentenced to work in a prison factory or farm until he has earned enough to pay his debt If the woman does not give the child up for adoption, she would be fully responsible for the care of the child after, say, it turns one year old Again, this is not the ideal solution (which would be two married parents caring for the child), but it moves toward greater fairness and responsibility

At the present time, the hardened rhetoric of the abortion debate is getting us nowhere The specific debates about when life begins and about how to treat it at various early stages can become very complex and divisive As followers of Jesus we should always err on the side of the weak and those with no voice or little power My own interests are in protecting both unborn children and vulnerable pregnant mothers in crisis I want to hold up both the sanctity of life and freedom of choice without sacrificing either value And I want a position that holds men just as responsible as women for the challenges of pregnancy

Most important of all, however, a Christian ethical position will promote responsible sexual behavior and adoption as the alternative to abortion and to having a child one cannot care for We need more and better sex education, more and better women's centers and houses, more male-on-male mentoring, more celebration of life and babies, more adoption [41] Only when we take such positive steps are we truly fulfilling the sixth commandment "You shall not murder" We do not fulfill the command when we merely shout "no" at those who are causing death

> Christian ethics values both the sanctity of human life and the human freedom of choice It is possible and necessary to affirm both of these values and to hold men just as responsible as we do women for the challenges and burdens of pregnancy. Christians must do what they can to stop the death of the unborn, but the best strategy includes promoting the gospel of life, creating supportive communities for pregnant women, advocating adoption and teaching responsible sexual behavior

The Extremely Ill Person: Can Euthanasia Be a Christian Ethical Practice?

Abortion tests our stance on killing at the very beginning of a life *Euthanasia* and *physician-assisted suicide* test our stance on killing at the end of life Our ethical starting point is the same it is wrong to take human life It is wrong to end a life rather than to leave the timing of the end to God Unfortunately, the issue of euthanasia is not going to go away but will instead become increasingly public and problematic

Euthanasia comes from the Greek terms for "good death" The ancient Hippocratic oath taken by physicians over many centuries forbids giving patients any death-inducing drugs, even if patients request them The physician's first duty is to "do no harm" Many today are insisting people have a right to a so-called death with dignity (Aren't there some deaths that can never be made "dignified"?) It is argued that patients have not only a right to competent health care, but also a right to die and perhaps even a right to be assisted in achieving their

---

[41]Lochman, *Signposts*, pp 97-101

death Doctors and nurses have traditionally believed their professional responsibility was to care for the patient's life and health and
that the patient's self-determination could not trump that mission A
doctor served the patient's health more than the patient's wishes

Most of us would agree that patients should not be forced to live indefinitely on life-support machines when they are unable to communicate, work or sustain meaningful relationships and when they clearly
have no hope for recovery Dying patients should not be forced to exist
indefinitely in indignity, misery and hopelessness Part of what motivates people to accept euthanasia or physician-assisted suicide is a fear
of not being allowed to die a natural death when the time comes There
is also a fear of being left alone to suffer a great deal Some patients also
fear that they will become a bother and expense to their relatives, in
which case a quicker death might be a relief to everyone

But I would contend that a serious line is crossed when a physician
or nurse moves from *allowing* someone to die to *causing* someone's
death Crossing this line—intending and causing death—violates the
sixth commandment, which prohibits the premeditated, intentional
taking of human life A traditional (but much challenged) distinction
has been made between what has been called "passive" euthanasia
(letting nature take its course) and "active" euthanasia, which is causing or accelerating the patient's death either directly (administering
the lethal treatment) or indirectly (e g , providing the means so that
the patient can end his or her life)

This is very complex territory, of course Letting nature take its
course (passive euthanasia) would not be right if we let die someone
whom we could save But all our lives must end sometime, and it cannot
be unethical to allow death to occur normally Being passive when we
could relieve pain and provide comfort to the dying would make us
guilty of callousness or unkindness, but not of murder Standing by when
a small child is drowning in a bathtub is certainly morally equivalent to
murder Actively administering strong pain-killing drugs to relieve the
suffering of a man dying from severe burns or cancer and to help him
sleep is not murder The Bible even recommends such comfort "Give
strong drink to one who is perishing, and wine to those in bitter distress"
(Prov 31 6) Giving anyone drugs with the intent of causing or accelerating his death, however, is a violation of the sixth commandment

Of course, these are very difficult issues It is often pointed out that giving strong pain-killing drugs can not only reduce pain but may also suppress or negatively impact critical life processes and death may come sooner rather than later The purpose of the drug is to relieve suffering, but a secondary, unintended but accepted effect is to shorten the patient's life Traditional Catholic moral teaching invoked a principle of "double effect " You intend a good effect but accept a secondary effect that, by itself, would be viewed as bad For example, radiation therapy to save a pregnant woman suffering from cervical cancer causes the death of the fetus I agree with this principle the intention was to preserve life or relieve suffering, and the secondary effect is a tragedy but not an evil or wrong thing

In contemporary secular medical ethics the supreme value is patient autonomy and self-determination, in light of which it is difficult to argue against a right to die For Christian ethics the supreme criterion is God's right to all life Our stewardship and responsibility over God's world is considerable but takes place within the boundary of "You shall not murder " The critical requirement is to find wisdom and discernment for specific cases in the company of others The community side of ethics is never more important than in these cases Patients, family members, doctors, nurses, pastors and others are most likely to do the right thing when they think, discuss and pray through crisis end-of-life matters together

Several other important concerns about euthanasia have been raised If patient self-determination is essential, how do we ensure that patients give their consent in a competent, unpressured way? Will presenting euthanasia as an option (instead of waiting for the patient to ask about it) create psychological pressure on terminal and severely ill patients to ask for it to relieve their family members of caretaking responsibilities and financial burdens? Will older or socially marginal patients fear being euthanized against their will at the hands of medical professionals and thus not go for medical care when they most need it? Doesn't offering euthanasia to all terminally ill patients introduce the risk that suicidal, suffering and depressed patients might choose to die when they likely might have chosen otherwise if given better treatment or support? Patients' conditions and attitudes often change Euthanasia is irreversible

Christians need to oppose euthanasia as strongly as they do abortion or any other taking of human life But we do not observe the sixth commandment just by voicing our objections Christians need to invade the health care system as sensitive professionals and volunteers, teaching a much better approach to pain, suffering, aging and death We need to provide hospice care and contribute especially to the research and development of pain relief Only when the church is providing such positive service and witness to life will its witness against death be credible

> For Christian ethics, euthanasia is no more acceptable than murder. But simply voicing our objections is not enough Christians need to provide a much better understanding of and approach to pain, suffering, aging and death than currently exists in the health care system, driven as it is by money and technology.

The Violent Attacker: Can Lethal Force Be a Christian Ethical Practice?

Finally, we need to ask whether Christians should engage in the use of *lethal force* as part of police units or as private citizens Here we are concerned primarily with threatening and using lethal force defensively Can an ethical Christian be a police officer? Or a member of a SWAT team? Is it ever justifiable to shoot to kill? The discussion of lethal force by police parallels the earlier discussion of warfare If the cause is just, the means are just and such force is a last resort, it may be morally justifiable to shoot to kill (e g , when a sniper is attacking an elementary school)

We must remember, of course, that some communities have suffered not just from gang or mafia violence but from police brutality This victimization is a serious problem, and in such communities we must discourage macho police use of lethal force Those who are armed and given badges can be seriously tempted to use lethal force excessively or out of bias It may be that some Christians are called to be "peace officers" on local forces and that their integrity and values can help police forces to operate effectively without succumbing to the temptations to abuse power

A companion issue is whether, in a world prone to violence, Christians should be among those who buy guns, guard dogs and other weapons What should ethical Christians think of the rise of vigilante militia, survivalist and supremacist groups in many parts of America? And where should the line be drawn between both public policy and personal choices? Should private citizens be permitted to arm themselves with vials of bubonic plague? With armored tanks and helicopters? No American's right to bear arms (or right to privacy or free speech) is unlimited It is one thing to ward off attackers and another to court opportunities to maim and destroy those who appear to you suspicious or hostile

It is interesting to explore the meaning of the right to bear arms, which is protected in the U S Constitution's Bill of Rights But let's not forget that Christian ethics are grounded not in the Bill of Rights but in Jesus and Scripture An extreme love of weapons manifests a terrible lack of freedom and faith in God [42] Whatever happened to trusting the Lord, turning the other cheek, loving your enemy and showing hospitality to strangers? Of course, Christians should be careful to avoid harm and unnecessary risk We should be careful about closing windows, locking doors, walking alone in dangerous places, carrying too much cash around and so on Turning the other cheek and accepting suffering are the ways of Christ—but so are avoiding and fleeing trouble

A much more challenging issue for Christians is how best to defend others, especially the weak I may turn my own cheek to my attacker, but if I see my mother being attacked, I don't think I will yell, "Turn the other cheek, Mom!" It is a Christian impulse that makes us want to defend the weak When defending ourselves and others, we need to use minimal rather than maximal force and remember that the "enemy" is someone redeemable by Jesus Christ

As in the preceding discussions, the bottom line is always discerning how to prevent the death of another and how to address—in a creative, positive way—the conditions that give rise to violence What is the gospel in this context? How can we be proactive rather than reactive?

---

[42]Michael Moore's Academy Award-winning film on America's obsession with guns, *Bowling for Columbine,* suggests that the real problem is not so much the presence of guns (since Canada has as many per capita), but rather the growing fear that dominates American culture and its media I couldn't help but recall all the biblical texts about the way fear has no place in the Christian life (e g , Josh 1 9, Mt 10 26-31, 1 Pet 3 14, 1 Jn 4 17-18)

The Broader Agenda

Not even the six special topics we have considered can exhaust the application and importance of the sixth commandment The entire spectrum of violence must be subject to the sixth principle [43] The principle is about valuing, protecting and nurturing life and health As Rabbi J H Hertz writes, "Jewish ethics enlarges the notion of murder so as to include both the doing of anything by which the health and well-being of a fellow-man is undermined, and the commission of any act by which a fellow-man could be saved in peril, distress, or despair "[44] Consider Luther's interpretation of this commandment

> Not only is murder forbidden, but also everything that may lead to murder   If you send a person away naked when you could clothe him, you have let him freeze to death If you see someone suffer hunger and do not feed him, you have let him starve Likewise, if you see anyone condemned to death or in similar peril and do not save him although you know ways and means to do so, you have killed him It will do you no good to plead that you did not contribute to his death by word or deed, for you have withheld your love from him and robbed him of the service by which his life might have been saved [45]

In the spirit of this classical view of the meaning of the command, I close this chapter with a few broader reflections on violence and Christian responsibility

Emphasizing the Gospel of Life: Ten Arenas in Which to Act

How can we proactively oppose and eliminate the conditions that so often result in the death of men, women and children? How can we proactively promote life, health and safety? Here are ten topics for thought and discussion suggested by the basic principle of the sixth commandment

1 Teach and practice conflict resolution Many people do not know how

---

[43]See David W Gill, "Violence," in David Atkinson et al , eds , *New Dictionary*, pp 875-79

[44]J H Hertz, ed , *The Pentateuch and Haftorahs Hebrew Text, English Translation and Commentary*, 2nd ed (London Soncino, 1988), p 299

[45]Luther, *Large Catechism*, p 35

to handle conflict and disagreement Mediate conflicts, teach conflict-resolution tactics and principles, help others "get to yes" before they explode in violence William Barclay presses the need to engage in reconciliation—of individuals, classes, churches "There is one special direction in which the worth and power of Christianity have to be demonstrated, and that is in the matter of reconciliation "[46]

2 *Tame the rhetoric* Let's remind ourselves, and teach others, to cut back on insults, name-calling and overheated rhetoric These just inflame feelings and polarize people on school grounds, on radio talk shows, in family arguments, during political campaigns and many other circumstances

3 *Provide shelter and safety* Let's create and support (financially and with our time) safe houses and shelters for battered women and children and for the homeless and hungry Let's provide counseling and teaching to help people get on their feet again financially, vocationally, physically, psychologically and relationally

4 *Provide healthy food and nutrition* People die all over the world because of inadequate food and unclean water The causes are multiple but avoidable if we will just commit to addressing them

5 *Offer affordable basic health care* Whatever your opinion on the role of government in health care (and this is an important area for Christians to be involved), we will always need private initiatives to bring basic, affordable, quality health care to people Do something for your community Do something for the world

6 *Promote healthy habits* We must fight against drug abuse, alcoholism, smoking and gluttony (a sin acknowledged by the church for centuries, which includes eating too much, eating too little and eating unhealthy foods) We must encourage others to develop healthy eating and exercise habits in our world of junk food and sedentary lifestyles

7 *Reduce, reuse, recycle* Are we contributing to the trashing of the earth, filling it with garbage on land, in the sea and in the air? This is

---

[46]William Barclay, *The Ten Commandments for Today* (Grand Rapids, Mich Eerdmans, 1974), pp 100-101

God's good creation, which should be reason enough for our being good stewards and caretakers But it is also the case that people get sick and die in polluted environments We must reduce our consumption of energy and generation of waste, and we must learn to repair or reuse things instead of throwing them away Christians who make excuses for not recycling must be counseled, loved, scolded or shamed into committing to this basic act of good stewardship

8 *Oppose media violence* We must oppose all sexist, racist, misogynist and vicious depictions and messages in popular music, film, video games, Internet sites and various print media We must not be intimidated or deterred by free-speech advocates We have no obligation to tolerate proviolence, hateful garbage in our deadly society any more than we have to tolerate someone who yells "fire" in a crowded theater

9 *Hold genetics and biotechnology accountable* God created a world of biodiversity and ecological balance Some geneticists, biotechnologists and eager capitalist investors tell you they can improve on creation with their genetically altered food, chemically enhanced meat, hormonally produced milk and so on Would-be Frankensteins in research labs and boardrooms must be held morally and criminally accountable for their actions Christians should be finding ways to support natural and organic food production as a way to preserve God's creation as he intended it Science and technology can certainly contribute to our life and health, but they must not be given an unlimited and unmonitored license for their plans to modify our lives

10 *Urge business to be prolife* Businesses offer services and products, and (in almost all cases) they must make a profit But as consumers, citizens, employees, investors and managers, we must insist that these businesses promote life, health and safety through their practices, services and products

I'm with Luther here The sixth commandment does not apply to only the action of pulling out a weapon and murdering someone It applies to just about anything having to do with our life and health It is about stopping the negative forces and promoting the positive conditions leading to life, health and safety Chouraqui argues that the abolition of violence must intervene on all levels, in all situations the individual level, family, social, national, international and even the relation among different animal species and different orders of the creation A society that would respect the life of other living beings—wouldn't it be better disposed to respect that of human beings? A society where women played a greater role—wouldn't it be more likely to save the lives of young people sent off to war?[47]

We are living in an age of increasing terrorism, suicide bombers, "shock and awe" warfare and nuclear threats Our cities and suburbs must deal with growing domestic violence, schoolyard shootings and street-corner murders These phenomena don't arise from nowhere, they result from spiritual, relational, political and economic causes and conditions Many people and nations react to this current situation by trying to crush all potential threats with overwhelming violence The great challenge to Christians is to move out into the world and into our neighborhoods with another message and another agenda—that of our Lord of Life and Prince of Peace

For Reflection and Discussion

1 Do you feel there are any forms of permissible violence or killing for followers of Jesus Christ? Describe what acts you think are permissible and in what circumstances they are justified, and then show how Jesus and the Bible support your argument

2 What is your opinion about whether Christians should own and prepare to use guns or other weapons against potential enemies? Do you feel comfortable with the trend toward "survivalism" and a personal arsenal?

3 Are you active in working for conflict resolution, reconciliation and peace in any way? How do we best model and teach these values in our families? in churches? in communities? among nations?

4 Which, if any, of the "Ten Arenas in Which to Act" are you involved in? Which do you think are most important? Would you restate or revise any of the author's descriptions or recommendations?

---

[47]Chouraqui, *Les Dix Commandements,* pp 173-74

9

Commitment Keeping

The commandment in the Decalogue against committing adultery follows the one prohibiting murder [1] Alphonse Maillot cautions that despite the special horror with which the church regards adultery, it is not *the* sin of sins, *the* mistake that stands above all others Adultery is very serious, but we must not lose sight of the other sins outlined in the commandments [2] Luther's opinion was that the "dearest" thing, one's life (protected by the sixth commandment), is followed by the "next dearest thing," one's spouse [3] Some people, of course, would disagree with Luther and say they would rather die than lose their spouse

Rather than argue about what is dearest, I prefer to say that life (existence) is the most immediate and fundamental requirement of our humanity, and that our close, covenanted relationships (symbolized above

---

[1] It is a mystery why the Septuagint translators reversed the order of the sixth and seventh commandments (which then affected Paul's list in Rom 13 9)

[2] Alphonse Maillot, *Le Decalogue Une morale pour notre temps* (Geneva Labor & Fides, 1985), p 112 Walter Harrelson is a bit too ambivalent about the seventh commandment He suggests that it is the "wise course" for married people not to commit adultery but then undermines his case by saying, "it cannot be claimed that this commandment should become an absolutistic and unbreakable norm, issuing in a commitment never to have sexual relations with anyone other than the marriage partner" *The Ten Commandments and Human Rights* (Philadelphia Fortress, 1980), p 130 William Barclay, on the other hand, devotes 82 of his 220 pages to the seventh commandment in his book *The Ten Commandments for Today* (Grand Rapids, Mich Eerdmans, 1974) As important as it is, I'm not sure the seventh commandment deserves a full third of our attention in the study of the Decalogue

[3] Martin Luther, *The Large Catechism* (Philadelphia Fortress, 1959), p 36

all by marriage) are the next circle of concern Alan Redpath sees the progression this way "As the previous commandment has to do with the sacredness of human life, so this one puts a flaming sword around the only relationship on earth which has power to bring life into existence "[4] We could also say that there is a "family triad" in the Decalogue The seventh commandment serves the sixth commandment in that marriage and sexuality are what produce new life (which is protected by the sixth commandment) Adultery threatens the fabric of the mother-father team (protected by the fifth commandment), which guards and nurtures that life Much violence and criminality (addressed by the sixth commandment) comes from situations where parenting (addressed by the fifth commandment) has been undermined by unfaithfulness (addressed by the seventh commandment) and marital breakdown It all works together

In its most original sense, the seventh commandment—"You shall not commit adultery" (Ex 20 14 par Deut 5 18)—meant that a man, whether married or single, was prohibited from having sexual intercourse with an *engaged or married* woman If a man, whether married or single, in ancient Israel had sexual intercourse with an *unengaged, unmarried* woman, he was expected to marry her, perhaps adding her to an already existing group of wives Note that this commandment was not a license for men to have irresponsible sex with single women, for any time they did so, they were required to marry the sex partner (cf Ex 22 16)

The term for *adultery (na'af)* is distinguished from the words for "sleep with" *(skb)* and "commit harlotry" *(znh)* Brevard Childs explains that

the punishment for adultery is death (Deut 22 22), while seduction or violation of a virgin requires the man either to marry the girl or offer a money equivalent (Ex 22 15, Deut 22 28f) It is clear from this evidence that throughout the Old Testament adultery was placed in a different category from fornication The command relates specifically to the former [5]

---

[4] Alan Redpath, *Law and Liberty A New Look at the Ten Commandments in the Light of Contemporary Society* (Old Tappan, N J Revell, 1978), p 80
[5] Brevard Childs, *The Book of Exodus A Critical, Theological Commentary* (Philadelphia Westminster Press, 1974), p 422

Adultery was specifically a matter of a violation of a marriage relationship

Rabbi André Chouraqui argues that a better way to express the meaning is the broader term "to adulterate"

The Hebrew *na'af* has a much larger meaning Adultery is one of the cases where that root can be employed, but it is not the only possible betrayal of the fidelity to which spouses are obligated This commandment condemns not only adultery but all *adulteration* of the conduct of the man or the woman, in their relations with others or among themselves [6]

Maillot translates the commandment as "You shall not break [Fr *briseras*] the marriage "[7] In short, the seventh commandment does have to do with sex, but its focus is on sexual conduct that violates, pollutes or breaks the covenant between a man and a woman

The Old and New Testaments often reinforce the basic message of the seventh commandment Much of Israel's law prohibited various sexual practices, including adultery, fornication, prostitution and bestiality (Lev 18, Deut 22—23) These crimes were so serious that offenders were to be put to death (Gen 38 24, Lev 20 10, 21 9, Num 5 11-31, Deut 22 22, Ezek 23 45) The book of Proverbs gives detailed warnings against the lure of sexual sin Adultery was not just sinful or criminal but colossally stupid "He who commits adultery has no sense, he who does it destroys himself" (Prov 6 32, see also Prov 5—7) The prophets repeat the warnings "When I fed them to the full, they committed adultery and trooped to the houses of prostitutes They were well-fed lusty stallions, each neighing for his neighbor's wife" (Jer 5 7-8, see also Jer 7 9, 23 14, 29 23, Ezek 16 32, 38)

> **Adultery is specifically a matter of violating, breaking or "adulterating" a covenanted marriage relationship. It violates the commitment to fidelity that was made before God**

The lesson is also taught in the stories of the Old Testament David's adultery with Bathsheba led to murder and untold sorrow There are

---

[6]André Chouraqui, *Les Dix Commandements Aujourd'hui* (Paris Robert Laffont, 2000), pp 177-78 The term covers all forms of disloyalty
[7]Maillot, *Le Decalogue*, p 112

also accounts of sexual heroism Joseph, for example, resisted Potiphar's wife's attempts to lure him into adultery and remained faithful even when falsely accused by his spiteful, rejected pursuer (Gen 39 6-20) The prophet Hosea heroically stayed with his unfaithful wife, and in so doing he became a model of God's faithfulness to his unfaithful people Israel What many biblical wives had to put up with also makes for heroic tales

The New Testament is as clear and consistent as the Old Testament that adultery is wrong It is on most of the vice lists and is the subject of many warnings Adultery cannot be part of the kingdom of God, and it is subject to the judgment of God John's Apocalypse describes unfaithfulness in the bleakest possible terms

Like Jesus, Paul hit hard at adultery (e g , Rom 2 22, 1 Cor 6 9-20) But when confronting the case of a man having sexual relations with his stepmother in the early Corinthian church (1 Cor 5 1-2), he urged that the penalty for such sexual misconduct was not death but excommunication Later on, Paul urged restoration of the erring parties to the fellowship following their repentance The message about adultery (and other sinful behaviors and attitudes) is "this is what some of you used to be" (1 Cor 5 11) That is, God forgives, restores and heals people of these mistakes God is not to be thought of as a vindictive, harsh judge Nevertheless, adultery must be repudiated and left far behind in the Christian life

Jesus and the Fulfillment of the Seventh Commandment

Jesus' own teaching intensified and broadened the prohibition of adultery by extending its application to even a lustful, adulterous attitude (Mt 5 27-30) Jesus also taught that anyone who divorced and then remarried was committing adultery (Mt 19 1-12) Thus it seems that here, as in the case of murder, Jesus makes the prohibition even more rigorous and difficult Who among us is not guilty? Furthermore, Jesus teaches about marriage, saying, "What God has joined together, let no one separate" (Mt 19 6, Mk 10 9) Adultery is not just an attack on a neighbor, it is an attack on a work of God—marriage

And yet, in practice, Jesus responded with grace and forgiveness, as he did to a woman caught in adultery and surrounded by accusers (Jn 8 3-11) Jesus also teaches, especially by his example, that relation-

ships with the opposite sex can be composed of love rather than lust
This is the revolutionary good news Jesus brings to the subject Christian ethics is not just about fenc-
ing off what is wrong, it is also
about pursuing what is right and
good Mary Magdalene, the sisters Mary and Martha, and the
Samaritan woman at the well are
four women to whom Jesus related in a constructive, respectful, loving way, and we can follow this example The negative
side of the law is to avoid adultery and even any flirtatious talk
or lustful fantasies The positive
message is to build respectful,
caring, loving relationships

**Jesus enlarges the prohibition against
adultery to include not just the act but
also the thought He presents it as a
grievous sin against what God has joined
together, not just against the people
involved But Jesus also extends great
grace and forgiveness to the guilty·
"Let anyone among you who is without
sin be the first to throw a stone at her,"
he tells the accusers And to the accused,
he says, "Go your way, and from now
on do not sin again."**

The Core Message: Relationships and Sexuality

We can look at the broader implications of the seventh commandment
in two ways First, we can ask how the commandment provides guidance for our sexuality Sexual health is more than just a matter of committing or not committing adultery Luther stressed this sexual side of
the seventh commandment

> Inasmuch as there is a shameful mess and cesspool of all kinds of
> vice and lewdness among us, this commandment applies to every
> form of unchastity, however it is called Not only is the external
> act forbidden, but also every kind of cause, motive, and means
> Your heart, your lips, and your whole body are to be chaste and
> to afford no occasion, aid, or encouragement to unchastity More-
> over you are to defend, protect, and rescue your neighbor when-
> ever he is in danger or need, and on the contrary to aid and assist
> him so that he may retain his honor Whenever you fail to do this
> (though you could prevent a wrong) or wink at it as if it were no
> concern of yours, you are just as guilty as the culprit himself [8]

---

[8]Luther, *Large Catechism*, pp 36-37

For Calvin, the seventh commandment "forbids us to lay snares for our neighbor's chastity by lascivious attire, obscene gestures, and impure conversations "[9] Lew Smedes reminds us that "old-time Reformed sermons on the commandment zeroed in on 'whatever may entice' short skirts, bobbed hair, the cinema, ballroom dancing, and lipstick— all came in for attack "[10]

Why is it that a sexual act is so important that it got into God's top ten list of don'ts? Sex can certainly threaten the place of God in our lives It can become something that people obsess about day and night, a raging and uncontrolled force It can destroy not just relationships, but also careers, ministries and churches Conversely, sex can express love It can provide physical expression of a union of two souls It can produce the miracle of new human life It is a powerful and amazing aspect of human life, and the seventh commandment prods us to reflect seriously on it The Bible speaks to our sexuality in a much wider sense than adultery and fidelity alone

But, second, we can also see that the seventh commandment is not just about sex It challenges us to look beyond sex and marriage to other interpersonal relationships, other covenanted partnerships I don't agree with Luther that this command is chiefly about preserving *chastity* I think it is chiefly about preserving

> **The ethical discussion of adultery covers not just our sex lives but, more broadly and deeply, our relational lives—just as the ethical discussion of murder led to the broader issues of health and peace**

relationships Earl Palmer has written, "Adultery breaks a commitment that has been made between two people and destroys a relationship, the family Far-reaching destructive results are the consequence of adultery in the lives of all those persons related to that family "[11] Rabbi Avroham Chaim Feuer explains that "the adulterer incites anger and animosity between the man and his wife and this arouses the anger of God "[12] Even

---

[9]Calvin *Institutes of the Christian Religion* 2 8 44

[10]Lewis B Smedes, *Mere Morality What God Expects from Ordinary People* (Grand Rapids, Mich Eerdmans, 1983), p 159

[11]Earl F Palmer, *Old Law, New Life The Ten Commandments and New Testament Faith* (Nashville Abingdon, 1984), p 107

[12]Avroham Chaim Feuer, *Aseres Hadibros The Ten Commandments, A New Translation with a Commentary Anthologized from Talmudic, Midrashic and Rabbinic Sources* (Brooklyn, N Y Mesorah, 1981), p 56

more directly, Jan Milič Lochman argues,

> What the Seventh Commandment is concerned with is not just
> minor details of our private conduct but the basic dimension of
> our human existence, our co-humanity For the man-woman
> relationship is *the basic form of co-humanity,* of human society,
> human solidarity   The man-woman relationship is the basic
> model of the co-humanity intended at the creation [13]

As we explore the basic map of Christian sexual ethics we must
keep in mind this broader "relational" message

Adultery as an Offense Against God

Adultery is a sin against a relationship that God has established The
second half of the Decalogue, just like the first, is about loving and honoring God Marriage is grounded first in creation Alan Redpath sees an
attack on a marriage as an attack on the image of God borne by the
couple "The unity and union of the man and the woman are the real
expression of God's image   not the man or the woman alone, but
male and female he made them, after his own likeness "[14] Chouraqui
also views marriage from the standpoint of creation "Biblical marriage
sacralizes life and love," he writes "It attaches itself to the creative will
of Adonai/Yahweh It thus participates in the mystery of creation, the
foundation of the universe and humanity "[15]

Maillot grounds his discussion of marriage and adultery not in creation but in the covenant established between God and Israel A Christian understanding of marriage should be guided not by our legal systems or traditions but by the covenant God makes with Israel

> He has delivered them to marry them in the desert and to give
> them a land that belongs to him With this nation God will con-
> clude a covenant—definitive, irreversible, exclusive—to which he
> will be eternally faithful and to which he hopes his people will
> simultaneously be faithful This fidelity *(hesed)* is the primary
> attribute of God—but it must also be the fundamental attitude of

---

[13] Jan Milič Lochman, *Signposts to Freedom The Ten Commandments and Christian
Ethics* (Minneapolis Augsburg, 1982), pp 107, 109
[14] Redpath, *Law and Liberty,* p 80
[15] Chouraqui, *Les Dix Commandements,* pp 178-80

Israel   We are called in marriage to experience here below the covenant of God with his people, the covenant of Christ with his church, to experience and to live the difficult "fidelity" of the famous *hesed*   This is also contained in the first commandment, which presents itself as an exclusive alliance "There will be no other gods beside me" means "There will be no other covenant with you but yours and mine You shall not break this marriage "[16]

Creation and covenant provide the general foundational truth, the specific truth about a given marriage is, as Jesus taught, "What God has joined together, let no one separate " Maillot warns, "I may not presume to be God of my brother, I may neither take his life   nor take the wife that   has been given him precisely by the Lord "[17] In short, undermining and attacking a marriage covenant is first and foremost an offense against God Even if the marriage is deeply wounded and all the parties are alienated and frustrated, and even if the adultery seems completely private, the Christian ethical road map says that this path is an offense and insult to God

> Marriage is not just a human tradition It bears witness to, and participates in, a new creation of God's—a man and woman becoming one flesh and bearing his image—and God's covenant of fidelity and love with Israel and the church. As we are reminded in the marriage vows, "What God has joined together, let no one separate."

Adultery as a Wound to Our Humanity

Adultery is not just a sin against God, however It is an illusion to think adultery can be a victimless crime, something consenting adults can commit without necessarily harming anyone else There is always a substantial price to be paid It is a brutal assault on people, beginning with the betrayed spouse It often destroys families and wreaks havoc on children It leaves painful wounds on the extended family and friends [18] And adultery is, for the adulterer, something like ingesting

---

[16]Maillot, *Le Decalogue*, pp 115-16

[17]Ibid , p 115

[18]We do not just marry a spouse, we marry a family and a community Marital breakdown shatters families and communities

poison There is no good to be found here

Adultery is an attack on a sacred trust between two people, a breech of a solemn covenant, a savage wound inflicted on one's partner "Adultery slashes the fabric of that fundamental but delicate human alliance called a marriage "[19] The couple vowed to be faithful to each other, and adultery breaks that promise Breaking promises undermines trust, betrays love and violates justice The wounds may heal, but the scars remain In adultery one takes back and gives to another what was already given to one's mate It is so easy to break trust and so hard to rebuild it Without trust, life withers and freedom disappears, leaving only anxiety, suspicion and jealous surveillance

Infidelity can corrupt relationships across the board, whereas fidelity liberates the self, the spouse and others to whom we relate In a truly eloquent passage, Walter Harrelson says,

> When a person is committed not to have sexual relations with anyone other than the spouse, such a commitment engenders trust, a freedom from anxiety, a readiness to deal with other persons who otherwise might be objects of sexual partnership in freer, more humane, less exploitative ways   "Thou shalt not commit adultery" is not an enslavement but a liberation, not a threat to freedom but a means to freedom, not a thwarting of life's flowering but an incentive to the flowering of human relations, including sexual relations [20]

Adultery is more than a wounding of the betrayed partner It also wounds those who engage in it God created our sexuality to flourish under conditions of monogamy and permanency This wound of adultery is not just about unwanted diseases or pregnancies Sexual fulfillment depends to a great extent on one's capacity to be vulnerable, unguarded and utterly open Each time we are sexually intimate with those to whom we are not married, we are undermining our capacity to be transparent, vulnerable and open with our mate If we have more than one partner, we must not—we cannot—give ourselves completely We must become guarded What adulterers give emotionally and spiritually is inevitably reduced even if the physical, animal side

[19]Smedes, *Mere Morality*, p 157
[20]Harrelson, *Ten Commandments*, p 187

of sexuality continues to provide a narcotic kick [21] Though it goes against the propaganda of our culture as well as against our animal instincts to say so, the bottom line is that adultery exacts a high price from its practitioners

Maillot points out the contradiction implicit in talk of "free love," sex without covenant

> There is no freedom without love and fidelity   There is no freedom in love if it is not freedom-together   the freedom of one for the other and the other for the one   Like art, love dies in an empty freedom   Israel cannot break its covenant without also breaking its deliverance and replacing it with servitude   One has only given oneself truly when one gives one's future and even one's eternity   The only love is to give one's life   There is no greater love   True freedom is to give fully, totally, once for all [22]

It is no wonder that Paul writes that "the fornicator sins against the body itself" (1 Cor 6 18) Other sins are outside the body, Paul writes, but this one harms our very self—body, soul and spirit Sexual intercourse "unites" us to another Adultery disunites us from God, the owner of our body, as well as from our mate, who is also the owner of our body (cf 1 Cor 7 2-5) Adulterers destroy their own souls (Prov 6 32)

When adultery breaks up or wounds a marriage, it usually devastates the children Children raised in single-parent homes, according to many studies, have an increased risk of poverty and violence Children of divorce often also have difficulty committing themselves or trusting the promises of others because they experienced firsthand the breaking of the promise their parents made

> **Adultery tempts us with its promise of a narcotic kick, but this high comes at a huge price It cruelly wounds those we betray It degrades and deforms our own capacity to truly make love. It usually shatters not just marriages, but also children, extended families and circles of friends It inserts a shame into our life story that cannot be easily edited out.**

---

[21] An adulterer is like a person who enjoys the taste of good food but only knows eating as a nutritional event rather than enjoying it as a social and relational event

[22] Maillot, *Le Decalogue,* pp 115, 117-18

to each other And when adultery breaks up a marriage, it usually fractures the extended family and the circle of friends This is a rupture with one's own history and story The seventh commandment is like a huge warning sign posted in front of a pit of bondage and death

Today's Challenges: Why It Is so Difficult to Avoid Adultery

Keeping the seventh commandment has never been easy As Chouraqui notes, "Adultery, as understood in our modern society, finds its basic cause in the fragility of man and woman exposed to the difficulty of honoring their promises of faithfulness "[23] Several forces play on this area of human fragility today

The Christian inclination to love. Oddly enough, our first challenge comes from within the Christian faith itself Sexual interaction with others, outside of the boundaries God establishes, is the most powerful temptation that many Christians will ever face (Maybe this is why the Septuagint translators reversed the order of the sixth and seventh commandments) Here is what I mean Most Christians don't feel especially violent, nor are they much inclined to steal Most Christians actually would like to enjoy better sabbaths, and most of us do not find cursing and lying very attractive There is a sense in which we are inclined toward obedience to these commands When we disobey them, we really feel the conflict with our new nature

In contrast, Christians may be somewhat inclined to break the seventh commandment Sex with other people can be very tempting, even if we are married to wonderful mates Why? Christians are sanctified for and educated to foster warm, nurturing, open, affectionate relationships We overcome a lot of the uptight, bitter insecurity of our pagan nature Our newer, warm-hearted feelings draw us toward others We see others in their true beauty In fact, ironically, *more* people may be attractive to us than before our conversion because now we appreciate others' uniqueness and reject the narrow, artificial standards of beauty and attractiveness proposed by the world We drop our preconceived worldly stereotypes of the perfect man or woman We learn how to be tenderhearted and vulnerable, open to one another, truly caring

All of this is good, but by letting down our emotional barriers, we

---

[23]Chouraqui, *Les Dix Commandements,* p 188

face the danger of crossing relational boundaries—first in our affections and feelings and thoughts, then in our words, then in our deeds But even the finest, sweetest, most innocent beginnings cannot temper the bitterness and the horror of the betrayal that come once we cross the line We must resist If we are already married, we need to invest our energy in our relationship with our mate and resist all temptations to fantasize or flirt with others We must be careful to avoid self-decep-

> **The struggle to be sexually faithful may be especially difficult for Christians who are taught to be vulnerable, open, tender-hearted, emotionally empathetic, caring and loving toward *all* others, not just toward the "beautiful people "**

tion about what's happening with our feelings and thoughts, and we must be sure not to grapple with our temptations in isolation We must seek help from friends who can counsel us and hold us accountable

The sexualization of contemporary life. The second special challenge we face is the intense sexualization that permeates our culture There is more to life than sex, but you would never know it from watching and listening to our advertising, music and movies Today's relationships, it seems, are only considered serious when they take on a sexual tone Homosexuality, for example, has become a huge public issue partly because sexuality itself saturates public culture and consciousness Homosexuals cannot very well be expected to show restraint when heterosexuals lead the way in sexualizing and vulgarizing our cultural landscape [24] People are constantly encouraged to dress and act in sexually seductive ways Products are sold by associating them with erotic images It is a little like taking God's name in vain, in which people borrow the power of the name, so too people borrow the power of sexual desire to strengthen the appeal of their product, from cigarettes to automobiles

The genitalization of sex. But it is worse than this Our third challenge is that sexuality is itself reduced to genital activity Sexuality ought to include the mysteries of our whole being, not just the sensa-

---

[24]It is hypocritical for Christian leaders to single out Gay Freedom Day parades and the like for censure, if they remain silent about heterosexual excesses at Mardi Gras, spring break and the like And in both cases why don't we light a candle rather than just curse the darkness?

tions in our genital area The reduction of sexuality to copulation and orgasm is a serious narrowing of its richness It is not surprising that children engage in genital play at ever earlier ages, that the relationship between a boyfriend and girlfriend has nowhere to proceed except to genital orgasm, that same-sex relations may also, if considered serious and intimate, lead to genital expression What other options are being given? Celibacy is proclaimed as the great *no* to the *yes* of genital activity But it is a little misleading to present things in this way because both extremes assume a narrow, genitalized view of life and sex Being a sexual person does not only mean engaging in activities that stimulate your genitals, but you would never know that in today's culture

The politicization of sexuality. A fourth challenge is the politicization of sexual issues (i e , posing them primarily or exclusively in terms of laws, campaign platforms, party politics and the overheated, simplistic rhetoric of mass media political persuasion) The politicization of sexuality is a socially destructive tactic Contemporary debates about homosexuality and sex education are cases in point, where propagandistic rhetoric merely hardens existing positions Bringing our differences of opinion about intimate, personal matters into the legislative arena usually has disastrous consequences The defeat of a political initiative is often interpreted as authorization for its opposite, the passage of a political initiative incites fear in the losers and excess in the winners The meaning of our sexual behavior is distorted when viewed primarily from the standpoint of rights and political power Sexuality is about relationships to other human beings, not relationships to laws

Not all virtue should be legally protected, and not all sin should be criminalized Some sins are less costly to the society than others and may be legally tolerated, some are nearly impossible to detect (lust, covetousness, hatred) and cannot be the subject of legal sanction While the cost to society of sexual misconduct is high (sexually transmitted diseases, children on welfare, etc), it may still be best not to criminalize all of the behavior that perpetuates these social problems Even if heterosexual marriage is a virtuous relationship worth protecting, it may be best not to encumber it with legal red tape

Christian ethics arises within a voluntary society and confessional community, and it derives its force from the community's living relationship to Jesus Christ For this reason, as well as the example of how

Jesus himself dealt with the society around him, Christians must speak and practice their truth in love and peace We must protect minorities (including homosexuals) in society and not seek to impose our standards on others Our calling is to be the salt of the earth and the light of the world, not to dominate and rule the world "for its own good " Except when the weak in our society are especially threatened (e g , by pedophiles, straight or gay), we should avoid thinking of the law as a major strategy to promote goodness and combat evil in our sex lives

The homosexual lifestyle sometimes presented in public education is no more antithetical to what I want my children to emulate than are the lifestyles of promiscuous heterosexuals, greedy hedonists, right-wing capitalists, left-wing Maoists or militant religious fanatics It is better to teach our kids to be in permanent critical tension with the world than to use the legal system to repress all alternatives We already have enough laws on the books to remove incompetent, predatory teachers

Isolated narcissists in a sexual wilderness. A fifth challenge is the atomization of people in today's culture, combined with their immersion in the propaganda of a right to sexual satisfaction Because of geographic mobility and other changes in economic and family life, more and more people live their lives as isolated individuals Deep, long-term, committed relationships are hard to come by Families struggle for survival In our boredom or loneliness, in our hunger for human touch and approval—for something more than the artificial or vicarious pleasures of modern technological society—we may reach out in the wrong way, misusing our sexuality While individual liberty brings with it some spectacular opportunities today for adventure and growth, its downside is that many of us are left extremely vulnerable We may make very unwise, reckless choices with our sexuality, with no one to talk to, support us or help us in our weakness

Meanwhile this isolated individual is overwhelmed by propaganda that views the satisfaction of personal appetites as the purpose of life and the fundamental right of all individuals But when sexuality is viewed primarily as a way to personal pleasure rather than a way to express a loving commitment to another person, it is fundamentally distorted and impoverished Narcissism, pathological self-absorption, is the undoing of sexuality Sex is about pleasing the other, about communicating tenderness and love, about physically consummating a relational commitment that already exists

The issue of a supposed right to sexual satisfaction is also not persuasive Most people, including married people, are sexually unsatisfied part, if not all, of the time That's life The notion that everyone has some kind of right to sexual (or other) satisfaction is perverse, it destroys our commitments and justifies selfishness

Biological and social determinism as excuses. Finally, our sexual struggles are not much helped by the tendency to define ourselves by our genetics or social conditioning, as though these factors are decisive in directing our values and behavior The issue of causation (nature or nurture) is a red herring The "constitutional" sex addict (whose powerful libido was unknown to primitive science) is no more justified in his unrestraint than is the constitutional liar, the violent-tempered person, the glutton or the drunk Part of being human is struggling with our history, our genetic inheritance, our environment, our cultural and parental conditioning We are called to transcend and master nature and culture—not submit to it We start with revelation (not observation) and redemption (not bondage) Our nature is not our destiny, it is not equivalent to the will of God

> A healthy sexuality is made difficult by the sexualization of life today, by the genitalization of sexuality, by the politicization of sex, by the isolation of individuals in a culture of narcissism and by the propaganda that says we must freely and authentically express our natural sexuality

The Good News: Getting Sexually Healthy

But we are missing a great deal if we think that Christian ethics has only a great big veto over our sexuality First of all, while we should not have sex with our neighbor's spouse (or fantasize about having it), we are free to try to have great sex with our own spouse In the Song of Songs and elsewhere in Scripture, married people are invited to explore the wonders and pleasures of a sexual life together

> Let marriage be held in honor by all, and let the marriage bed be kept undefiled (Heb 13 4)

Rejoice in the wife of your youth   May her breasts satisfy you
at all times, may you be intoxicated always by her love (Prov
5 18-19)

Do not deprive one another except perhaps by agreement for a
set time, to devote yourselves to prayer, and then come together
again (1 Cor 7 5)

The gospel at the heart of the seventh commandment is an invitation to give sexual pleasure to your mate This is a lifelong privilege
and responsibility

Sex was God's invention, after all It was not a mark of the Fall or an
invention of the devil Sexual intercourse is intended to be enjoyed between a man and a woman married for life It is a concrete, physical,
joining of two into one flesh, a total and complete intimacy in the context of a total and complete commitment At its best, sexual intimacy
and intercourse are the supreme expression of oneness, of the bonding
and interpenetration that happen when two beings become one, it not
only reflects the unity that already exists, but augments and fortifies
that unity Sexual intercourse gives physical expression to a lifelong,
total, uninhibited giving of spouses to each other, to something greater
than the sum of the two individuals

Some Christian leaders and teachers, notably Saint Augustine, have
taught that sexual relations even within marriage are only for the purpose of producing children, not for mutual pleasure But as Bill Hybels
points out, "Scripture seems to indicate that God created human sexuality primarily for pleasure Procreation appears to be a secondary purpose God first spoke of man and woman 'becoming one flesh' within
the context of ending Adam's isolation and loneliness (Gen 2 18-25),
the role of procreation is not mentioned until later "[25] Marital sex is a
gift of God

Sexuality is about our created need and capacity for intimate human relationship God separated Eve from Adam in the creation In
sexual intercourse "two become one" that is, they are reunited Sexual
intercourse is the supremely intimate physical connection of two peo-

[25]Bill Hybels, *Laws That Liberate* (Wheaton, Ill Victor, 1985), pp 80-81, Walter C Kaiser Jr has a long and helpful section on the positive meaning of sex in Scripture in *Toward Old Testament Ethics* (Grand Rapids, Mich Zondervan, 1983), pp 192-95

ple and in the Old Testament is often communicated by the verb "to know" (e g , "now the man knew his wife Eve," Gen 4 1) Sex is participation, experience, union, nakedness and vulnerability Total sexual intimacy is coordinated with total life commitment You can't be fully "known" if you have learned to put up an emotional shield in your sexuality (as must happen when you have multiple partners)

> **Following a Christian sexual ethic is not just about saying no to the wrong things, but about saying yes to God's gift of sex used in the right way. It is not just about avoiding bad relationships, but about developing strong, life-affirming, committed partnerships.**

The relationship between freedom and boundaries in sexuality is key Sexual relations are intended to express uninhibited freedom, but they cannot flourish in the absence of covenant and commitment

These two concepts, "freedom" and "covenant," are vital for any understanding of the Seventh Commandment The command "You shall not commit adultery" is not simply a disciplinary legal measure in the area of human sexuality Genuine liberation achieves its goal in human relationships only when there is fidelity, a fidelity which is *voluntary and free,* of course, not one which is externally imposed and legally enforced [26]

This is why sexual intimacy in the absence of a covenant (fornication) or in violation of a covenant (adultery) is harmful to the self and others—physically, emotionally, socially and spiritually

The seventh commandment is also wrongly interpreted if we think the alternative to adultery is have nothing at all to do with your neighbor's spouse While our culture seems to say that serious relationships end up either in bed or nowhere, the Christian gospel disagrees Instead of sexual misconduct, there is friendship—a relationship of respect and love that builds up our neighbor even as it enriches our own life and relational commitments

Such friendships may even include affection and some kind of physical expression, from hugs to handshakes to holy kisses (e g , 2 Cor 13 12) Our problem in this domain is that we lack models and guide-

---

[26]Lochman, *Signposts,* pp 110-11 (italics in original)

lines on these matters [27] Affectionate touching may get abused or mis-interpreted, of course, so caution is in order But we are physical and emotional beings and need to connect, safely, on this level It is not only athletes who need to high-five, pat and hug each other

In summary, the negative prohibitions are clear do not have sexual intercourse in violation of a (marriage) covenant, whether yours or the other person's In fact, do not even think about it Do not speak flirtatiously or act suggestively with your neighbor's spouse Positively, learn to regard your neighbor's spouse as your brother or sister and cultivate a relationship that nurtures his or her life along with yours If marriage is part of your calling in life, express your sexuality in fidelity and love to your mate

The seventh commandment is built on the first six commandments The most critical movement is to make sure the Lord is our God and our guide in every domain of our lives, including our sexuality and our relationships As we embrace this perspective, we learn to see all people (including those we find attractive) as made in the image of God and thus unique and irreplaceable (not as objects to be used and discarded) We see too that they are living, growing beings (not stereotypes or sex objects) who deserve our respectful communication (instead of flirtation or harassment) and so on This perspective gives us a rich, holistic texture for managing our sexuality—nothing like the superficial sexual mythology of our decadent era

Area Principle 7 Never act, think or communicate in any way, sexual or otherwise, that violates or threatens covenanted, committed relationships Rather, regarding such relationships as God's creation, do whatever you can to support fidelity, loyalty and commitment

We will now look briefly at six different topics in Christian sexual ethics sexual attitudes, sexual talk and behavior, sexual practices within marriage, divorce, unmarried sexual behavior, and homosexuality Because there is almost uniform consensus against the following practices, I will not discuss them here bestiality (sex with animals), incest (sex with close relatives), rape (sex imposed against the other person's con-

---

[27] I like the French tradition of greeting friends with a kiss on each cheek but never on the mouth These are warm contacts without sexual ambiguity

sent), prostitution (sexual acts for money) and sadomasochism (sex accompanied by cruelty or pain inflicted on the self or the partner)

Sexual Attitudes: From Admiration to Lust

Since Jesus warned that even one who merely looks on another and wishes to commit adultery is guilty of committing adultery in the heart, it is essential to reflect on our attitudes Our attitudes are the seedbed of our words and actions Save a place for racist attitudes in your heart and mind, and racist speech and action will eventually be manifest But just as being *conscious* of someone's race is not equivalent to being racist, being conscious of someone's sexual identity is not equivalent to being either sexist or lustful

The cultural environment in which we live seems to be more blatantly sexual every year While we need to choose wisely the kinds of cultural stimuli we see and hear, it is not possible to completely escape or be shielded from all sexually provocative phenomena After all, our calling is to be in the world as God's ambassadors, not to escape it Since a complete environmental purification is impossible, we will need to work on our attitude and thinking

First of all, there is nothing unnatural, sinful or ethically wrong in admiring the femininity, masculinity or beauty of God's creatures If you and the object of your admiration are single (but *only* in that case), it can be appropriate to move beyond admiration to desire In fact, if it were not for such attraction, admiration and desire, the human race would come to an end

The boundary conditions are these First, we must not view someone's sexuality in isolation from her or his whole being (It is wrong to view people narrowly as sexual objects) Second, we must not be obsessive or excessive in our focus (Such idolatry narrows and corrupts our life and spirit) And third, we must not allow ourselves to desire others if we have a marital commitment to another or if those others are already in committed relationships

The Christian gospel here is that our minds are not just supposed to turn away from evil and be disengaged but rather to think actively and intentionally on whatever is pure and excellent and lovely (Phil 4 8) Neither a lustful mind, nor an empty mind, but a mind focused on what is pure and excellent is what God desires we have In a culture that pushes our thoughts and attitudes in less healthy directions, it is important to pray for God's help and also crucial that we share our struggles with a small group of covenanted friends who can support and hold each other accountable Remember that Jesus' first temptation (of his hunger) took place when he was alone in the desert We need to avoid

> Admiring another's beauty is fine, provided it does not become obsessive or lead to an improper desire. Attitudes are the seedbed of actions, so we must learn to think of others in respectful, positive, holistic ways if we are to have quality interactions and relationships.

being isolated and alone with our struggles, for that is when we are most vulnerable

Sexual Talk and Behavior: From Flirtation to Harassment

It is one thing to work on our attitude, and another to examine our talk and behavior What are the boundary conditions and positive guidelines here? What should we think about how we speak and act around the sexes, about nudity, about the way we dress and our bodies are displayed, and about portrayals of nudity and sexuality in advertising, entertainment, education and art?[28]

What guidance do we get from Christian ethics? Where does our freedom to express ourselves conflict with our responsibility for our effect on others? We need to distinguish between sexist treatment, sexual harassment vis-à-vis acceptable flirting, and sexually responsible dress and behavior

Sexist talk and behavior stereotype and discriminate against females or males based on their sex Sexism is treating women or men as though they are fit only for certain roles or speaking to or of them

---

[28]Kaiser, *Toward Old Testament Ethics*, p 192 "The Bible has no such legislation on nakedness as such More frequently it is used figuratively of being discovered (Job 26 6) or being 'disarmed' (Jer 49 10) or literally of a person who is shamed when he or she is taken into captivity by a conqueror The man and woman were 'naked' without shame (Gen 2 25) while the serpent was 'crafty' Obviously there is a kind of pun being made on these two terms perhaps the guileless simplicity of their nakedness is being contrasted with the subtle wiles and entrapments of the evil one " Kaiser also cites more than twenty verses where "nakedness" is a euphemism for genitalia (many of these are in Lev 18 and 20) Or it may, per the NIV, be a euphemism for sexual relations

in a disrespectful way Sexism turns gender into an ideology Sexism unfairly and unjustly stigmatizes people based on their sex Sexism is an offense against God, who created both women and men in his own image and likeness No less than racism or other "isms," Christians should unequivocally reject and oppose all forms and expressions of sexism

> Christians ought to be in the forefront of all resistance to sexism (and most other "isms"). There is no room in Christian ethics for stereotyping, for making images or for unfairness

Sexual harassment has been defined in various ways

- "unwelcome sexual advances, requests for sexual favors, and other verbal or physical conduct of a sexual nature" (Equal Employment Opportunity Commission)
- "sexual attention imposed on someone who is not in a position to refuse it" (Catherine MacKinnon)
- "deliberate or repeated unsolicited verbal comments, gestures, or physical contact of a sexual nature which are unwelcome" (Alan Campbell)

Sexual harassment is about both sexual threats or offers and hostile or offensive sexual conduct

At stake in sexual harassment is the safety of those being harassed, their dignity as whole persons who deserve respect and their freedom to work, move about and live without fear or threat Organizations must create policies and processes for individuals who are being sexually harassed, such as the following

- Make it clear to any offenders that their behavior is unwanted and that no means *no* Unless the behavior is unambiguously out of line (e g , grabbing, vulgarity), it is unethical to start a whistleblowing strategy of accusation without first confronting the offender
- Create a paper trail, documenting the harassment
- Share your concern and experience with trusted colleagues, and try to get them to witness the inappropriate behavior for themselves
- Complain to a supervisor
- Go to someone who can force some significant change (e g , a law-

yer, a journalist, a spouse, a pastor)

We live in a vulgar, aggressive culture where many people seem to believe they have a license to say outrageous things, to stalk and even intimidate others, and to inflict their sexually offensive music or behavior on others The harassment-free offices and organizations of our time stand in stark contrast to the vulgarity portrayed in media and reenacted in many public places today Christians must stand against this trend and be models of respectful speech and behavior

We also need to reflect on *sexually responsible dress* and *behavior* Matters of dress are partly cultural, partly contextual and partly individual Some cultures have found it scandalously racy to expose a face or a bit of ankle to the opposite sex Others are not particularly enflamed even by shorts and a tank top Some individuals can view without temptation paintings, sculptures and films containing some nudity or sexuality For others any exposure to such things is a stumbling block It is important not to sit in judgment of others, but rather to help one another and to not put a stumbling block in front of any weaker brothers or sisters

How we dress, dance, move, gesture, touch and look at others—all send out messages to other people Nothing justifies another person's harassment of you, but the Bible urges us to be wise and to stay on the modest side (rather than work the extreme edges) of what is acceptable in our culture

It is not right for Christians to speak in a disrespectful or a harassing manner to others made in the image of God. And it is both wrong and foolish to dress and act in ways that would likely elicit sexual come-ons from others

Dress and behave in ways that are certain to send out positive, healthy messages rather than wearing or doing something that may send out the wrong message Take personal responsibility, pray and get some advice from others about your choices

Sexual Practices Within Marriage

Aside from the obvious prohibition (i e , no adultery), are there any ethical boundary conditions or guidelines for sexual expression within a marriage? Saint Augustine believed that husbands and wives should avoid sexual desire for each other and rigorously keep the coital act under the control of their will, but his position owed a lot more to his wild preconversion sex life and to his Neo-Platonic philosophical training than to the Bible Who can read the Song of Solomon without sensing that God approves of marital sensuality and sexuality? Paul himself argues that married partners' bodies belong to each other and that they should not deprive each other except for periods set aside for prayer (1 Cor 7 2-5) Thus, the only constraints on sexual expression within marriage are the broader themes that guide all of our relationships no violence, cruelty, harm, oppression, selfishness or dishonesty Whatever is done with love, fidelity, mutuality, gentleness, kindness, service and joy is acceptable

Divorce and Remarriage

God's basic attitude toward divorce is summarized by the prophet Malachi "I hate divorce" (Mal 2 14-16) [29] In the brief controversies over divorce in the Gospels, Jesus makes it clear that divorce can only be justified in the most extreme circumstance—where one's partner has broken the covenant by committing adultery Anyone who otherwise divorces a spouse and remarries is himself committing adultery So "what God has joined together, let no one separate" (Mt 19 6, see also Mt 5 32, 19 3-9, Mk 10 2-12, Lk 16 18) Paul may be providing a second justification for divorce in his counsel that after one's conversion, one could let one's unbelieving spouse leave the marriage if he or she insists (1 Cor 7 15)

The heart of the matter, however, does not lie in a legalistic attempt to condemn or exonerate individual cases Maillot says that what the letter authorizes, the spirit rejects Jesus did not defend principles or ideas but *people* in these controversies [30]

The fact is that we are broken people living in a broken world Unquestionably, those who divorce can find grace and forgiveness and healing even in the ugliest of circumstances But the end of a marriage,

---

[29] The frequency of divorce among Christians is now about the same as the general population Some conservative evangelical and charismatic churches are now accepting divorce and remarriage, even among their ministers Those who disregard clear biblical standards on divorce and then hold a rigid line on other biblical sexual standards should realize that they don't have much credibility

[30] Maillot, *Le Decalogue*, p 119

no matter how "justified," is always a tragedy (even if a tragic relief in some cases) and represents a death in a profound sense As a type of tragic, premature death, a divorce deserves a "funeral" and a time of mourning, just out of simple respect When leaders fail in their marriages, no matter who was at fault, it is important to honor the importance of marriage by stepping out of leadership and public roles for a significant period of time Not to do so sends a terrible message to the Christian community and the world

Our understanding of the tragedy of life and our reliance on the immeasurable grace of God should not blind us to the damage that is often done by divorce Laura Schlessinger has boldly argued, "The *fact* is that at least two-thirds of divorces are unnecessary, that is, not founded in violence, addictions, or infidelities These divorces are more destructive to the children than two people staying together 'for the sake of the children,' in spite of a lack of desire, fulfillment, or happiness "[31] The lifelong devastation and loss usually inflicted on families and children by divorce is as grievous a sin as adultery The lost romance, friendship and sexual fulfillment that often are invoked to justify a divorce are challenges for virtually all marriages to greater and lesser degrees and for those spouses who persevere as well as those who give up and divorce More often than not, the same problems recur in the second, third and fourth marriages of divorced people Hang in there and work at matters with your first spouse if at all possible

Divorce is sometimes a tragic necessity to escape violence, infidelity, abandonment or cruelty Other times divorce is a pitiful, narcissistic, desperate act of betrayal Most often it is a mixture of many reasons, causes and excuses In all cases, there are painful consequences—scars and wounds both to others and the self In all cases, God's grace and healing are available to those who come to him in humility and need The Christian community needs to work hard at the right balance of maintaining the high standards of fidelity and incarnating the immense graciousness of the gospel

Christians must do a much better job of preparing people for marriage and sustaining them through its challenges We don't have to di-

---

[31] Laura Schlessinger and Stewart Vogel, *The Ten Commandments The Significance of God's Laws in Everyday Life* (New York HarperCollins, 1998), p 51

vorce and remarry when things get tough! We can commit ourselves to
a renewal of our union, companionship and common life with our family and friends Our leaders need
to show us how to persevere by
modeling this in their own marriages, not just by preaching
about it

Singleness and Sexual Practices

What about the sexual expression and practices of unmarried
people? Some of this is culturally contextual Holding hands
or kissing a cheek might have
been an erotic and compromising behavior in some cultures
Today's Western culture almost
assumes that all single people
will be sexually active before
marriage (which may never
come), that unmarried couples may live together for a while and that a
person may have several sexual partners over the course of a life We're
not going to get a lot of help from this culture

> Divorce is always a tragedy on the order of death In many cases it is wholly unjustified And in every case, even those that are justified, people—not just the divorcing spouses themselves but their children, family and friends—are seriously hurt, though it sometimes takes years for the damage to be fully visible Of course, there can be forgiveness and healing through God's grace, but spouses need to resist choosing divorce as long and as often as possible To avoid the trauma of divorce, Christians must work much harder at helping spouses build strong marriages

Christian ethics recognizes and affirms that single people are not
asexual beings, nor are they subhuman if they have not married or engaged in sexual intercourse As Lochman writes, "Marriage is not the
only form the man-woman relationship can take, still less the only
commanded form   Branding the *unmarried* as 'disobedient' or ab-
normal people [is] a value judgment for which there is no support
whatever in the Bible The fact that, at the very center of the New Testament, we find an unmarried person presented as 'true man' speaks
for itself "[32] Jesus was fully human and yet was single

In Jesus' discussions of marriage, the disciples expressed the opinion that marriage may be so difficult that it is better to stay single (Mt
19 10) Jesus replied, "There are eunuchs who have been so from

---

[32]Lochman, *Signposts*, p 113

birth, and there are eunuchs who have been made eunuchs by others, and there are eunuchs who have made themselves eunuchs for the sake of the kingdom of heaven" (Mt 19 12) Whether one is married or a eunuch, Jesus teaches that we are to accept what we are able to, what our gift is Eunuchs were literally castrati, men incapable of having sex and reproducing Metaphorically, I believe, Jesus was alluding to singleness and a life without sexual intercourse Some are single from birth (as a result of genetic programming), some made so by others (through socialization) and some by personal choice for a higher purpose All of these are honorable and valid situations

If one has a powerful libido and sexual appetite, the chances are that this person is called to marriage, not singleness As Paul says, "It is better to marry than to be aflame with passion" (1 Cor 7 9) In my opinion, Christians should be promoting early marriage rather than promoting an unrealistically extended period of celibacy well into one's twenties (if not longer) The arguments that people are not ready—that they don't yet "know themselves"—until sometime after finishing college or even graduate school are not very persuasive It doesn't seem wise to require that most men and women abstain from sex during the ten or fifteen years during which they experience their most intense sexual desire (to say nothing about their being the optimum age to bear children)

In any case, it is dangerous to be sexually obsessed or active outside of a marriage covenant Total intimacy should be coordinated with total commitment Physical as well as emotional and spiritual damage result from our failure to respect the marriage relationship To try to keep intimacy and commitment in equilibrium, it is better to try and fail at marriage than not to try at all and just sleep around without any commitments

Short of marriage, how much kissing and touching is appropriate? How much fantasizing and dreaming? How much flirting and romance? The clear boundary is no fornication—no sexual intercourse without total commitment (within marriage) to each other Beyond that, single people should avoid activities that tempt or harm themselves or others Cultivate relationships with whole persons, not just the sexual side of people Sublimate sexual energy into other channels Stay connected to God and put God at the center of your relationships with others Stay accountable in a small group with whom you can honestly share the struggles and opportunities of life

Homosexuality

Homosexuality is one of the most controversial topics of our time Statistics vary, but it seems that somewhere between 2 and 5 percent of men and women are practicing homosexuals Homosexuals in previous eras usually kept their sexual orientation as well hidden as possible and were viewed with a combination of pity, revulsion, fear and condemnation Known homosexuals have often been treated as unnatural, deviant, mentally ill, spiritually lost, morally reprobate and even criminal Even if one disapproves of homosexual behavior, one cannot justify the appalling cruelty and hatred that have been directed at gay and lesbian people over the centuries Especially for Christians, there is no excuse for such treatment

In our era, perhaps uniquely in history, the pendulum in attitudes toward homosexuality has swung way over to the other side Society is being asked not only to decriminalize and tolerate homosexuality as an option for private sexual practices among consenting adults, but to grant special recognition and legal protection to homosexuals as a minority just like African Americans, women and the disabled Many lobby for homosexual relationships to be recognized in law and language as authentic "marriages", they advocate also for homosexuality to be presented as an option (alongside traditional heterosexuality) in sex education classes and for homosexual relationships and activities to be mainstreamed and normalized in television programs, movies and other media

Christians should certainly take a leading role in protecting the privacy and freedom of all people, including gay people However, it is more problematic for Christians to be asked to approve of homosexual practice While Christians have said many foolish and ignorant things about homosexuality, it remains the case that heterosexual monogamy is the biblical standard and model for genital sexual relationships, from beginning to end All of the *specific* biblical passages that mention homosexuality condemn it [33] That these condemnations are linked with

---

[33] For example, Lev 18 22, 20 13 (condemnation of homosexual relations in context of OT ritual law, cultic defilement, idolatry), Gen 19 1-29, Judg 19—21 (violence, rape, inhospitality), Rom 1 18-32 (violations of nature and of God's will), 1 Cor 6 9-10, 1 Tim 1 8-11 (vice lists)

other sins (e g , violence, inhospitality) or with ritual laws or with primitive psychologies does not constitute sufficient grounds to accept homosexual practice today as legitimate All biblical teaching on all subjects is culturally linked and is not for that reason alone dispensable The burden of proof is on those who want to argue for a change in this perspective

Homosexual practice (like heterosexual promiscuity, divorce, sadomasochism, incest, bestiality, etc) is wrong in Christian ethics because it harms those who engage in it (even if this harm is not immediately apparent) It violates God's plan for sexuality, relationships, love and freedom Nobody ever said it would be easy to deny ourselves what we desire, of course Just as physical fitness demands some pain and self-discipline, so too sexual fitness requires some self-discipline

Traditionally, most theologians have argued that homosexuality is an abomination which must be firmly rejected by the church and punished by civil law More recently, some theologians see homosexuality as a tragic falling short of the orders of creation and redemption, deserving care and sympathy but not acceptance or legitimacy Still others believe that homosexuality may be an irreversible effect of the Fall and that celibacy or at least faithful monogamy are the best morality possible under the circumstances

Other Christians today urge a radical change in the traditional stance a full acceptance of homosexual practice In this view, homosexuality is morally neutral, like left-handedness It is, they hold, a condition that was simply not understood before our century and that is not really addressed by Scripture As with other issues (including slavery, monarchy, divorce and the subordination of women, to name four cases where the mind of the mainstream church has changed), we should not assume that a change in position toward homosexuality is inconceivable for biblical Christians

While the debate and controversy continue, a compelling case has

---

> Homosexual practices violate the basic meaning and pattern of sexual relations presented throughout the Bible, and every specific text that refers to homosexual practice condemns it We should note that in the Bible, the sins of adultery, divorce and heterosexual fornication are emphasized even more frequently than is homosexual practice

not yet been made to biblical, evangelical Christians for reversing the traditional position on homosexuality (any more than for reversing the stance on polygamy and polyandry as an option for those with naturally high libidos) Homosexuals need to understand that many (if not most) Christians who disagree with their sexual practices are driven to their position not by homophobia but by their study of Scripture and by careful thought Similarly, traditional, heterosexual Christians must understand that many proponents of a revisionist, gay-affirming position also want to affirm faithful monogamous relationships and a Christ-centered, biblical discipleship

Despite having considerable sympathy for gay and lesbian Christians, I find myself unable to affirm homosexual sexual practice from a biblical Christian standpoint Even so, heterosexual Christians should all make efforts to reach out in care and friendship to homosexuals (who may well be among our friends and family and who are always our neighbors) We must be in the forefront of efforts to defend the spiritual value, human dignity and basic social-political rights of all people, including those with whom we disagree The compassion shown by Christ should also drive us to seek cures for AIDS or any other afflictions suffered by homosexuals Homosexuals should be welcomed into the care and discipline of the church, no more or less than promiscuous heterosexuals, embezzlers and white-collar criminals Church leaders, who are held to a stricter standard, must avoid all appearance of evil—including both the evil of homophobia and that of gay sexual practices

Christian ethics cannot approve homosexual sexual behavior—nor can it approve homophobia.

Relationships: Keeping Our Commitments

As with the other commandments, the seventh one is representative of something bigger than the initial topic It is not just about adultery and not just about sex This deeper theme is human relationships of the covenanted sort The broader message is about keeping our commitments Marriage, symbolized and actualized in sexual union in both its commitment and its intimacy, is the primary symbolic form of covenanted cohumanity Adultery is the most blatant attack on that relationship and is, therefore, a terrible evil

The Bible testifies throughout that relationships are crucial Remember the only negative comment made by the Creator in Genesis 1—2 "It is not good that the man should be alone" (Gen 2 18) Remember, too, the Trinity "Let us make humankind in *our* image" (Gen 1 26), male and female are created in the image of a God who is three-in-one We can't be fully human without relationships Remember the great covenanted friendships in the Bible David and Jonathan, Ruth and Naomi, Peter and Mark, Paul and Timothy, Jesus and his disciples

Sex may not be crucial to everyone, but committed relationships certainly are Jesus and Paul had full rich lives without sex, but not without intimate friendships Authentic human life is *koinonia* life (shared life, community) Not just casual but intentional relationships are essential for discernment and growth, for good thoughts and actions

Because relationships—whether between spouses, between parent and child, between siblings or between friends—are crucial to a good human life, breaking them up or even threatening them with sins such as gossip is terrible Stirring up strife or "sowing discord" (Prov 6 14, 19) among friends or family is the moral equivalent of adultery The seventh commandment prohibits any threatening of covenanted relationships among ourselves and others

Lew Smedes says that the seventh commandment "calls us to make a deep decision, not simply about sex, but about the meaning and purpose of human life " Are we going to be "covenant-keepers" or "self-maximizers"?[34] The messages of the seventh commandment are "Keep your commitments" and "Protect the relational commitments of others " The feelings people have when they discover that their spouse or lover has betrayed them and had sex with someone else are the same as the feelings you have when you discover that a close friend has betrayed you

We must carefully observe the moral boundaries of not adulterating, compromising, threatening or betraying our commitments or those of

> Sex may not be crucial to everyone, but committed relationships certainly are. Jesus and Paul had full rich lives without sex, but not without intimate friendships. Authentic human life is *koinonia* life Not just casual but intentional relationships are essential

[34]Smedes, *Mere Morality,* pp 160-61

other people And we must nurture and encourage such friendships and relationships wherever and whenever we can The sixth commandment teaches us that people have a right to life and health, a right not to be harmed physically by anything we do or make The seventh commandment teaches that people have a right to form associations with others and to not have those relationships attacked or harmed by others We care for others not just by protecting their health, but also by protecting and encouraging their friendships and relationships

The seventh commandment challenges us to evaluate what we are doing to support marriage It also challenges us to determine whether we are nurturing faithful, meaningful friendships We should do everything in our power to encourage and reinforce both casual and covenanted friendships and to care for and repair such relationships amid the contradictory messages and influences of our culture In business, for example, moving employees without concern for how this might break up their personal networks of friends might be a sin, not just a management strategy

> The Christian church must *teach* the practice of covenanted friendship along the lines of Ruth and Naomi and David and Jonathan and should *celebrate* such commitments with congregational ceremonies

Clearly, we need some vastly improved friendship education The church could be playing an important role here There is so much in the Bible about committed friendship—its bases, its outlines, its behavioral possibilities Where are the sermons on the friendship covenants of David and Jonathan, Ruth and Naomi, and Jesus and his disciples? One interesting aspect of many of these friendships is that they are same-sex relationships And yet they involve the kind of lifelong covenant and intimate sharing and support that we usually think of only as we talk about marital ideals

Both church and society have suffered a great loss by failing to affirm and nurture such same-sex relationships Males often have no close male friends with whom to celebrate, commiserate, discuss or share their struggles Relationships among men tend to be temporary and function- or task-driven (e g , golf partners or work associates) rather than long-term and holistic Only athletes, so it seems, can enjoy the intense male camaraderie, physicality and emotional expressiveness craved by many and needed by all men The phenomenon of male "buddies" is increasingly rare And as more and more women conform (by choice or necessity) to the hectic lifestyle traditionally associated with men, they too suffer the loss of intimate, same-sex friendships

An irony should not be lost here gay and lesbian couples often demonstrate the sort of deep, intimate same-sex relationships we all need One can find beauty and goodness in such relationships We would be terribly mistaken in assuming a necessary connection between same-sex friendships and a homosexual orientation It is our *human* orientation that requires such intimate same-sex friendships Eroticizing such relationships is unnecessary and even harmful, but the basic relationship is often a beautiful thing

Christians should not only encourage friendship, they should support the recognition of "covenanted friendship" in the church Ruth and Naomi's pledge—"Where you go, I will go   Your people shall be my people, and your God my God" (Ruth 1 16)—is often quoted in heterosexual wedding ceremonies, but *originally it was a pledge between two women* David and Jonathan "made a covenant" before God to care for each other, to encourage each other, to care for each other's offspring if one of them died before the other (1 Sam 18 1-3) Jesus and his disciples covenanted in loyal friendship with each other

Frankly, we need both a renewed teaching and a way celebrating our commitments of loyal friendship before God and the church We treat it as casual and unimportant, and it becomes so in practice But it is not good for one to dwell alone! Jesus sent his disciples out two by two, not one by one (Mk 6 7) The church has failed to teach the crucial importance of lifelong friendship, sealed by vows, manifested in a pattern of shared life In a world crying for meaningful relationships, the church has failed to answer with its message of the possibilities of true friendship We have treated it as a casual, transient, unimportant option

Despite the concerns many raise about such a practice, creating new ceremonies of covenanted friendship in the church is not a move to endorse sexual relations outside of marriage To yield to the fear that this will implicitly endorse homosexual behavior actually does just the opposite it acquiesces in the popular culture's message that all "serious" relationships lead to bed We have everything to gain by affirming covenanted friendships in ceremonies of commitment

Outside of the church, in the political arena, I strongly support what are often called "domestic partnership" or "civil union" laws because our society suffers from a lack of commitment, not an excess There is every reason to be in favor of formal as well as informal covenants among men and women Marriage (i e , the covenant between a man and a woman) is one, but not the only, legitimate form of domestic partnership in society[35] Two (or more) individuals should be able to commit themselves to each other in a legally recognized bond New laws should be written for these purposes

> **Any domestic partner or civil union legislation that encourages human bonds and responsible caring for others is to the good. Christians must not yield to the cultural message that committed partnerships necessarily are sexual**

Making agreements to care for each other, to buy and tend property together, to merge economic opportunities, to share responsibility for finances, debts, loans, health crises, transportation and so forth—these are good and praiseworthy things It is a terrible mistake to assume or imply that domestic partnerships are necessarily eroticized and sexualized Why should the only options be traditional marriage and traditional singleness? The purposes served previously by extended families could in some important ways be sustained by such bonds Why shouldn't two (or more) older (or younger) men or women be able to enter into such a relationship in which they create a common life before the law?

Why does sex necessarily have anything to do with our debate about the desirability of such civil unions? The desirable factor of such partnerships is the serious form of community that is created in a world of isolated and vulnerable individuals Of course, such domestic partnerships have always existed My wife's family had an aunt and two uncles who never married and lived together in an informal domestic partnership well into their eighties Unfortunately, the law only saw them as

---

[35]Given the recent controversies over legalizing civil unions or gay marriages, Christians might ask what competence any worldly government has to define and regulate anything more than some sort of civil union Perhaps the church should define and regulate Christian marriage for itself and promote its beauty and desirability to all who wish to hear, perhaps the state should get out of the marriage business and confine its interest to civil unions

three individuals with the same address

Legally recognizing domestic partnership and religiously recognizing covenanted friendship will contribute to the stability, peace and health of both our society and our church Those disinclined toward heterosexual marriage will have two important options for forming seriously committed relationships in our cold world

Rabbi André Chouraqui has said,

The Ten Commandments do not pretend to heal people of their pathologies They aim only to transform the old man in us, slave to his instincts, into a being respectful of others and of the self There exists only one remedy universally effective in the life of couples it is love Love is the foundation of the union of two beings When love dies, the couple dies [36]

Friendship, forgiveness and generosity are the major ingredients of such love

I have often said that the best moment in marriage is when you suddenly realize that it is your best friend who is there beside you So too, the weakness of a marriage is usually related to a failure to build it as a friendship at its core Marriage is a special form of friendship, adultery is a special form of the sin against friendship The best preventive against adultery may be to reinforce the concepts of covenant and friendship

For Reflection and Discussion

1 How do you avoid the temptation of romantic entanglement with someone who is already married? What are the danger signs and exit strategies in such a situation?

2 What do you find are the most helpful guidelines for dating and sexual expression between unmarried Christian people?

3 What do you think of the author's suggestion that celibacy through one's twenties is not necessarily realistic or healthy and that earlier marriages may be desirable for most Christians?

4 How do you nurture and keep your relational commitments? How

---

[36]Chouraqui, *Les Dix Commandements,* p 191

have you built meaningful friendships?

5 How do you respond to the author's ideas about promoting covenanted friendship in the church and civil unions (domestic partnerships) in society? Can they be promoted without endorsing sexual
   behavior in these relationships? What do you think of the idea of
   having governments regulate only the civil-union side of relationships and churches regulate marriage as they see fit?

10

Stuff Stewarding

Our basic human existence requires not only life and health (protected by the sixth commandment) and committed relationships (covered by the seventh commandment), but a minimum of "stuff," a basic material infrastructure for life food, clothing, shelter, tools and so on That is why the eighth commandment declares, "You shall not steal" (Ex 20 15 par Deut 5 19) Luther saw this as a continuation of a progression from your life (as the dearest thing), to your spouse (the next dearest thing) and now to your property (the next dearest after your spouse) [1] My own way of describing the progression is that one's life is the most basic, immediate reality of our existence, this is followed by our covenanted partnerships and then our material property Viewed from the other direction, we can see that shelter and material resources (addressed by the eighth commandment) make it possible to have a marriage (covered by the seventh commandment), which in turn makes it possible to generate and protect life (protected by the sixth commandment)

When the text says we should not steal, it is prohibiting the taking of someone else's property Rabbi André Chouraqui explains that the original term "signifies 'theft' in Hebrew Theft consists of fraudulently subtracting from the property of another, including not only the action of stealing but also kidnapping, robbery, piracy, larceny, fraud and any

---

[1] Martin Luther, *The Large Catechism,* trans Robert H Fischer (1529, Philadelphia Fortress, 1959), p 39

other actions that tend to subtract fraudulently the goods of another "[2]
Brevard Childs points out that "the particular nuance of this word *[gnb]*
which distinguishes it from other types of misappropriation such as *lqh*
or *gzl* is the element of secrecy "[3] Stealing is "taking by stealth "

Some scholars have argued that the focus of this commandment was
originally confined to kidnapping, to stealing a person There are few
crimes more horrible than kidnapping In ancient Israel, anyone who
kidnapped a person, no matter what happened to the victim, was to be
put to death (Ex 21 16) All of America was in a state of shock when the
child of heroic transatlantic-flight pioneer Charles Lindbergh was kidnapped in the 1930s In the 1970s, Patty Hearst's kidnapping by the
Symbionese Liberation Army gripped the public's attention While kidnapping is a terrible violation of the eighth commandment, Dale Patrick
cautions us that "there is no warrant for such narrowing in the wording
itself "[4] The prohibition against theft goes far beyond kidnapping

The Bible has a great deal to say about theft, with punishments
carefully tailored to each form of stealing [5] In ancient Israel, if someone stole an ox and slaughtered or sold it, he must pay back *five* oxen
If he stole and sold or killed a sheep, the penalty was to pay back *four*
sheep If he stole an animal and it could be returned alive, he still paid
double to the owner (Ex 22 1) If a thief confessed his crime before being caught, he would pay the victim full restitution plus one-fifth (20
percent), a lighter penalty (Num 5 5-7) If a thief could not pay for
what he had stolen, he could himself be sold into slavery to pay the
debt, although every sabbath (seventh) year slaves were to be set free
and debts remitted, so this was not a permanent disaster

Not only were you not to steal, you were not to stand by passively
watching while others were robbed of their possessions or even while
their possessions drifted away by accident (Ex 23 4-5, Deut 22 1-3)

---

[2] André Chouraqui, *Les Dix Commandements Aujourd'hui* (Paris Robert Laffont,
2000), p 196

[3] Brevard Childs, *The Book of Exodus A Critical, Theological Commentary* (Philadelphia Westminster Press, 1974), p 423

[4] Dale Patrick, *Old Testament Law* (Atlanta John Knox Press, 1985), p 41 See also
Childs, *Book of Exodus*, p 423, on why the commandment should be read as forbid-
ding more kinds of theft than just kidnapping

[5] See, e g , Lev 19 11, Prov 6 30-31, Is 1 23, Ezek 18 10-13, 22 29, 33 14-15, Amos
3 10, Zech 5 3

Usury (charging interest on loans) was another practice forbidden among the Israelites, though it was allowed in transactions with non-Israelites (Ex 22 25-27, Lev 25 35-38, Deut 23 19-20, 24 6, 10-13, 17) To charge interest to someone in need and without resources was seen as akin to theft [6]

Israel was also supposed to leave the edges of its crop fields and vineyards unharvested—they were not to pick the plants clean—so that the poor (the alien, orphan and widow) could have something to eat (Deut 24 19-22) And Israelites were to pay wages to poor and needy laborers daily, before sunset (Deut 24 14-15, Lev 19 13) Every third year the tithes were made available to Levites, poor, aliens and orphans (Deut 14 28-29) Every seventh year all debts were canceled, and credit histories started over with a clean slate (Deut 15 1-11) Not to follow these economic practices was like stealing from the poor Merchants were also warned that dishonest scales and weights were an abomination to the Lord, whereas just balances and scales were his delight (Prov 11 1, see also Lev 19 35-36, Deut 25 13-15, Prov 20 10, 23, Amos 8 4-6) On the other end of the spectrum from the robber and exploiter of the poor, "Whoever is kind to the poor lends to the LORD" (Prov 19 17)

In addition to its laws and counsels, the Bible raises the subject of theft by way of its stories Jacob, the father of the Israelite nation, ripped off his brother Esau on two occasions and deceived his father-in-law, Laban (Gen 25 29-34, 27 1-40, 30 25-43) Jacob's wife Rachel stole her family's idols when she ran off with him (Gen 31 19-20) Per Moses' instructions, Israel began its national history by borrowing heavily from the Egyptian masters and then running off with the plunder (Ex 12 35-36, from which we get the phrase *spoiling Egypt*) Achan's theft of booty from the defeated enemy Jericho (after the troops had been warned not to take anything) resulted in his being put to death (Josh 7) Jezebel had Naboth murdered so she could take pos-

---

[6] It is like theft because you are taking material things from someone when you should not It is not by stealth, though, so it is more like robbery than burglary Of course, these laws regulated transactions in a simpler direct-exchange and barter society and concern cases of basic survival needs We must rethink matters in a monetary and credit economy, above all in cases of loans for business purposes beyond basic personal needs Still we must strive to avoid any unethical loan practices or interest rates

session of his vineyard for her husband, Ahab (1 Kings 21 1-16) Sometimes these stories of theft give clear warnings not to steal, other times, the story doesn't take a strong editorial position but leaves us to think it through

The New Testament clearly denounces stealing as wrong The eighth commandment is quoted in various contexts In a powerful statement Paul says, "Thieves must give up stealing, rather let them labor and work honestly with their own hands, so as to have something to share with the needy" (Eph 4 28) James (repeating the theme of Deut 24) severely warns those who fraudulently withhold pay from their laborers (Jas 5 1-6) Thieves and robbers are also condemned in various biblical vice lists (1 Cor 5 11, 6 10)

Jesus' Economics

Jesus explicitly affirmed the commandment not to steal, in answer to a question about the way to life (Mt 19 16-18) Think also of how Jesus overturned the tables of the moneychangers in the temple and rebuked them for turning God's temple into a "den of thieves" (Mt 21 13 KJV) [7]

> Jesus' many warnings against greed, covetousness and the desire to be rich can be seen as the interior side of the prohibition against theft. It is significant that Jesus had more to say about wealth and poverty than about heaven and hell, adultery, homosexuality or many other topics we think important.

It is also interesting and highly symbolic that Jesus was crucified between two thieves, one of whom expressed faith in him before dying (Lk 23 32-43) Thieves are not without hope when Jesus is near

Just as Jesus broadened the prohibition against murder to include angry, murderous thoughts—and the prohibition against adultery to include adulterous, lustful thoughts—so Jesus' many warnings against greed, covetousness and the desire to be rich can be seen as internal applications of the prohibition against theft More broadly, it is significant that Jesus had more to say about wealth and poverty than about heaven and hell, adultery, homosexuality or many other topics we

---

[7] The "thieves" are merchants and moneychangers, not just pickpockets and petty criminals

think important His teaching on economics has its share of warnings and denunciations against materialism, greed and dishonesty, but its main focus is on simplicity, gratitude and generosity among the diligent stewards of God's creation

The Core Message

In Israel's rabbinic tradition, the eighth commandment prohibits excessive profit-taking interest on loans to fellow Jews, failing to respond when someone greets you, representing someone else's ideas as your own and misleading someone into being grateful to us when we do not deserve it [8] Some of these applications may seem a bit stretched, but it is this kind of reflection that drives to the heart of the principle

Luther wrote that "thievery is the most common craft and the largest guild on earth If we look at mankind in all its conditions, it is nothing but a vast, wide stable full of great thieves   We are commanded to promote and further our neighbor's interests, and when he suffers want we are to help, share, and lend to both friends and foes "[9]

It is difficult to improve on Calvin's comprehensive grasp of the meaning of the commandment

> There are many kinds of theft One consists in violence, as when a man's goods are forcibly plundered and carried off, another in malicious imposture, as when they are fraudulently intercepted, a third in the more hidden craft which takes possession of them with a semblance of justice, and a fourth in sycophancy which wiles them away under the pretense of donation   If an agent or an indolent steward wastes the substance of his employer or if   a master cruelly torments his household, he is guilty of theft before God [10]

Therefore, Calvin says, "Let it be our constant aim faithfully to lend our counsel and aid to all so as to assist them in retaining their property   And not only so, but let us contribute to the relief of those

---

[8] Avroham Chaim Feuer, *Aseres Hadibros The Ten Commandments, A New Translation with a Commentary Anthologized from Talmudic, Midrashic and Rabbinic Sources* (Brooklyn, N Y Mesorah, 1981), p 57
[9] Luther, *Large Catechism,* pp 40, 43
[10] Calvin *Institutes* 2 8 45

whom we see under the pressure of difficulties, assisting their want out of our abundance "[11]

While kidnapping and slavery are extreme examples of theft, they do not exhaust the meaning of the eighth commandment, which concerns the whole material infrastructure necessary to life and under the stewardship of your neighbor It is not wrong to receive a gift from your neighbor, nor is it wrong to receive goods, money or service in a fair exchange But it is wrong to take another's possessions in any other way Jan Milič Lochman invites us to think of "theft from above" and "theft from below "[12] The former refers to theft by the rich and powerful who overcharge and underpay The latter is the conventional appropriation of another's property

Why Is Theft Wrong?

Stealing is wrong because it attacks and harms our neighbor Our neighbors need some basic material things (e g , food, clothing, shelter) just to survive But my neighbors have a *right* to, not just a need for, their property It is transparently *unjust* and unfair to steal property placed under the stewardship of our neighbors Even the threat of theft is wrong because it reduces our neighbors' freedom and increases their anxiety Owners can leave their property unguarded if they know that we observe this command

Alphonse Maillot gives a compelling account of how our being is dependent on our having and how human freedom is impacted by theft

> Habitually I cannot "be" without a minimum of "having " Without this minimum "having," I depend absolutely on others I become their thing, their property, their slave It is the same whether these others are the clan, a class, the tribe or the state This command intends to safeguard this minimum of "having," which guarantees to each his freedom to "be" and avoid becoming an object Thus, this command prohibits me from attacking this minimum "having "
>
> It is not thus a defense of some abstract and theoretical "divine right to property" that does not take account of circumstances, nor

---

[11] Calvin *Institutes of the Christian Religion* 2 8 46

[12] Jan Milič Lochman, *Signposts to Freedom The Ten Commandments and Christian Ethics* (Minneapolis Augsburg, 1982), pp 129ff

is it a defense of a right to equality, also theoretical It intends to protect a right to a real individual freedom, a freedom that can only be guaranteed to the extent that I retain the right to have for myself certain goods that belong to me [13]

Lochman also links the ideas of "having" and "being"

> There is no biblical basis for considering property as demonic "Having" is obviously integral to human "being" in history, part of its built-in biological defense against need   We human beings can only survive by fabricating our basic necessities of life from our environment and possessing the elementary equipment for life In this sense, personal property is an indispensable condition for the development of human life [14]

Lew Smedes argues that if property is important enough to be protected by this commandment, then it must be wrong for people to own nothing, to have no property at all [15]

Theft is unfair and unjust to many neighbors beyond just the one from whom the material has been stolen For example, all of us have to pay higher prices in stores to compensate for shoplifters and thieves All of us pay higher insurance premiums because of the cheats and thieves who make fraudulent claims We pay for expanded police protection and other security measures—all because of the thieves out there

But theft is bad for the thief as well as for the victim To begin with, stealing is an evidence of bondage, of a lack of freedom The thief is in such slavery to the material object that he cannot resist reaching out and seizing it Theft begins in the heart—in envy, greed and covetousness The thief has an unquenchable desire to possess A free person has the power to walk away from temptation Thieves are powerless slaves before the object they must steal

Stealing is also a degrading violation of the thief's humanity All of us were created in the image and likeness of our Creator, with a nature that is expressed and fulfilled by making good things and contributing

---

[13] Alphonse Maillot, *Le Decalogue Une morale pour notre temps* (Geneva Labor & Fides, 1985), p 128

[14] Lochman, *Signposts,* p 129

[15] Lewis B Smedes, *Mere Morality What God Expects from Ordinary People* (Grand Rapids, Mich Eerdmans, 1983), p 185

positively to others Thieves go against their own nature in taking the forbidden thing, and in so doing they undermine their pride and sense of wholeness Thievery is a shameful, sleazy, subhuman activity that corrupts and degrades its practitioners Theft also invariably complicates life and poisons relationships Known or suspected thieves are shunned and mistrusted They must always look over their shoulders to see whether their pursuers have caught up with them They must lie to cover up their acts

If the negative effects of stealing—both on the thief and on the victims—are not enough reason already to avoid theft, a final argument is that theft is an attack on God We may think that God has a claim on a tithe (10 percent) of our stuff In reality, God owns the "cattle on a thousand hills" and is the true and final owner of the whole earth (Ps 50 10) When we steal, we are usurping God's place as the owner and distributor of his property When we steal, we are taking from God, first of all, not just from the human owners of the property Even if those owners have acquired the property in a questionable way and our Robin Hood instincts to more justly redistribute the goods are aroused, there are other strategies than theft to bring about justice

> **Theft harms not only the victims, but also the thieves, who have become enslaved to objects they cannot resist taking Thieves are further degraded and shamed by their incapacity to compete, survive or win in a fair competition. Thieves must also cover their tracks, always looking over their shoulders and living in a complex web of lies**

People can *directly* steal from God by failing to give him the first fruits of their income in the form of tithes and offerings (Mal 3 8-10) Alan Redpath extends the range of stealing from God beyond our material things to our very selves We may be stealing from God by denying him his ownership and use of our abilities and gifts "It has much to do with robbing God of his rightful ownership of life and not allowing him to possess his inheritance in his people, and at the same time our robbing him of our availability by failing to press home for our inheritance in him "[16] Redpath continues,

---

[16]Alan Redpath, *Law and Liberty A New Look at the Ten Commandments in the Light of Contemporary Society* (Old Tappan, N J Revell, 1978), p 92

This commandment is   broken in failure to make a total consecration and commitment of our lives to him   He wants your
brain to think through, your hands to work through, your feet to
run and walk for him, your heart to radiate his love He wants the
talents and gifts you possess for they are his They belong to him
because he created you and them To hold those talents to yourself he regards as stealing   The cross is God's great plea   as
you realize you are *bought* The Lord does not say that he has
"kept" you or "made" you but that he has "bought" you [17]

We belong to God and must not steal what belongs to God

Why Are We Tempted to Steal?

We live in a materialistic culture of consumption We have lost our
bearings and are now practicing the theory Jesus so decisively rejected that life consists of the abundance of things that we possess
"He who has the most toys wins," says a bumper sticker "Greed is
good," argued the business leader in the popular film *Wall Street* Consumerism and materialism appeal to our basest appetites and most
selfish inclinations But in an atmosphere of spiritual poverty, mammon can also be substituted for God as the central focus of our life It
appeals to our craving for concrete, material things (i e , our need for
idols) Of course, people have always had such appetites, but our culture, as none before it, has figured out how to fan those desires into an
unquenchable fire

Imagine what our culture looks like to God or what it will look like in
the broader frame of world history Even the poor in America are
wealthy by world standards Those of us in the middle class are fabu-
lously wealthy The richest 2 or 3 percent of the American population
have the sort of wealth that has previously been available only to author-
itarian monarchs of empires The obsession with *more* that has led some
of our top corporate (and political and nonprofit) chieftains to steal millions of dollars, the miserly attitude about paying taxes, the pathetic
record of charitable giving—frankly, it boggles the mind But these dramatic examples illustrate the reason why we must pay careful attention
to the eighth commandment in the church Convenience store holdups,

---

[17]Ibid , p 94

pickpocketing and car break-ins are only the most superficial aspect of the challenge Nice, well-scrubbed, affluent, churchgoing people are immersed in a culture of theft as much as those petty thieves

What is wrong here is an imbalanced obsession with things and with personal wealth creation We become workaholics, shoppers, consumers and financial planners occupied not just with responsible saving for the future but with maximizing our net worth We suffer from a lack of faith and trust in God and a lack of community, so we are driven to be as financially independent as possible From our imbalanced lives we are getting imbalanced values In such a skewed environment, wealth and material things move toward the top of our priority list

But as Paul wrote, "Those who want to be rich fall into temptation and are trapped by many senseless and harmful desires that plunge people into ruin and destruction For the love of money is a root of all kinds of evil, and in their eagerness to be rich some have wandered away from the faith and pierced themselves with many pains" (1 Tim 6 9-10) Jesus warned how hard it is for the rich to enter the kingdom of God—harder than for a camel to enter the eye of a needle (Lk 18 24-27) The pursuit or even the possession of great wealth can create a distracting anxiety that chokes out more important things (Mt 13 22, Mk 4 19, Lk 8 14) Too much wealth can lead one away from dependence on God and into a false sense of strength and

> It is hard to see theft (wrongful appropriation of property) for what it really is when we are immersed 24/7 in a culture of materialism, consumerism, advertising, celebrity, image, glamour, narcissism and idolatry. It is easy for Christians to get caught up in the surrounding culture of acquisition, consumption and wealth and call it "God's blessing "

virtue Instead of relying on God, we rely on what our money and power will produce

Getting Healthy in Our Economic Lives

It is easy to confine the application of this commandment to an interpersonal level that doesn't get much beyond the criticism of petty thievery, shoplifting and embezzlement To help us go deeper, and then to get healthier in this area of our lives, we need to explore the broader fabric of a biblical theology of things—of wealth and poverty What does the Bible teach us about economic matters? How do we practice these ancient principles in our era?

The starting point for all discussions of Christian economic questions is the affirmation that "the earth is the Lord's and all that is in it, the world, and those who live in it, for he has founded it   and established it" (Ps 24 1-2) All property is first of all God's property—not primarily our neighbor's or our own Whether a formal title to this or that property designates us as *owners* or *renters* is not terribly important by comparison to God's designation of us as the *stewards* of his property Stewardship is the key, foundational concept in Christian economic philosophy and ethics

Stewardship is when one manages property on behalf of its true owner The distinguishing trait of all Christian economic thinking is that economics is subordinated at every step to a higher power and purpose The enemy is not economy but autonomy Jesus put it best "No one can serve two masters

You cannot serve God and wealth" (Mt 6 24) "Strive first for the kingdom of God and his righteousness, and all these things will be given to you as well" (Mt 6 33) "All these things" refers to food, clothing and other "stuff " Serve God as you steward his stuff

> The organizing, foundational principle of any authentic Christian approach to economic life is *stewardship*. Everything belongs to God, and our business is to care for God's property and God's people in God's way

If the first concern of Christian economic thinking is to serve God, the second is to serve and care for our neighbors Lochman explains, "Objectively property is misused whenever it turns into an instrument of power over our fellow human beings instead of being an aid to ensure human life and development   The subjective aspects of the misuse of property [are those that] destroy the humanity not only of the poor but also of the rich "[18] Greed and its companion vices assail and cripple our humanity

The eighth commandment is not just about refraining from theft, but

---

[18]Lochman, *Signposts,* p 130

about actively protecting and preserving our neighbor's property The
Israelite law required the people not just to abstain from stealing each
other's animals but to return animals to their owners (even an enemy
owner) if they were found straying (Ex 23 4-5, Deut 22 1-4) Paul draws
out this positive agenda when he says, "Thieves must give up stealing,
rather let them labor and work honestly   so as to have something to
share with the needy" (Eph 4 28) John challenges us, saying, "How
does God's love abide in anyone who has the world's goods and sees a
brother or sister in need and yet refuses help?" (1 Jn 3 17) Work is
about empowering us to share things with people in need

Of course, the Bible insists that we provide for the material needs of
our own households Paul writes that "whoever does not provide for
relatives, and especially for family members, has denied the faith and
is worse than an unbeliever" (1 Tim 5 8) It is not God's will that we become poor and homeless God blesses our work and intends that it go
well with us and that we live long in the land the Lord gives us (Deut
5 16, 33) The Proverbs counsel
us to work hard and provide for
ourselves and our households
(e g , Prov 10 4-5, 13 22, 31 10-
31)

But Christian economics is
not just about defining *mine* and
yours It is also about under-
standing *ours*—learning how to think about common possessions,
common responsibility and common stewardship The New Testament
Greek word for *community* (sometimes translated "fellowship") is
koinōnia The early Christians came together and had all things in common [*koinos*] (Acts 2 43-47, 4 32-33) As any among them had need,
the others would help provide out of the things they had They took offerings to send to brothers and sisters in need when they heard of it
The use of language is really striking here early Christianity was about
koinos (sharing in common) replacing *idios* (thinking in terms of "my
own," the root of our term *idiot*) The coming of the Holy Spirit at Pentecost (and his presence with us ever since) makes people more com-
munity-oriented It is not God's Spirit but another, alien spiritual force
that stimulates our individualistic selfishness

> Christian economics is not just about
> *mine* and *yours* but about *ours*.
> The Holy Spirit replaces *idios* with
> *koinos*—individualism with community
> thinking and behavior.

So Christian economics is about serving God, serving others and sharing in community But is that all? Is there any place for individual industriousness and success? for wealth and beauty? Both the Old and New Testaments frequently commend industriousness and condemn laziness Jesus' parable of the talents has multiple layers of meaning, but at one level it certainly praises the stewards who invested profitably, doubling what they were given, but is very critical of the timid investor who buried his treasure and had no gain to show the boss (Mt 25 14-30)

Is it a sin to be rich or to aim at prosperity? The Bible's harsh words for the wealthy are not because they have wealth, per se, but because of their idolatry, arrogance, injustice or miserliness toward those in need The biblical descriptions of the afterlife, heaven, make it sound like mansions, feasts and luxury are part of God's plan We see clearly in creation that God created and values beauty, not just utility We must not forget that our Lord's first miracle was the creation of excellent wine for a wedding feast

Some of the famous and heroic biblical characters were rich Abraham left his home and heritage in Ur of the Chaldees, going out in obedience to God without knowing where it would lead He became wealthy enough to have a personal army of six hundred men Job was very wealthy, then impoverished, then wealthier than ever The royal family of David and Solomon became very rich, although David started out as a modest shepherd boy Joseph of Arimathea's wealth allowed him to provide a tomb for the crucified Lord

If wealth is acquired and used in a righteous way, if those who have wealth see themselves as stewards rather than allowing wealth to corrupt them, then I don't see how it can be criticized It may well be the blessing of God For a philosophy of personal or community economics, however, it is hard to beat the middle way advocated in Proverbs "Give me neither poverty nor riches, feed me with the food that I need, or I shall be full, and deny you, and say 'Who is the LORD?' or I shall be poor, and steal, and profane the name of my God" (Prov 30 8-9) In the same spirit, Paul knew "what it is to have little, and   what it is to have plenty" (Phil 4 12) and urged "godliness combined with contentment" (1 Tim 6 6-8) Those who advocate extreme positions are almost certainly wrong both the "health and wealth, name it and claim it" gurus with their gaudy lifestyles and gilded television sets—and their grim-faced, killjoy counterparts who make ugliness, poverty and melancholy into virtues

On the other end of the spectrum, is poverty a virtue? Are the poor more admirable than the rich? Jesus did say, "Blessed are you who are poor" (Lk 6 20) But poverty, neediness and emptiness are never presented in the Bible as intrinsically valuable conditions Poverty, like the cross, may have an *instrumental* value in that it is the means to an end It was blessed to be poor, Jesus said, because it meant one had room to receive the kingdom of God So too, choosing to live very simply and in a condition of poverty can be very valuable Life can be less complex and one may have fewer worries One can identify with, come alongside and serve more of the people of the world if one is poor Our dependence on God as well as our community increases when we are poor So voluntary poverty does not automatically confer virtue and sainthood on its practitioners, but it may be an admirable and holy path to take

The Law, the Writings and the Prophets all show a constant concern for those who are poor and needy *involuntarily* Against those who thought that observing religious ritual fasts was all it took to please God, the Lord said through Isaiah,

> Is not this the fast that I choose to loose the bonds of injustice,
> to undo the thongs of the yoke, to let the oppressed go free, and
> to break every yoke? Is it not to share your bread with the hun-
> gry, and bring the homeless poor into your house, when you see
> them naked, to cover them, and not to hide yourself from your
> own kin? (Is 58 6-7)

We must not let our spirit of entrepreneurship degenerate into what the prophet Micah denounces in Micah 2 1-2 "Alas for those who devise wickedness and evil deeds on their beds! When the morning dawns, they perform it, because it is in their power They covet fields, and seize them, houses, and take them away, they oppress householder and house, people and their inheritance "

The most powerful words come from the mouth of the prophet Amos

Therefore because you trample on the poor and take from them levies of grain, you have built houses of hewn stone, but you shall not live in them, you have planted pleasant vineyards, but you shall not drink their wine For I know how many are your transgressions, and how great are your sins—you who afflict the righteous, who take a bribe, and push aside the needy in the gate (Amos 5 11-12)

Alas for those who lie on beds of ivory, and lounge on their couches, and eat lambs from the flock, and calves from the stall, who sing idle songs to the sound of the harp, and like David improvise on instruments of music, who drink wine from bowls, and anoint themselves with the finest oils, but are not grieved over the ruin of Joseph! (Amos 6 4-6)

Hear this, you that trample on the needy, and bring to ruin the poor of the land, saying, "When will the new moon be over so that we may sell grain, and the sabbath, so that we may offer wheat for sale? We will make the ephah small and the shekel great, and practice deceit with false balances, buying the poor for silver and the needy for a pair of sandals, and selling the sweepings of the wheat " (Amos 8 4-6)

Jesus' appropriation of the economic liberation and care themes (e g, Lk 4 16-21) and his warnings to the rich, especially in the parables and the synoptic apocalypse, reinforce these same themes We must never set aside others' basic needs in our quest for wealth or success Paul and Peter and the New Testament church were exemplary in their concern for the poor

Luther shared the biblical passion for helping the poor

Beware how you deal with the poor, of whom there are many now If, when you meet a poor man who must live from hand to mouth, you act as if everyone must live by your favor, you skin and scrape him right down to the bone, and you arrogantly turn him away whom you ought to give aid, he will go away wretched and dejected, and because he can complain to no one else, he will cry to heaven   Such a man's sighs and cries will be no joking matter   for they will reach God [19]

---

[19]Luther, *Large Catechism*, p 42

In short, the way that we get healthy in our economic lives is to let the challenge of the eighth commandment prod us to review our whole philosophy of economics and material things When we do this, we discover that stewardship and *koinonia*, not free enterprise and individualism, are our foundational concepts We may choose voluntary poverty We may be blessed with great wealth We may seek a balanced, middle way between wealth and poverty In all three cases our concern is the same to glorify and honor God with our property and resources, always maintaining a special concern to protect and care for the poor of our world

---

Area Principle 8· Never take or accept anything that belongs to others if it is necessary to their survival or if the means by which you acquire it are unjust. Rather, regarding yourself as a steward of God's possessions, work to care not only for yourself, your household and community, but also for the poor and needy of the world.

How Shall We Then Steal?

It is difficult to confine oneself to a short list of the ways theft is carried out in today's world Chouraqui writes that the various methods of thieves "could inspire several encyclopedias   One finds them in banks, mayor's offices, governments, councils, command posts The facility with which they carry out these misdeeds is astonishing— and it is still more astonishing how passively the world accepts it "[20]

Maillot also writes about the many actions included in the idea of theft

At what point do the profits of an enterprise become money stolen from the workers who have made it happen? Or again the proceeds about which I dissimulate on my tax return—is this a theft from society? And reciprocally, the state that always considers me a potential thief and makes me support the games of reporting accounts of others, isn't it an accomplice of thieves, and thus a thief itself? Here's a last example that which I have

---

[20]Chouraqui, *Les Dix Commandements*, p 201 Genetically manipulating nature, cloning, turning it into a commercial market, selling and buying organs—these are, Chouraqui believes, violations of the command, thefts of what belongs to God See pp 206-7

not given in the offering, which I subtracted from the collective church to which I pretend to belong, is this also a theft?[21]

Maillot's last point reminds us of Jesus' challenge to people who excuse their lack of financial support to their parents by saying that they are offering this money to God instead (Mt 15 3-6)

The adjacent list describes some of the ways we may be stealing today It is only a brief sample of what could be a lengthy list

This list hardly begins to raise important questions about what we might call structural theft systems and policies that take money or property from one group and give it to others in an unjust way Part of the problem is that to define *theft*, we need to clarify what constitutes legitimate ownership and property Our challenge today is exacerbated by the vast and growing numbers of very needy people, the increasing scope of their needs and an economy that is just not doing the job Something is wrong when a relative few have so very much while masses of people have hardly anything The problem cannot be blamed only on a few crooks here and there The economic system

HOW MANY WAYS CAN WE STEAL?

- keeping the change we receive from a cashier when we have been given too much
- remaining silent when we are not charged enough on a bill
- failing to report all our income and to pay taxes on it
- filing insurance claims or accepting settlements we don't deserve
- taking office supplies for personal use
- unauthorized personal use of office or church phones and computers
- failing to work during time for which we are being paid
- replenishing our kitchen supplies with restaurant supplies
- overcharging customers or providing them with poor service or products
- overbilling third-party payers (e g , insurance companies)
- underpaying employees
- undertipping service personnel (at restaurants, airports, etc)
- presenting someone else's ideas or creations as our own or failing to give credit where it is due
- accepting a salary raise or bonus for work that was not ours alone when the other contributors are not also given raises or bonuses

---

[21]Maillot, *Le Decalogue*, p 124 As Maillot points out, we can easily fall into a hair-splitting casuistry here and miss the basic spirit

itself is broken, but the elite beneficiaries of the system have developed hard hearts and blind eyes

Let us look briefly at several challenges to our economic thinking What are the Christian contributions to these discussions? What are Christian ethical practices in these different areas?

The Corporate Capitalist System

With the demise of the Soviet Union and the end of the Cold War at the end of the 1980s, corporate capitalism vanquished Marxian socialism in the battle of economic systems Now Russia and even China are adopting free-enterprise capitalist systems and practices to a significant degree And modern capitalism is not just a national phenomenon Enabled largely by developments in transportation and communication technologies, the global linking of economies and the extension of corporate-style business operations are viewed by many as the one great hope of combating world poverty Economic development today means lowering or eliminating national trade barriers, standardizing manufacturing and management techniques, attracting capital investments from around the world, and joining in the activities and purposes of the global economy

Biblical Christians have a strong orientation toward creativity, innovation and hard work—core virtues of capitalism Freedom, initiative and personal responsibility strike a more biblical chord than does the obedience to centralized planners in distant bureaucracies that is typical of state socialism Strangers joining in corporations to work together on common purposes rings true to Christian values And, finally, a readiness to reach across barriers of land and sea, of culture and language, and of nations and ethnic groups in a positive global perspective is very much in accord with the Christian vision

Nevertheless, there are other aspects of global, corporate capitalism that can trouble a Christian mind For a faith that looks forward to a New Jerusalem into which "people will bring   the glory and honor of the nations" (Rev 21 26), the relentless extension of a standardized, global mass culture that comes at the expense of cultural diversity is not very appealing For a movement that believes in servant leadership, *koinonia* and contentment, the specter of greed and self-serving opulence among so many corporate leaders is revolting For a move-

ment that is aware of the corrupting power of selfishness and pride, the
intensifying concentration of power in fewer and fewer hands is omi-
nous Corporate scandals (e g , Andersen, Enron, Tyco, WorldCom,
Global Crossing) can no longer be excused as exceptions resulting from
a few "bad apples " They are entirely predictable instances of the corrupting effects of power, greed, wealth, opportunity, lack of accountability and immersion in a club of kindred spirits Lord Acton's dictum
is as true in business as in politics and religion "Power tends to corrupt, and absolute power corrupts absolutely "

Christians must reject the theory that people pursuing their self-interest in unregulated markets (or any other time or context) will produce the best, fairest economic results for everyone [22] Historically, we
have seen the "invisible hand" before (such as with the late nine-
teenth-century American robber barons), and it is not a pretty sight
When an ideology of free competition is used to justify a system that
leads to monopolies and the suppression of competition, we must object An allegedly free market sets allegedly just prices that, in actual-
ity, unjustly ignore the externalized costs of production that must be
borne by neighbors and future generations (e g , pollution, destruction
of social and natural environments, disposal of worn out products)

We cannot create a perfect economic system, but we can learn a lot
from the ancient Israelite economic system, which preserved elements
of free enterprise within a set of socially progressive laws and institutions and which prevented both debt and power from getting out of
hand I believe some form of capitalism is probably the best economic
system in today's world, but it must be held in check, held responsible
for its true costs, for example, by governments and popular associations (labor unions, churches, consumer groups, etc) or it will destroy
the planet

While governmental responses are also needed, Christians can begin
to address the economic challenge by demanding that their brothers
and sisters with executive-level jobs respond to the leadership of Jesus
Christ rather than that of the market alone But how many Christians
in corporate leadership could provide even the most basic summary of

---

[22] Adam and Eve acted on self-interest in a free, unregulated market when they harvested that first "apple "

the economic teaching of Jesus or any other part of the Bible? Now you
see the problem A Christian business leader might be capable of offering a prayer before a meal at a business summit, but that is about all
many of them have to give

The question we must face is whether we are accomplices in a system and an economy that are sometimes stealing basic necessities from
the poor of the earth? Christians sometimes worry about being accomplices to sexual sin by making birth control available to unmarried people We ought also to worry about whether we are accomplices to murder if we object to weapons controls And, in the present context, we
need to ask whether we are accomplices to theft by our support of the
more predatory manifestations of capitalism We must never forget how
God feels about the poor and about those who mistreat or ignore them
To whom much is given, much is required (Lk 12 48)

The point of this brief discussion is not to choose one of the world's
economic theories to support, it is to challenge Christians to think biblically, critically, creatively and redemptively about the economic policies, practices and institutions of our time The Christian economic
"theory" is stewardship The guiding principle is to avoid taking anything or any profit that rightfully (i e , in the eyes of God) should belong to someone else and, rather than focusing on personal gain, to
seek to give to those in need

Wages and Prices

How should wage and compensation levels be decided? I have inter-
viewed quite a few CEOs (most of them non-Christians, as far as I
could tell) and asked them whether CEO compensation is an ethical issue or just a market issue The answer has always been that it is a market issue Supply and demand set compensation levels, they say This
is certainly true for workers, for example, when corporations close
American manufacturing sites and build factories in Mexico so as to be
able to hire cheaper labor, it is true again when Mexican plants are
closed and new ones open in China where laborers can be paid still
less Investors like the bigger quarterly earnings, consumers like the
lower prices, and the CEOs love their multimillion dollar bonuses—but
is this invisible hand the hand of our Creator and Redeemer at work? I
don't think so

It is hard for followers of Jesus' teaching and example to fathom board members deciding to add millions of dollars to an already super-wealthy executive's compensation even as, under that CEO, benefits packages of ordinary employees are being trimmed back, department staffs (including long-term employees) are being "downsized," remaining workers are being encouraged or required to work extra long hours, and (despite these cuts) stock values and annual reports (adjusted to put the best face on everything) show operating losses—again This scenario is not an exaggeration

The fact is that it is not a free market setting these compensation levels, it is boards of directors, stocked with cronies who share similar values, chaired by the CEO, and accountable only to each other Until this generation, executive leaders of companies often took reductions in pay to help their companies through hard times, and the differential between executive and employee pay was one-hundredth of what it is today The old values of loyalty, equality, fairness, compassion and the like are in short supply as each person grabs for everything they can get Executive compensation is certainly not about justice, and it has only a remote and inconsistent relationship to corporate performance

Of course, the world of professional sports and entertainment has similar discrepancies between the compensation of superstars and that of ordinary players Why don't the beneficiaries and perpetrators of this scene think of lowering ticket prices and minimizing the "all advertising, all the time" ballpark experience instead of generating all possible revenue so as to pay exorbitant player salaries? The same question should be asked of famous musicians and film superstars The answer seems to be that enough people are willing to pay $60 for an upper-deck ticket to see a pro football game or a concert and to accept meekly, if not actually enjoy, the advertising blaring from the colossal Diamond Vision scoreboard

Let us consider another business model, the one put forth by warehouse retailing leader Costco Their model follows these ironclad policies First, the wages paid to store workers, anywhere in the world, must be higher than what comparable companies in the area are paying their workers And second, the prices they charge customers are never more than 14 percent above what Costco paid for the item How is it that Costco is able to refuse to let the market dictate how much they charge for merchandise or how little they pay employees? I don't know enough about Costco to be able to say this is an exemplary company in other respects, but their wage and price policies show that it is possible to follow principled, value-driven policies and still succeed in the marketplace This example (and there are others) should encourage Christians in business to stand up for their values and principles and not cave in to market rhetoric

At various times in church history, topics like usury (interest on loans), fair prices and just wages have occupied the thinking of Christian thinkers At various times Christians, such as Lord Shaftesbury and John Woolman, have placed Christian principles above market demands and expediency When slavery was legal and the market supported the institution handsomely, such Christian leaders resisted and opposed it No matter how profitable, slavery was wrong It was theft, though most business leaders of the time didn't call it that

The time for us to renew that spirit and challenge the institutionalized greed and theft of today's global economy is long overdue Our calling as Christians is not to simply be naysayers railing against greed and oppression We need some brave and articulate prophets, but still more we need a new generation of thinkers and leaders to show a third way in economics

Taxes

Saint Augustine is famous for saying that governments are not much more than successful, victorious robber bands Extracting money and labor from people against their will is called *theft*—unless the thieves are in power Then it is called *taxes* and *civilian service,* so the argument goes In formal democracies (Augustine lived in the late Roman Empire, not in a democracy), those who authorize taxes are voted (more or less) into power, and thus we endorse their decisions to some extent, but it may still be legitimate to raise the question of whether taxes ever qualify as theft We can ask, Is the tax money being collected and recorded fairly and honestly? Is the revenue being used properly and honestly? Unfortunately, there is graft, dishonesty and corruption in government, just as in business

Further, are the tax policies themselves fair to citizens, or do they grant special favors? The wealthy sometimes complain that the higher

tax rates they pay on income are unfair and may even qualify as theft
Inheritance taxes have been criticized (by some of the wealthy) as an
unjust double taxation, as taking away a family's property Tax code re-
visions in recent years have been criticized for the opposite reason or-
chestrating a large transfer of wealth to the richest echelons of the population at the expense of the middle classes in this generation and the
next (as a result of a huge and escalating national debt)

But the other side of the issue is that taxes are the way we collectively pay for our common needs and interests, such as representative
government (which we don't want limited to independently wealthy
people), police and fire services, armies of defense, roads and other basic infrastructure Many societies also use tax revenues to make some
provision for education, health care, safety regulations, scientific research, the arts and assistance to the poor Remember what Paul said
about the Roman Empire (not about Calvin's Geneva or Kuyper's Neth-
erlands or Quaker Pennsylvania) "For the same reason [i e, con-
science] you also pay taxes, for the authorities are God's servants
Pay to all what is due them—taxes to whom taxes are due, revenue to
whom revenue is due, respect to whom respect is due, honor to whom
honor is due" (Rom 13 6-7) Jesus once urged his disciples to pay a tax
simply to avoid giving offense to others (Mt 17 24-27)

Thus, despite all the reasons Christians might find to object to tax
policies, the other side is that we must not steal from the government
by failing to pay the taxes we owe And to put it more positively, we
should be willing to pay taxes to help support the common good
Haven't we seen before what happens to the poor and the environment when everything is left to private charities, such as churches?
It is a terrible situation How much better it is to live in a society that
makes provision for its people and its environment, even though this
is done imperfectly

Charitable Contributions

Nevertheless, no matter how progressive a government might be, society will always need private charity and initiative Christians and
churches have a major role to fulfill here and cannot just look to the
state But how much should we give? Alan Redpath asks, "Does New
Testament grace allow a lower standard than Old Testament law? God

forbid "[23] Christians commonly say that they are not bound by the formal requirements of Israel's law We are set free to live by grace, but does this mean we are free to do less? Or are we instead free to do more? The ancient Jews tithed off the top (i e , they gave 10 percent of their first fruits) and then made *additional* offerings They were not particularly wealthy This was the standard for all Jews, wealthy or poor

The prophet Malachi asked, "Will anyone rob God?" and then charged the people with robbing God by failing to donate their tithes and offerings (Mal 3 8-10) Even the poor in America's urban and rural areas are well off in comparison to most people in the rest of the world The middle and upper classes are rolling in wealth in comparison to others Not to give generously—and for most of us that means giving 10 percent or more of our gross income—is a scandal Of course there are exceptional circumstances when we cannot make this goal, and we then remember that we serve a gracious, understanding God But as the years roll by, our normal, usual pattern should exceed that minimal tithe standard

We must also be attentive to how our charitable contributions are used Not just business and government but charitable organizations have sometimes operated irresponsibly and fraudulently Leaders (e g , pastors, priests, bookkeepers, accountants, fund managers and heads of organizations) have siphoned off money from disaster-relief funds or other accounts for their own purposes More respectably, but no less questionably, some nonprofit organizations have irresponsibly wasted financial donations on lavish salaries, travel and entertainment Some have placed friends or relatives on payrolls though they contributed little or nothing to the organization The "theft" we endure when we decide to buy an admission ticket at an exorbitant price is one thing, the theft perpetrated by scoundrels who take people's sacrificial donations is a special outrage

Certainly, Christians who are involved in overseeing finances and determining policies for charitable organizations need to try to influence the organizations to operate in a responsible and ethical manner Despite these problems, our primary emphasis must be on the positive

---

[23]Redpath, *Law and Liberty,* p 56

potential of charitable giving by Christians From their earliest years, our children need to discover the joy of giving to others Christians and the churches need to become unending sources of creative and redemptive activities and programs, both near and far, and give generously and sacrificially to support these good works Historically, Christians have been known as generous people practicing a generous faith We need to make sure we earn and maintain that reputation

Gambling

Conservative pundit and author of *The Book of Virtues,* William Bennett, turned out to have a long-time addiction to gambling, often for very high stakes Is this an acceptable and ethical hobby for a Christian to have? Redpath doesn't think so "The whole habit of gambling is the very essence of theft for the reason that by gambling a person comes to possess something which is a total violation of labor and love A gambler receives money for which he does not work, and by doing so he robs the one through whom he receives it "[24] Bennett, of course, did not *technically* steal from any particular person, and he is wealthy enough to continue providing for his family despite his losses

It is no secret that the gambling tables and machines are all programmed in favor of the casino or the sponsoring venue Gambling entertainment comes at a price, and who is paying? The gambler's family is often the hardest hit, but churches and charities may also lose out as one's money flows into the gaming houses

One of the worst developments of the past thirty years has been the proliferation of government-sponsored lotteries, which encourage the hapless and hopeless to spend their dollars buying a chance at winning millions of dollars Governments often persuade skeptical electorates to approve state lotteries by promising that the proceeds will support public education, which they do But the skeptics were right after all once lottery revenues began to flow in, educational support from conventional tax sources began to erode, usually leaving the schools no better off Of course, state-promoted lotteries do not just financially support education through schools, they directly engage in the education of the people with their billboards and massive advertising cam-

[24]Ibid , p 93

paigns They have one lesson they constantly teach "You don't need to save, study or work hard anymore to achieve your dreams Just buy lottery tickets—this is the pathway to untold wealth and happiness'"

This is theft The government is blatantly lying to steal a dollar here, a dollar there, from the poor, uneducated, desperate and vulnerable (who buy most of the lottery tickets) Lotteries undermine the thrift and the work ethic that are the true path through school and into business and into the housing market

Native Americans have discovered in recent years that they can make large amounts of money by building casinos on reservation lands, exempt from federal gambling restrictions While anyone familiar with the history of America's treaty violations and theft of Indian lands has to feel that some kind of justice is being exacted as foolish palefaces are now relieved of their money on these reservations, it remains the case that economic development based on proceeds from gambling is hardly ideal

As outrageous as gambling and lotteries may strike us in a Christian ethic, the best response is not just to oppose them, but to propose constructive alternatives Investing in better education, job creation and small-business development that touch the lives of those prone to turn to gambling (either as providers or consumers) has to be the Christian agenda

Reparations

A few years ago my Japanese brother-in-law received a check for $25,000 as reparations for having been born in an internment camp in Utah toward the close of World War II His family had been unjustly taken from their home in Berkeley and interned in a camp because the government feared that Japanese and Japanese American people living on the West Coast might collaborate with a Japanese invasion Many of those interred lost their businesses and property during this process It is a shameful episode in American history

But it does raise the question of whether reparations should be paid to other people groups which have been robbed, injured or exploited in the past A significant movement among African American leaders is demanding reparations for slavery, that is, for labor that was never compensated Do African Americans deserve reparations? Well, yes

The problem is that Native Americans deserve reparations as much as African Americans do So do Mexicans, from whom California and much of the American Southwest was essentially stolen But then Mexicans would have to sort through how much they owe the Native Americans in California, from whom they took the property It gets further complicated, because there was a fair amount of intermarriage among the Spanish and Indian peoples in Mexico and in California

Then there is the problem of assigning financial responsibility to people like me, whose ancestors were working-class people in Germany, Sweden and England until they immigrated to Minnesota and Oregon in the late nineteenth and early twentieth centuries What do we owe? We certainly have benefited from being of European ancestry, though we never thought about it or talked about things that way We were all too busy looking for work or working at whatever jobs we found

The core issue is whether people who have been robbed should be paid back The answer is yes, if at all possible But once we move beyond clearly established names, dates and episodes of theft (such as the forcible relocation of Iwawaki family from Berkeley to Utah in 1943), it gets increasingly difficult to find a just, fair or feasible way of carrying out a repayment plan Everyone can see the absurdity of having most of us present-day white Americans paying any reparations to wealthy African Americans such as Michael Jordan, Halle Berry, Janet Jackson, Clarence Thomas, Barry Bonds, Willie Brown or Condoleezza Rice

So although there is an imbalance in the historical scales of justice, race-based reparations cannot be justly carried out The Bible always links justice and mercy There can be no perfect justice, so if we want to move forward, we must practice mercy and grace along with justice Because our history is too complicated to unravel now, a better approach to reparations is to ensure that the descendents of slaves (and of immigrants, and of Native Americans, etc) receive financial assistance based on their need for example, money for education, microloans, funding for new small-businesses and health care subsidies Such assistance would provide the foundation we all need to live well A needs-based assistance program will ensure that no one descended from groups exploited in the past will fall through the cracks

America's minority and immigrant populations deserve our recognition, our gratitude and (usually) an official apology (The populations of which I am thinking include the Irish, Italians, Jews, Chinese and others whose labor built our cities and railroads, often in appalling conditions and for terrible wages) Realistically, though, we cannot sort through them, group by group, to determine what reparations should be paid to whom, and it is divisive, distracting and counterproductive to do so Better to pull together as a people and pool some resources to help needy applicants to get education, jobs and health care

And there is no reason why Christians and churches should await government action on these issues We should initiate programs as soon as possible to address these needs It will be nothing new Christians have engaged in education, health care and job creation for centuries, always with a special concern for the poor

Lifestyle Choices

The preceding discussions focused primarily on institutions businesses, governments, churches and other nonprofits In closing, we need to focus also on issues of personal choice and responsibility Does one's choice to drive a gas guzzling SUV contribute to a theft from future generations who may bear the costs of this choice? Is one's coffee-drinking habit at all responsible for the economic changes in Latin America that take away people's farms and traditional livelihoods? Does one's purchase of certain clothing or athletic gear amount to stealing an Asian child's time and educational opportunities? Are the stores one shops at providing cheap goods because they are failing to pay a living wage to their employees or not compensating their suppliers fairly?

We don't have satisfying answers to these questions The issues they address are not simple, yet we must summon the courage to raise these questions and to explore the effects our lifestyle choices have on others Learning more about where things come from and how they are made is an eye-opening experience We must not live in a manner that, however indirectly, deprives other people of the necessities of life, for that would be theft

In the Sermon the Mount, Jesus discussed three ways by which we practice our piety and religion before God (Mt 6 1-18) One way is to pray, we are all familiar with this text because it contains the Lord's Prayer A second way is to give alms to the poor The third is to fast, to abstain from food for a time All three of these practices are helpful as we reflect on the ethics of the eighth commandment First, we ought to pray about this area of our life and to resist market forces and cultural trends as we seek to do God's will on earth as it is done in heaven Second, we need to give—regularly and sacrificially—to those in need Third, we need to cut back, even fast, regularly Saying no to our appetites and desires is an important discipline that helps us gain proper perspective on ourselves as well as on others who have no choice but to fast

> The three disciplines Jesus teaches in the Sermon on the Mount are helpful as we work out the right thing to do with our stuff *pray* about the issues, that God's will be done, *give* as generously as we can; and *fast* to gain self-discipline and awareness as well as to experience temporarily what the poor experience all the time.

In Search of a New Paradigm

Our reflections on the eighth commandment can be as uncomfortable and problematic as those on any other of life's basic arenas No, most of us do not steal in any overt sense Most of us wouldn't cheat on our taxes or appropriate somebody's intellectual property without credit But when we let the commandment act like a searchlight that ranges over our lifestyle, our business and our politics, when we think not only in terms of what we have done but what we might have left undone (sins of omission), we get closer and closer to the truth

God is full of grace and forgiveness, and I don't think we should lay a guilt trip on ourselves or others, especially about questions of indirect and complex economic factors The point, though, is that we not grant ourselves a quick "pass" on this commandment, but allow God to question us—and then to rise up in creative faithfulness and provide salt and light in a world of so much need and so much possibility

For Reflection and Discussion

1 Have you ever personally had someone steal from you? How did you feel and what did you do about it? How could it have been prevented?

2 In your view, what are the best ways that wealthy people can be responsibly generous to those in need? How would you define *wealthy* today?

3 How can Christians impact business policies and practices that seem to exploit people in other parts of the world? Have you brought your Christian values into your business and career life? How did it go? How might Christians make a stronger impact on today's business scene?

4 What should local, parish churches be doing to teach both youth and adults the economic values of Scripture and how to resist the consumer culture?

11

Truth Telling

We've gone from discussing life to relationships to property—and now we turn to communication The ninth commandment declares, "You shall not bear false witness against your neighbor" (Ex 20 16 par Deut 5 20) The term used in the Exodus passage *(shaqer)* means "lying" or "untrue witness " The term used in Deuteronomy *(shaw)* means "empty," "vain," "insincere" or "frivolous witness"—the same word that is used in the third commandment, which forbids an empty, vain use of God's name These terms provide us with two angles on the same problem communicating wrongly *about* our neighbor

Old Testament scholar Brevard Childs explains, "The commandment is directed primarily   against the threat of false accusation The original commandment is, therefore, not a general prohibition of lying but forbids lying which directly affects one's fellow "[1] French Reformed theologian Alphonse Maillot writes, "One only becomes truly a liar in the Old Testament when one seeks to deceive the other, to lead him off into false ways, or when one seeks publicly the eyes and ears of others to give a false image   The lie, the truth, is *relational* "[2]

Again, we want to notice this commandment's location in the Decalogue Protecting the truth about someone, their reputation, is the next priority after protecting their material property Luther argues, "Be-

---

[1] Brevard Childs, *The Book of Exodus A Critical, Theological Commentary* (Philadelphia Westminster Press, 1974), p 424
[2] Alphonse Maillot, *Le Decalogue Une Morale pour notre temps* (Geneva Labor & Fides, 1985), p 138

sides our own body, our wife or husband, and our temporal property, we have one more treasure which is indispensable to us, namely our honor and good name, for it is intolerable to live among men in public disgrace and contempt "[3] My own way of putting it is that communication about a person is a little less concrete and immediate, a little more distant, than are their hearth and home (but more immediate than the sphere of thought and attitude addressed by the final commandment)

Alan Redpath sees a link between the two commandments concerning communication "The Third Commandment forbids taking the name of the Lord in vain, which governs our relationship with him This Ninth Commandment means that our relationship with other people should be governed by the same principle "[4] In my view, these two communication commandments are not just about God (cf the third commandment) and people (cf the ninth commandment) but about "false or vain communication *to*" (the third commandment) and "false/vain communication *about*" (the ninth commandment)

Dale Patrick suggests that the ninth commandment "constitutes something of a conclusion to the preceding ones Following the proclamation of prohibitions of crimes and torts, it protects the citizen from being convicted of any of these falsely and the court process itself from becoming the vehicle of murder or theft "[5] We could also see it as a kind of foundation for what precedes it a bad reputation (addressed in the ninth commandment) can disqualify one from buying or renting property or from getting credit, or maybe it could even drive one to steal (violating the eighth commandment) That can lead to the rupture of relationships and families (protected in the seventh commandment) and maybe even end in frustration, violence and the loss of life (addressed by the sixth commandment)

The ninth commandment is not just about randomly spouting false information It is about *harming our neighbor* through our falsehoods The big problem here is the offense against our neighbor, not just the offense against the facts Calvin emphasizes the relational aspect in its

---

[3]Martin Luther, *The Large Catechism,* trans Robert H Fischer (1529, Philadelphia Fortress, 1959), p 43

[4]Alan Redpath, *Law and Liberty A New Look at the Ten Commandments in the Light of Contemporary Society* (Old Tappan, N J Revell, 1978), p 100

[5]Dale Patrick, *Old Testament Law* (Atlanta John Knox Press, 1985), pp 56-57

positive form "For the legitimate observance of this precept consists of employing the tongue in the maintenance of truth, so as to promote the good name and the prosperity of our neighbor "[6]

Both the "lying witness" of Exodus and the "empty or vain witness" of Deuteronomy relate first to legal disputes and trials, that is, to perjury [7] More broadly, the commandment covers all forms of slander, libel, gossip, talebearing, insinuation and insult of one's neighbor Luther shows its breadth "It forbids all sins of the tongue by which we may injure or offend our neighbor [including] false witness, corrupt teaching [and] the detestable, shameful vice of back-biting or slander by which the devil rides us "[8] Redpath says it includes talebearing, innuendo, failing to speak up to oppose false witness and even flattery [9]

> The ninth commandment is not just about randomly spouting false information. It is about *harming your neighbor* through your falsehoods The big problem here is the offense "against your neighbor," not just the offense "against the facts."

Rabbi André Chouraqui stresses the importance of the notion of *witness* Peter was reproached for witnessing falsely that he did not know Jesus Christians who died for the faith were called *martyrs,* a term based on the Greek word for witness *(martys)* [10] The ninth commandment is part of a broad biblical condemnation of the sins of speech (and a correspondingly vigorous promotion of speaking the truth) If a malicious, false witness was found out, he was sentenced to suffer whatever he had intended for the accused by his false testimony to suffer (Deut 19 15-21) The Leviticus Holiness Code instructed the people "You shall not lie," "You shall not defraud your neighbor," "You shall not swear

---

[6]Calvin *Institutes of the Christian Religion* 2 8 47

[7]Against those who see a broad application of the commandment, Walter Harrelson, *The Ten Commandments and Human Rights* (Philadelphia Fortress, 1980), p 143, restricts its meaning to "speaking truthfully in public, not about truth-telling in general " It is about public testimony in trials, social and commercial dealings, and public worship

[8]Luther, *Large Catechism,* p 44

[9] Redpath, *Law and Liberty,* p 101

[10]André Chouraqui, *Les Dix Commandements Aujourd'hui* (Paris Robert Laffont, 2000), p 212

falsely by my name, profaning the name of your God," "You shall not go around as a slanderer among your people," and "All who curse father or mother shall be put to death" (Lev 19 11-12, 16, 20 9)

While false and deceptive witness were clearly and repeatedly condemned, several famous stories indicate that the rule was not always strictly observed, even by the heroes of the faith For example, Abraham twice provided a deceptive, half-truth that Sarah was his sister, rather than boldly admitting that she was his wife (Gen 12 18-19, 20 2-12) His son Isaac bore similar false witness about his own wife Rebekah (Gen 26 6-11) Jacob was frequently engaged in deceptive witness, including to his own father (e g , Gen 27 1-40) More understandably, the Hebrew midwives deceived Pharaoh to save their babies, Rahab bore false witness to protect the Israelite spies, and Samuel deceived some of Saul's people when he went to anoint David as Saul's successor (Ex 1 15-22, Josh 2, 1 Sam 16 1-5)

Despite this inconsistent performance by biblical characters, the teaching of Scripture is constant The book of Proverbs is especially full of counsel about our speech For example, two of the "six things that the Lord hates" and that are an abomination to him are "a lying tongue" and "a lying witness who testifies falsely" (Prov 6 16-19)

With their mouths the godless would destroy their neighbors
Whoever belittles another lacks sense, but an intelligent person remains silent (Prov 11 9, 12)

A faithful witness does not lie, but a false witness breathes out lies   A truthful witness saves lives, but one who utters lies is a betrayer (Prov 14 5, 25)

Scoundrels concoct evil, and their speech is like a scorching fire
A perverse person spreads strife, and a whisperer separates close friends (Prov 16 27-28)

A false witness will not go unpunished, and a liar will not escape (Prov 19 5)

Do not be a witness against your neighbor without cause, and do not deceive with your lips (Prov 24 28)

Argue your case with your neighbor directly, and do not disclose another's secret (Prov 25 9)

The reason for all of this is that "a good name is to be chosen rather than great riches" (Prov 22 1) Falsely attacking someone's reputation is a horrible thing to do

The prophets blasted the people for their sins of speech In a classic and typical passage, Jeremiah writes

They bend their tongues like bows, they have grown strong in the land for falsehood, and not for truth   Every neighbor goes around like a slanderer They all deceive their neighbors, and no one speaks the truth, they have taught their tongues to speak lies, deceit upon deceit   Their tongue is a deadly arrow, it speaks deceit through the mouth They all speak friendly words to their neighbors, but inwardly are planning to lay an ambush Shall I not punish them for these things? says the LORD, and shall I not bring retribution on a nation such as this? (Jer 9 3-9)

Jesus' advice to those who bear witness was to avoid swearing oaths assuring one's truthfulness Keep it simple "Let your word be, 'Yes, Yes' or 'No, No ' " (Mt 5 33-37) Another kind of false witness against which Jesus warned was claiming him as Lord but not acting like it or not doing God's will (Mt 7.21) Jesus himself was condemned to death on the basis of false evidence (Mt 26 59-60, Mk 14 55-59) He was subjected to insults and falsehoods but did not respond in kind

Paul exhorts us, saying, "Putting away falsehood, let all of us speak the truth to our neighbors" (Eph 4 25), and "Get rid of   slander, and abusive language from your mouth Do not lie to one another" (Col 3 8-9) James says in a famous passage "How great a forest is set ablaze by a small fire! And the tongue is a fire   No one can tame the tongue With it we bless the Lord and Father, and with it we curse those who are made in the likeness of God   Do not speak evil against one another" (Jas 3 5-10, 4 11) In short, the biblical teaching on ethical speech to and about our neighbors is a rich and thorough commentary At its heart is the principle of the ninth commandment do not bear false or vain witness against your neighbor

The Positive Counterpart to False Witness

The flip side of this broad condemnation of false witness and the sins of speech is the equally extensive praise of truthful witness and the positive power of our speech After all, God's creation was brought forth by his word, and his word declared that it was good The commandments are themselves a true witness to God and to his covenant with Israel The psalmist urges us to "laud" and "declare" God's great works to others (Ps 145 4-7) Proverbs commends wise, noble and true words "All the words of my mouth are righteous, there is nothing twisted or crooked in them" (Prov 8 8) "Death and life are in the power of the tongue, and those who love it will eat its fruits" (Prov 18 21) "A word fitly spoken is like apples of gold in a setting of silver" (Prov 25 11)

Jesus often used the phrase, "Truly, truly, I say to you" (e g , Jn 3 3 RSV) Truth mattered to him "The truth will make you free," he said (Jn 8 32) The master theme of Jesus' message was not condemnation and bad news but truthful "good news" *(evangelion)*, and he commissioned his followers to be his faithful, true witnesses throughout the world No wonder "the crowds were astounded at his teaching" (Mt 7 28)

Paul urged that we speak the truth in love (Eph 4 15) It is not good enough to spout true facts, we must speak with loving, constructive purposes, to build one another up, not tear one another down "Let your speech always be gracious, seasoned with salt, so that you may know how you ought to answer everyone" (Col 4 6) "The Lord's servant must not be quarrelsome but kindly to everyone" (2 Tim 2 24) The truth must be told Jesus and the prophets and apostles boldly laid out the truth, even when it was difficult Their witness was true and necessary, never vain, empty or pointless

Jean Milič Lochman explains the nuances of some of the vocabulary for truth

> The Greek word for truth *aletheia* means truth in the sense of a theoretic insight into the structure of reality Its purpose is the discovery of the hidden, the unveiling of phenomena, and the conceptual grasp of the true ontological realities The Hebrew term *emeth* on the contrary, refers to the trustworthiness, reliability, validity, and binding character of a personal behavior, but above all, in a concentrated form, the demonstration of fidelity between persons [11]

---

[11] Jan Milič Lochman, *Signposts to Freedom The Ten Commandments and Christian Ethics* (Minneapolis Augsburg, 1982), pp 142-43

Again, the commandment is about our neighbor It is a relational matter

Luther calls for the positive counterpart to false or empty witness against one's neighbor "A person should use his tongue to speak only good of everyone, to cover his neighbor's sins and infirmities, to overlook them, and to cloak and veil them with his own honor It is a particularly fine, noble virtue always to put the best construction upon all we may hear about our neighbor "[12] Our challenge has to do with *how* we bear witness Is it true or false, empty or significant? Is it all negative, or do we bear positive witness when we can? A second challenge is how we interpret the witness we hear from others about a third party Luther's advice is superb there is always room for interpretation Put the *best* possible spin on what you hear, not the *worst*

> **Area Principle 9· Never communicate false or irrelevant information in a way that could harm someone's life or reputation. Rather, regarding truthfulness as an essential, core attribute of God's character and presence, communicate truthful information and wisdom that helps people and situations.**

Why False Witness Is Wrong (and Truthfulness Is Right)

All of us live not just in a material world of behavior and things, but within an environment of communication—of words, truth and falsehood, information, gossip, slander, joking, compliments, praise and instruction But is this information true (in accord with reality) or false (an inaccurate description of reality)? Terrible consequences can result from a lack of truth This is really at the heart of the scientific and philosophical quest to discover the truth, to expand our knowledge

Mistakes and errors are bad, but intentional falsehoods are even worse A lie can be defined as "the communication of a falsehood with intent to deceive " False (or empty, vain, baseless) witness against our neighbor is wrong, first of all, because of its harm to the victim False witness can ruin one's reputation and may put one's property, relationships and life itself in danger "For honor and good name are easily

---

[12]Luther, *Large Catechism*, pp 47-48

taken away, but not easily restored "[13] Just think about the harm done to people by false accusations Even if vindicated, the damage has often spread so far that it is not completely reversible Think of how vicious rumors and innuendoes have hurt people By contrast, telling the truth can help our neighbor by warning him of danger, by edifying, building up, comforting, and encouraging him It can provide others with a clear, accurate and helpful picture of our neighbor The truth can redeem bad situations and bring hope and new life

The direct victim is not the only person harmed by false witness False witness and lies harm society in general They undermine confidence and foment cynicism about information and about people "Who can you believe anymore?" we ask with resignation False witness often provokes lies of retaliation, creating an ugly social order in which we no longer expect to tell or hear the truth Laura Schlessinger has argued that truth is also "a precondition of justice Only when we have a clear picture of how things are can we discern how to behave appropriately If we don't have a clear or true picture of how things really are, we are more likely to behave in a way that is ultimately unjust "[14]

Lies and false witness are also wrong because they harm the one who speaks them Lies create an internal contradiction that destroys personal integrity and wholeness, you know the truth but say otherwise This poisons your mind and soul in the same way that your body is poisoned when you know something is inedible and harmful and you eat it anyway Lies also harm the liar by necessitating a continuing web of deception to cover one's tracks One lie is rarely enough What a foolish, exhausting distraction to have to always be thinking about how to cover up for one's lies And when found out, liars have great difficulty ever reestablishing their trustworthiness False witnesses create enemies who may be desperate and angry enough to do serious harm in retaliation

But false witness is also wrong because it is a major offense to God The Bible puts it very graphically lying is a direct participation in the realm of Satan and a betrayal of the God who is truth The original sin in the Garden of Eden followed the serpent's questioning God's word

---

[13]Ibid , p 45
[14]Laura Schlessinger and Stewart Vogel, *The Ten Commandments The Significance of God's Laws in Everyday Life* (New York HarperCollins, 1998), p 271

("Did God say, 'You shall not eat from any tree in the garden'?") and then his flatly denying it ("You will not die", Gen 3 1-5) The biblical Satan/devil is a deceiver, a liar and the father of lies, according to Jesus (Jn 8 44-47) The Hebrew word *Satan* and its Greek translation *devil* both mean "accuser"—one who hurls a lying accusation across at a foe Satan "accuses [our comrades] day and night," the Apocalypse says (Rev 12 7-11) The command against false accusation is not a lighter weight command It takes us to the very essence of evil in an important sense Babel, or Babylon,

> False witness is a cruel attack on our neighbor, whose reputation is a valuable and essential factor It also degrades and demeans the false witness, who lives in a web of lies and internal contradictions Finally, false witness and lying take us out of the reality of God, who is the truth, and into that of the devil, who is a liar and the father of lies.

another symbol of hardcore evil in the Bible, is the place of human arrogance and of confusion of tongues It is the exact opposite of all that is good and true in human communication

God created the world "very good" by his Word, and God has redeemed the world by the Word made flesh (Gen 1 31, Jn 1 14) "Grace and truth came through Jesus Christ" (Jn 1 17) Jesus said, "I am the truth" (Jn 14 6) When the promised Holy Spirit comes, he guides people into all truth (Jn 16 13) The Spirit makes possible the Pentecost miracle in which Babel is reversed and communication among different language groups can once again occur Thus, lies and falsehoods are offenses against God, not just against our neighbor Christians are followers of the God of the Word and of truthful good news False witness pollutes and corrupts the communication sphere of human life, which God wishes to inhabit

Maillot's insights into this commandment are helpful

> The Word   is the clearest sign, the most obvious, that we are made in the image of God It can also be the clearest sign that we seek to take the place of God   The problem of language always remains the primary problem in philosophy   Language is always incantation, that is, one does not speak merely to describe   but to act   Thus, one cannot say with impunity that someone is an imbecile, that is to act on him   We must

not pose as the God of our brother   At its simplest, when one
speaks of others, avoid using the verb "is/be " The verb "is/be"
belongs to God alone   Paradoxically, one assassinates people
with the "being" verb [15]

Maillot says that when we bear false witness against someone and
say something like "Joe is a crook," we are pretending to be God, who
alone has the right to declare what a person truly is

Today's Communication Context: Truth Against the Flow

Unfortunately, our contemporary culture gives permission and support
to false and empty witness Speaking the truth in love is, frankly, coun-
tercultural People bear false, lying witness about their own lives by epidemic cheating on tests and papers in school, by inflating or blatantly
misrepresenting their accomplishments on resumes, by cheating on
tax returns and insurance claims, by adopting pseudonymous personas
in communications and by lying to friends and family members People
bear false witness about others not just by courtroom libel and slander
but by contributing to gossip, stereotypes, unfair grading or inaccurate
reference-letter writing Gossip rags like the *National Enquirer* call out
to shoppers checking out of stores What a world!

One basic problem is how to define and uphold the distinction between truth and falsehood in our postmodern, relativistic era, in
which everyone has a presumed right to define truth as they wish
False witness gets trivialized to mean little more than being false to
your own feelings and perception Such relativism is so widely taken
for granted that writers and producers have no hesitation about modi-
fying aspects of historical accounts to add interest and (they hope)
market share [16] Journalists and even official government sources are
sometimes also found to be fabricating story lines and details Television interviewers in hot pursuit of the latest headline story frequently
ask questions along the lines of "How did you feel when Johnny was
killed there in front of you?" It's not about facts and truths but about
subjective feelings The half-truths of advertising could fill a book all

---

[15]Maillot, *Le Decalogue,* pp 138, 141
[16]The "improved" life story of John Nash, the schizophrenic mathematician portrayed in the film *A Beautiful Mind,* is a good example

their own All of this breeds cynicism about our ever being able to make real distinctions between false and true witness

A second factor is the speed and fluidity of life We are always busy, always in a hurry We need summaries, sound bites, headlines *USA Today* and the Headline News Network typify the dumbed-down, abbreviated news many in our culture live on But people and their lives are much more complex than such accounts can portray Bearing faithful witness takes time Evaluating true and false witness also takes time Unfortunately the negative sound bite seems to stick in our minds better than the positive one High-speed false witness is all around us

A third factor is the volume of information that surrounds us and bombards us We are inundated by a firehose-like stream of information and data We suffer from "infoglut" and "infotrash " Almost any topical search on the Internet turns up more time-wasting trivia and error than truth (And the error is only recognizable as error if one already brings some critical tools and background to the search, and how many searchers are likely to be in that position⁹) While it is true that never has so much information been so widely available, the ironic result is a world of half-informed and misinformed people who don't even know their weaknesses The ridiculous disinformation so rampant on the Internet, which is uncritically passed on by so many, is a very bad omen Think of all the false alarms about computer viruses It is fertile ground for false witness

> Our cultural and communications context is false-witness-friendly. The ease of anonymous, unaccountabe and inexpensive smearing of people's names, spreading rumors and half-truths, is ominous Of course our new technologies can also be used to spread true witness, but are people today prepared to recognize the difference⁷

Communication technologies (personal computers, the Internet) have radically transformed our information environment in the past decade Certainly the possibilities of better, more frequent communication with others are enhanced by e-mail and the Internet At the same time, these same technologies can leave us swamped with e-mail messages, pop-up ads and unwanted spam It takes tremendous discipline to use these communication tools in a constructive, balanced way

Rebuilding a Healthy Communication Arena

How do we recover truth and faithful witness in a world of falsehoods? Chouraqui suggests that

> the only reasonable solution is the return of the individual in his interiority and his profound truth It is in himself that he must reestablish the truth   When man ceases to lie to himself about his sensations, feelings and thoughts, he will no more lie to others The lucidity of the individual is the guarantee of transparency in human relationships and relations among groups [17]

But how and why will such self-consciously truthful individuals arise? Maillot stresses the importance of listening to others

> First of all, [true witness] consists of listening to and believing others Certainly it does not mean a blind belief but an open belief We could say that it is a matter of eliminating suspicion the suspicion   where we do not listen to what the other says but where unceasingly we think, "You say this, but you think that," or "You say this but it is because of this thing or that other person or because of your own interests or because of your education "[18]

But how and why will we overcome this suspicion, cynicism and paranoia?

When facing such an overwhelming task as this, I often think of how Jesus faced the culture of his day Jesus found himself confronted by the imperialistic presence of Rome, the various, competing schools of philosophy (Platonists, Stoics, Epicureans, etc), the divergent interest groups in Israel (Herodians, Sadduccees, Pharisees, Zealots), the crowds of the poor and hungry, and the endless stream of physically, mentally and spiritually ill people While he did give some public speeches and engage in some mass action to combat hunger, most of his energy was channeled into a band of twenty or so men and women, whom he trained to be a different sort of community with a different philosophy of life, a different lifestyle and a different outlook on life, truth and history

---

[17]Chouraqui, *Les Dix Commandements,* pp 226-27
[18]Maillot, *Le Decalogue,* p 142

In a similar fashion, our wisest response to today's challenges is to work on ourselves, our households and our communities (e g , church, business, school) One of the first priorities is simply building up our human relationships and the quality of our community life together Now more than ever, critical thinking and discernment are best pursued in the company of others We can help each other clarify and weigh what we hear and say and think We can practice listening and communicating with each other Weaknesses in my knowledge and skills are compensated by your strengths, and vice versa While Chouraqui has an important point about recovering our inward spirit of truth, this individual renewal also requires community

We must strive to rebuild more balanced lives and not try to keep up with what is coming out of the information fire hose We need a balance of quiet and sound, of thinking and conversation, of listening and speaking, of time alone and time with others In our reading, watching and studing, we need a balanced variety of perspectives—contributions from different political, geographic and national views and from people of different ages, sexes and ethnicities We need less trivia and more depth

Jacques Ellul often urged people to concentrate on two things First, to look for the "maincurrents," the trends and trajectories in our culture that lie under the chaos of daily headlines and current events This will mean reading books, longer articles, magazines and journals and watching television news programs that devote large time segments to careful, historical analysis (instead of the worthless popular shows, featuring talking heads and panels of screaming pundits) Second, Ellul says, we should seek to understand reality through conversations with our flesh-and-blood neighbors They are much more real than the statistical table on the cover of *USA Today* In our churches and communities, we can organize reading and discussion groups about important maincurrent issues in our culture To combat our vulnerability to false witness about individuals, we can create opportunities for people to share who they really are their history, interests, questions and plans

One of our culture's biggest weaknesses is the demise of what are called the grand narratives of life and its direction and meaning Marxism was one of these alternatives in the past Islam is a present-day metanarrative of great power and attraction for many Without a cogent story like this as a foundational framework, people have little to help them evaluate events and ideas The most convenient substitute narrative is consumerism, which holds that the meaning of life is to acquire stuff and to feel good, and if people try to stop you, keep on trying anyway

Recovering healthy, truthful communication is best pursued by small communities of kindred spirits who (1) work together to understand the main forces and trends affecting our spiritual, political and cultural landscapes, (2) value flesh-and-blood conversation and relationship, and (3) work at rebuilding and elaborating a robust Christian worldview and philosophy of life

Christianity has a powerful alternative story of life, its meaning, purpose and direction One of the most important endeavors our churches and study groups can undertake is to teach the Christian worldview and philosophy of history and life more intentionally From childhood onward, Christians need to maintain this alternative way of looking at truth, relationships, the past and future, work and rest, beauty and pain, and so on As I said earlier, it is hard to evaluate truth and falsehood when we have no reliable standards against which to measure them Christians have an answer—a story, a philosophy of life—that can help do just that

Silence

Refusing to speak to or about someone can be an insult or a harmful, irresponsible act On some occasions we must overcome our fear or laziness and raise our voices for the truth and for our neighbor To stand by quietly and allow a miscarriage of justice or an innocent person to be slandered is to be guilty What would you want others to do if you were being slandered in a similar circumstance?

On the other hand, as Ecclesiastes says, there is a time to speak and a time to refrain from speaking Some ethical dilemmas seem to force us to tell a truth that will cause a lot of harm, or to tell a lie that will cause less harm How can we deal with that dilemma? We cannot always remain silent or evade commenting, but sometimes that is what we can and should do We are not compelled to comment or pass public judgment on everything

Being silent puts us in a better position to listen and to reflect By undertaking a sort of "verbal fast," we may have our senses renewed so that we hear and speak more effectively and sensibly It is a good thing to set boundaries and create balance in our lives, including our communication

Gossip

We live in a society of gossip and talebearing, we are a society of "whisperers," to use the biblical term (e g , Prov 16 28) Society gossip columnists in major publications, the *National Enquirer* and its competitors, and so-called news shows featuring celebrity gossip pander to people's curiosity And how much ordinary conversation among people would be left if we removed talk about the weather and gossip about others? Maillot, as we saw earlier, believes that gossip about someone is a form of usurping God's privilege to designate the reality of a person's character A stereotyped, dismissive statement about someone is false witness because it doesn't allow for the fact that people change and grow [19] Luther was even more emphatic "Learning a bit of gossip about someone else, they spread it to every corner, relishing and delighting in it like pigs that roll in the mud and root around in it with their snouts "[20]

The only justifiable reason for passing on information of a personal nature about others is that doing so promises to help those people If sharing information about others leads to more prayer or more care, then it is probably legitimate We must be sure what we pass on is true, and that means we must interact with the person concerned Even if something is true, however, it may not be legitimate to share with others It is even worse to speculate on people's actions, tastes, relationships and attitudes It is bad enough to *think* about such things in a negative way, it is an abomination to God to pass on such speculations to others, for gossip destroys lives

What are some practical steps to take to avoid spreading untruths? To start, when someone wants to share gossip with you, cut him off and say, "I don't want to hear about that " When someone pries and probes for your information about someone else, decline to tell her anything Refuse to read gossip about celebrities, boycott celebrity gossip televi-

---

[19]Ibid , p 140
[20]Luther, *Large Catechism,* p 45

sion shows and magazines Set a good example for others This may seem like a small matter, but it is intensely important, and we must stand up and fight against this community-breaking, life-destroying pattern of communication

Telling the Truth to People

Rather than gossip about someone, if we know someone has a problem, we should speak about it to God in prayer and speak to that person directly (in the form of exhortation or counsel), rather than gossip *about* it This is faithful witness about someone *face to face* This is how change and improvement are possible Exhortation, unlike gossip, is faithful, positive and true witness But even this must be accompanied by humility, listening, wisdom and love We must be slow to speak and to condemn or judge and quick to listen (Jas 1 19) We must always speak the truth in love, in a way that redeems and liberates and builds up the other Otherwise, we should be quiet

Stereotypes

One of the most insidious forms of false witness is the stereotype "Oh, he's a Stanford-type," we used to scoff at UC Berkeley We might say, "Ah, a fundamentalist!" or "It's just those feminists (or those liberals, right-wingers, etc) " Stereotypes of women, men, blonds, Blacks, Chinese, Jews, Poles, children, Republicans—these kinds of things are almost always invidious (negative in their impact) Chouraqui points out that for two thousand years some Christians, including leaders, have accused the Jews of deicide, of killing God This false witness has led to untold suffering [21]

This is akin to the problem of idolatry discussed earlier it is replacing a living reality with an image—a lying, false image at that Stereotypes are, at best, a misleading and partial witness Often they are blatantly false and unfair When we hear them we must protest and immediately introduce evidence to undermine the power of the stereotype Conspiracy and hate groups promote these stereotypes, as do the media We should reject stereotypes and prejudices as vigorously and unequivocally as we reject gossip, for they destroy souls and communities

---

[21]Chouraqui, *Les Dix Commandements,* pp 215ff

Editorializing and Reporting in the News Media

When are news sources reporting the facts of a story objectively, and when are they interpreting and evaluating it? It is difficult to differentiate between reporting and editorializing these days No one, of course, can be totally objective Even one's choice of *what* to report is already value-laden, we all speak from a certain perspective or standpoint, so we see things differently Nevertheless, we can attempt to describe situations, events and people in a fair and full way To deliberately put an editorial spin on a story (or a history) and then present it as a fair and balanced report of the facts—without acknowledging one's interests— is bearing false and deceptive witness Our ideological interests and authorial perspective should always be acknowledged—and resisted when the purpose is factual reporting It is important to read a variety of sources, deliberately chosen to include diverse perspectives

Advertising, Evangelism and Political Campaigning

Where should we draw the line on false witness when we are not just reporting but recruiting? Where is the line when we are trying to persuade people to buy a product, vote for our candidate or convert to our faith? When does our witness become false? It seems unethical to fail to disclose the failures or negative features or costs of the product, candidate or faith Unrealistically inflating the positive promise, hopes and possibilities also seems unethical We must not say that people who believe in Jesus (or buy a BMW or wear Calvin Klein jeans or vote for the Republican candidate) will be happy all the time, or that their problems will disappear or that they no longer need to take their medicine To some extent, of course, when people know that we are playing the role of salesperson and the context and our agenda is clear (sales' conversions' votes'), we do not need to accompany every positive statement with a counterbalancing qualification

Whistle-Blowing

Whistle-blowing is when we make a public issue of something that has not been resolved privately It is a term used most often in a business context to describe when someone exposes an ethical or legal transgression, usually by going "over someone's head" or going public Before we blow the whistle, it is critical that we exhaust all other internal, existing channels (e g, confrontation or discussion), that we have compelling evidence of wrongdoing (not just a guess or hunch) and that we act to address a serious problem (not a trivial matter) which will, if left hidden, significantly harm others Whistle-blowing can destroy careers, so we must be exceedingly careful to ensure that it is not false witness (about bribery, sexual harassment or whatever)

Free Speech and Censorship

Should we take action to restrict in advance the potential for false or empty witness? Should we favor any sort of censorship or abridgement of free speech? Once false witness is made, it is often difficult to contain the consequences Completely unfettered free speech is not, of course, a real possibility For example, we do not allow people to yell out "Fire!" in a crowded theater Slander and libel and blatant misrepresentation cannot be allowed if we seek to maintain any semblance of justice or peace

John Stuart Mill argued persuasively for erring on the side of uncensored free speech His argument was, first, that we may be proven wrong, and those we wish to censor may turn out to be right, second, that few opinions are completely right or wrong, so we cannot draw a clear line between those which are right and those which are wrong, and third, that even if our opponents are wrong, they play a positive role in that truth is always more strongly held when it is confronted by error and opposition John Milton's famous essay "Aereopagitica" also advocated letting "truth and falsehood grapple " Milton asks, "What has truth to fear in a free and open encounter?" In every era we need to review how we can best protect truth as well as freedom, knowing that allowing freedom necessarily entails the risk that falsehoods will live alongside the truth

Protecting children and other vulnerable audiences has to be one important concern of Christians in this arena We do not want to subject them to propaganda, lies or corrupting influences On the other hand, it is only by facing opposition that we can develop discernment, so we don't want to be overly protective And finally, Christians can best bear witness to their faith in a political system that guarantees free expression History teaches us that restrictions on free speech will seldom be helpful to the Christian gospel

Sports, Jokes and White Lies

Perhaps there are some situations in which lies, deception and false witness are acceptable because of agreements among the participants or because the consequences seem trivial Thus, some would say that, in at least some contexts, it is acceptable to joke in a way that everyone understands is funny but not completely true Within a game, such as poker or football, all participants agree to certain forms of faking and deception within defined limits (e g , no slipping extra cards up your sleeve, no drugging one's opponents) And within human relationships some would say it is acceptable to compliment a meal or dress or decoration insincerely in order to avoid hurting the feelings of the host Such "white lies" are, however, an unfortunate habit that can help condition us to larger, more serious untruths The question of what is permissible with jokes is more serious if the humor perpetuates stereotypes and misunderstandings in society (which jokes often do) The trickery in sports and games is not a problem so long as the rules of the game and the expectations of the participants are clearly defined and accepted by all

Deceptive Witness in Statecraft and Relationships

Is there a place for deception or false witness when the stakes become much higher? Must governments disclose their intentions to one another? Would it have been wrong for the Allies to try to deceive the Nazis through false witness of some sort in order to win the war and liberate the death camps? Should a physician describe in detail the likely suffering of a dying burn victim when asked by the victim or family members? These are very difficult questions Remember, first, that choosing silence and evasion is probably better than introducing falsehood because the consequences of such a choice on the social (and diplomatic or professional) fabric of trust are less drastic than are the consequences of lying Second, lies, false witness and deception should only be justified as a last resort, not as the normal pattern of life

> False or empty witness comes in many forms Gossip, exaggeration, stereotyping and talebearing are some classic examples In the vast quantity of information moving through cyberspace and in our communication lives, we must be vigilant to protect our neighbor from false witness.

In the end, I conclude again that while Christians must take a stand against false and empty witness in all of its multiple forms today, our primary tasks will be to proclaim truthful, edifying witness to and about our neighbors In personal conversation and in business, professional and civic activities, Christians must be bearers of truthful good news While Christians have never faced such a challenge as we have in the modern communications arena, neither have we ever had as much opportunity to represent the truth

For Reflection and Discussion

1 Is there such a thing as a permissible untruth? Can we justify white lies? jokes? diplomatic or military deception?

2 How can we work against gossip and false witness in the Christian community?

3 What instances of falsehood trouble you most in the surrounding culture?

4 Do radio and television talk shows such as those of Rush Limbaugh, Laura Schlessinger, Jerry Springer, Maury Povich, Bill O'Reilly and others practice false witness in your view? Explain

12

Attitude Aiding

Still less concrete and immediate than the things people are saying about you are the thoughts they are thinking about you The final commandment addresses that area of human life the attitudinal and spiritual atmosphere in which we live and to which we contribute The biblical approach to ethics understands something very basic our words and our actions have their roots in our attitudes

The tenth commandment says, "You shall not covet your neighbor's house, you shall not covet your neighbor's wife, or male or female slave, or ox, or donkey, or anything that belongs to your neighbor" (Ex 20 17 par Deut 5 21) [1] What exactly is *covetousness*? It is a yearning for something that belongs to someone else [2] Dale Patrick adds that "'coveting' here is not merely an inward state but a driving force that produces schemes and overt action "[3] A complete (three-part) definition goes something like this Covetousness is (1) a desire for someone

---

[1] The Deuteronomy passages reverses the order of house and wife, and adds *field* The Lutheran tradition sees this as two commandments the ninth concerns coveting the spouse, and the tenth concerns coveting everything else Luther maintained ten commandments by joining the first and second commandments

[2] The Exodus version of the commandment uses the Hebrew word *hamad,* the Deuteronomy version uses both *hamad* and *hitawweh* OT scholar Brevard Childs explains the difference in nuance "The emphasis of *hamad* falls on an emotion which often leads to a commensurate action, whereas the focus of *hitawweh* rests much more on the emotion itself " *The Book of Exodus A Critical, Theological Commentary* (Philadelphia Westminster Press, 1974), p 427

[3] Dale Patrick, *Old Testament Law* (Atlanta John Knox Press, 1985), p 58

or something that (2) belongs to another, (3) accompanied by thinking and scheming how to acquire that object

The biblical story of covetousness begins in Genesis, with Adam and Eve deciding that the fruit of the forbidden tree was "desired to make one wise" (Gen 3 6) This covetousness led to the act that shook the world But the story of covetousness has many chapters As Israel took possession of its Promised Land, the people were cautioned about the idols and images left behind "Do not covet the silver or the gold that is on them and take it for yourself, because you could be ensnared by it, for it is abhorrent to the LORD your God" (Deut 7 25) Achan's covetousness for the expensive spoils of the war with Jericho led first to his theft and then to his death (Josh 7 20-26) David's covetousness for Uriah's wife, Bathsheba, led to adultery and then to murder (2 Sam 11) Ahab and Jezebel coveted Naboth's vineyard and had him killed so they could seize it (1 Kings 21 1-16)

The Prophets and Writings repeatedly condemn covetousness "A heart that devises wicked plans" is "an abomination to the Lord" (Prov 6 16-17) The prophet Micah warns, "Alas for those who devise wickedness and evil deeds on their beds¹   They covet fields, and seize them, houses, and take them away" (Mic 2 1-2) Proverbs also warns against coveting other people's spouses "Do not desire her beauty in your heart, and do not let her capture you with her eyelashes" (Prov 6 25)

In the New Testament, Paul stresses the importance of the interior life "You were taught to put away your former way of life, your old self, corrupt and deluded by its lusts, and to be renewed in the spirit of your minds" (Eph 4 22-23) "Be sure of this, that no   one who is greedy (that is, an idolater) has any inheritance in the kingdom of Christ and of God" (Eph 5 5) Much of the apostolic teaching is about replacing malice, anger, lust, greed, jealousy, envy and other bad attitudes with humility, forgiveness, compassion, kindness, tenderheartedness and joy

Paul described his own personal experience with the tenth commandment "If it had not been for the law, I would not have known sin I would not have known what it is to covet if the law had not said, 'You shall not covet ' But sin, seizing an opportunity in the commandment, produced in me all kinds of covetousness" (Rom 7 7-8) The commandment articulated a moral standard, a measuring stick, that both awakened Paul's desire to do the forbidden thing and convicted him that it was wrong

James gives a substantial explanation of the dangers of this bad attitude

One is tempted by one's own desire, being lured and enticed by it, then, when that desire has conceived, it gives birth to sin, and that sin, when it is fully grown, gives birth to death   For where there is envy and selfish ambition, there will also be disorder and wickedness of every kind   Those conflicts and disputes among you, where do they come from? Do they not come from your cravings that are at war within you? You want something and do not have it, so you commit murder And you covet something and cannot obtain it, so you engage in disputes and conflicts   You ask and do not receive, because you ask wrongly, in order to spend what you get on your pleasures (Jas 1 14-15, 3 16, 4 1-3)

Finally, 1 John argues that "the love of the Father is not in those who love the world, for all that is in the world—the desire of the flesh, the desire of the eyes, the pride in riches—comes not from the Father but from the world And the world and its desire are passing away, but those who do the will of God live forever" (1 Jn 2 15-17) Here again, as with all of the previous nine commandments, the message of the commandment is a central teaching throughout the Bible

Jesus

Jesus' teaching puts great emphasis on our hearts and our attitudes In the Sermon on the Mount, Jesus said, "Blessed are the pure in heart," and he intensified the prohibition against murder to include anger and the prohibition against adultery to include lust (Mt 5 8, 21-22, 27-28) "Take heed, and beware of all covetousness," Jesus warned (Lk 12 15 RSV) He repeatedly emphasized that our external actions are rooted within

For out of the abundance of the heart the mouth speaks The good person brings good things out of a good treasure, and the evil person brings evil things out of an evil treasure (Mt 12 34-35)

What comes out of the mouth proceeds from the heart, and this is what defiles For out of the heart come evil intentions, murder, adultery, fornication, theft, false witness, slander These are what defile a person (Mt 15 18-20)

Woe to you scribes and Pharisees, hypocrites' For you clean the outside of the cup and of the plate, but inside they are full of greed and self-indulgence   You are like whitewashed tombs, which on the outside look beautiful, but inside they are full of the bones of the dead and of all kinds of filth So you also on the outside look righteous to others, but inside you are full of hypocrisy and lawlessness (Mt 23 25-28)

Christians, like the Pharisees, have sometimes focused too much attention on the right words and deeds At other times, Christians have focused almost exclusively on interior faith and good intentions Jesus provides a balanced emphasis, stressing the importance of both a good attitude and a good spirit, of (outward) words and deeds that conform to one's (interior) heart and will Reading Jesus' words and other biblical teaching, it is strange to consider how we could become so unbalanced in one direction or the other

The Heart of the Matter

Let's try to better understand the profound nature of this challenge The problem occurs in our attitude Alphonse Maillot compares this commandment to the others

The nine other commandments are the "possible" commandments   We can know when we obey or transgress them The "objective" and external sins can be recognized, and we can admit that our will has given consent   But with the tenth commandment, we are present before a sin that is not "at hand" but in the heart,   a sin that is subjective, interior and   [over which] we have no power, it is a sin outside our will [4]

Perhaps we can best understand the problem by comparing covetousness to some other attitudes we have toward other people and other things First of all, *admiration* is not the problem To admire your

---

[4]Alphonse Maillot, *Le Decalogue Une Morale pour notre temps* (Geneva Labor & Fides, 1985), pp 147-48

neighbor or your neighbor's spouse, children or property is fine To admire is to recognize beauty, value, accomplishment and worth In fact, being insensitive to such beauty and value or being incapable of admiring people, nature and things is an indication of an arrested, deformed personality Maillot writes, "The commandment does not suppress our saying 'Wow, what a beautiful house' Wow, what a pretty woman'" The commandment thus becomes the lens that allows me to see the beauty which has been given to me and that helps me to see rightly in front of me "[5]

Admiration is not necessarily an attitude that wants to possess, take over or exploit Of course, admiration can go wrong by crossing over into *jealousy* or *envy* Jealousy and envy focus on the owner more than on the stuff

> Admiration is a normal, healthy response to beauty and value It only goes wrong if it becomes envy, jealousy, obsession or idolatry

she owns (e g , I envy the owner, but I covet her car) Envy and jealousy are the fruit of spiteful attitudes toward someone else A jealous person overlooks her own blessings and wishes she were the other person Sometimes covetousness grows out of envy and jealousy, but the admiration that originally led to envy is not to blame

Admiration can also go wrong by turning into *idolatry* or *obsession* We can become fixated on what we admire, thinking of it too often, organizing our thoughts, time and energy around it, or becoming completely unbalanced in our perception of it The object of our admiration then "possesses" us, even if it (or he or she) has no idea that this is happening Covetousness often grows out of this sort of obsession

Admiration can legitimately become *curiosity* to know more and then *desire* to have This can be a good when two conditions are met first, the object of your desire is rightly available (e g , the woman or man is single, the house or land or car is up for sale or rent) and, second, you are free to proceed to act on your desire (e g , you are not already married, it is not irresponsible to purchase or rent this house or land or car)

The concept of desire is also important to understand in this discus-

---

[5]Ibid , p 154

sion The movement from *admire* to *desire* is significant and good
much of the time Rabbi André Chouraqui argues that desire, per se, is
a deeply human and constructive emotion, to be distinguished from
covetousness "Man and woman cannot live and survive without having
desires and without satisfaction I hunger and thirst—these desires
push me to eat and drink Desire can be defined as a call to live It
presses us to protect our life, to satisfy our need to invent, to build, to
learn and to teach Thus desire is a function of life "[6] As Jan Milič
Lochman has also written, "The Tenth Commandment is certainly not
prohibiting all impulses, longings, desires, and passions   The notoriously 'lukewarm' [do not] have a particularly good press (cf Rev
3 16) "[7]

In the Middle Ages, Christians tried to avoid what they called the
"seven deadly sins " Pride, envy and anger (the first three) were viewed
as perverted love or desire Sloth was viewed as a defective love, a lack
of desire Avarice, gluttony and lust were viewed as vices of excessive
love or desire—for possessions, food and sex, respectively Covetousness, we can see, is most closely related to the latter three forms of excessive love or desire

Sexual desire, to narrow the focus a bit, is part of God's creation
For all of the warnings against illicit sex, Proverbs also has this to say

Drink water from your own cistern, flowing water from your own
    well
Should your springs be scattered abroad, streams of water in
    the streets?
Let them be for yourself alone, and not for sharing with strangers
Let your fountain be blessed, and rejoice in the wife of your
    youth, a lovely deer, a graceful doe
May her breasts satisfy you at all times, may you be intoxicated
    always by her love
Why should you be intoxicated, my son, by another woman
    and embrace the bosom of an adulteress? (Prov 5 15-20)

---

[6]André Chouraqui, *Les Dix Commandements Aujourd'hui* (Paris Robert Laffont,
2000), p 236
[7]Jan Milič Lochman, *Signposts to Freedom The Ten Commandments and Christian
Ethics* (Minneapolis Augsburg, 1982), pp 150-51

These are the words of someone who praises appropriate sexual admiration and desire

And as rigorous and disciplined as the celibate Paul was, he also wrote this

The husband should give to his wife her conjugal rights, and likewise the wife to her husband For the wife does not have authority over her own body, but the husband does, likewise the husband does not have authority over his own body, but the wife does Do not deprive one another except perhaps by agreement for a set time, to devote yourselves to prayer, and then come together again, so that Satan may not tempt you because of your lack of self-control (1 Cor 7 3-5)

Desire for the opposite sex is a creation of God, not of the devil Desire for sexual fulfillment is God's invention The issue is whether that desire is properly directed and expressed and whether it is in balance

It is not a violation of the tenth commandment when a single man or woman finds a member of the opposite sex attractive and desirable and wishes to meet that person Certainly, the person feeling such desire must not be obnoxious, harassing or rude toward the one desired But such desire is not, in the absence of such negative features, bad in itself It is a natural part of God's good creation for men and women to be drawn together into relationships and marriage

So, too, the desires for a better house, farm, education, job, salary or church (or even for a better golf score or wardrobe) are not necessarily bad things Such ambition can be a powerful force for good Ambition to prosper through hard work and wise investments is not improper, if we take seriously Proverbs, Jesus' parables and apostolic teaching A lack of drive and ambition, whether

> **Desire is a normal, healthy human drive toward relationships, growth, accomplishment and excellence**
> **Desire needs to be disciplined and directed much more than quenched**

from fear or laziness, is not an admirable trait But these desires, just like our sexual desires, can go off track by becoming obsessive and idolatrous or by leading us into covetousness

For the tenth commandment, the problem is that the object of our

desire *belongs to someone else* and is not available to us Our desire
can thus only lead to frustration (if we don't get what we want) or theft
(if we do wrest it away from its owner) Chouraqui says, "The boundary between desire and covetousness is traced in the Bible by the object permitted or prohibited to pursue "[8] Luther describes covetousness as a "scheme to despoil his neighbor of what belongs to him
having designs upon your neighbor's property, luring it away from him
against his will, and begrudging what God gave him "[9] The object of
covetousness, as opposed to desire, is something that belongs rightfully
to someone else "It is not wrong to desire a wife, but it is wrong to desire the wife of another man "[10] Lochman says, "The specific concrete
focus of the Tenth Commandment is the '*sidelong glance*'—the envi-
ous comparison we make between ourselves and others   Covetousness finds expression in an effort to catapult ourselves into the other
person's position "[11]

> **Covetousness is a desire, accompanied by some scheming, to acquire someone or something that rightfully belongs to another It is rooted in our failure to accept ourselves as we have been created and our restlessness to be and have something else, to play God for ourselves.**

Covetousness is not just about
lusting to possess the spouse of another It is about wanting *whatever*
belongs to our neighbor "The second part of the tenth commandment reflects a traditional type of
list, common to the Ancient Near
East   The function of the list is
to be all-inclusive and to rule out
any ambiguity as to the extent of a
man's property "[12] Your neighbor's
house and spouse are included, but so are your neighbor's intellectual
property and friendships The list is comprehensive Don't covet *anything* that belongs to your neighbor

The final stage of the development of covetousness is when we begin
concocting a *scheme in our mind* to acquire that forbidden object To

---

[8]Chouraqui, *Les Dix Commandements*, p 236
[9]Martin Luther, *The Large Catechism*, trans Robert H Fischer (1529, Philadelphia
Fortress, 1959), pp 49-50
[10]Alan Redpath, *Law and Liberty A New Look at the Ten Commandments in the
Light of Contemporary Society* (Old Tappan, N J Revell, 1978), p 111
[11]Lochman, *Signposts*, pp 150-51
[12]Childs, *Book of Exodus*, pp 427-28

covet is not only to desire what belongs to another, but to begin fantasizing, intriguing or plotting how to get it Rabbi Avroham Chaim Feuer says, "Whoever desires his friend's house, wife, or possessions transgresses *you shall not desire* from the moment he begins to meditate on how he can achieve his goal "[13] Bill Hybels describes how admiration can lead to fantasy and covetousness

> All of us notice attractive members of the opposite sex now and then Attraction and stimulation are normal reactions for sexual beings, such as we are Obviously, that normal reaction does not constitute the lust to which Jesus referred in Matthew 5 No, it's not the first, casual look that constitutes lust Nor is it the innocent appreciation of a muscular physique, a shapely body, or a pretty face It's the second, third, or fourth look—the look that's accompanied by an imagined seduction, a mental undressing, and a conscious fantasy of having a sexual relationship with that person—that defines lust That is what Jesus forbade [14]

We have seen that admiration and desire are, by themselves, positive aspects of what it means to be a human being So what is it that causes these positive things to go astray? The root of covetousness, Maillot argues, is our discontent with ourselves and our wish to be in God's place

> It is not a question of resignation, which, in advance, refuses all change It is not a prohibition of changing houses, professions or parishes Still less is it prohibited to try to become more intelligent or qualified, or to help my children work better, or to ask my wife (or husband) to be more gracious (or loveable) Simply, with this command God wants us to learn how to love reality   The desire for change is absolutely not wrong in itself [15]

The challenge is to balance self-acceptance, contentment and trust in God's care with a constructive and appropriate ambition This is not easy in a culture such as ours

---

[13] Avroham Chaim Feuer, *Aseres Hadibros The Ten Commandments, A New Translation with a Commentary Anthologized from Talmudic, Midrashic and Rabbinic Sources* (Brooklyn, N Y Mesorah, 1981), p 60
[14] Bill Hybels, *Laws That Liberate* (Wheaton, Ill Victor, 1985), p 90
[15] Maillot, *Le Decalogue*, pp 152-53

Why Covetousness Is Wrong

Area Principle 10 Never allow yourself to covet what belongs to someone else Rather, regarding your thoughts and attitudes as belonging to God, cultivate gratitude for what you have and a positive appreciation for what your neighbors have

The logic is pretty simple if the action itself would be wrong (adultery, theft, murder, etc), then fantasizing about it and wanting to do it are also wrong, because our attitude can lead to actions We form a plan or a vision in our mind, and then we act on it If we repeatedly, obsessively rehearse an act in our minds, we are preparing ourselves to do it Almost every bad thing that was ever done was conceived first in someone's mind Not all lustful thoughts lead to adultery, but all adultery begins with lustful thoughts Not all greed leads to theft, but all theft starts with greed Not all anger and envy lead to murder, but all murder begins with anger and a bad attitude

Coveting something can lead us to lie, cheat and then steal Coveting someone can lead to flirtation, intrigue and adultery Envy can lead to violence and murder or theft, or to lies and gossip These actions harm others That is why they are wrong And that is why plotting to do them is wrong, even if you don't carry out the plot "When we covet something 'out there,' something that is available and waiting to be claimed, we limit most of our destruction to ourselves But when we covet what belongs to others, we bring those people into the situation, and jeopardize our attitudes toward them and our relationships with them "[16]

The tenth commandment is in some respects the least concrete and least immediate ethical concern on the list It can seem so harmless to covet And yet it can be seen as the foundation, the root, of all the problems addressed by the other commands Again, Chouraqui elaborates

> Think about the practical consequences of covetousness The sister of jealousy, it could well deserve to be called mother of all vices   The commandments are organically related one to another in their living unity The non-respect of one leads to the violation of the others This solidarity of the parts at the heart of all is the fundamental intuition of the Lawgiver [17]

---

[16]Hybels, *Laws That Liberate*, p 127
[17]Chouraqui, *Les Dix Commandements*, p 229

I think it is also fair to say that our attitudes have an effect on others, even if they do not lead to overt wrongful acts How can this be? Covetousness is unseen but nevertheless has a reality that poisons the atmosphere An atmosphere of covetousness, greed and lust is like an oppressive fog for those who must live near or within it Martin Buber writes,

> There is one attitude, however, that destroys the inner connection of the community even when it does not transform itself into actual action, and which indeed, precisely on account of its passive or semi-passive persistence, may become a consuming disease of a special kind in the body politic This is the attitude of envy The prohibition of "covetousness"   is to be understood as a prohibition of envy The point here is not merely a feeling of the heart but an attitude of one man to another that leads to a decomposition of the very tissues of society [18]

As Hybels says, "When we covet what belongs to someone else, we displace the owner In our minds we kick him out of the game, or out of the job, or out of the marriage "[19]

Covetousness is not just wrong because it harms, or could harm, others It is also wrong because it harms the coveter Covetousness is a selfish desire that poisons the soul and the spirit of the coveter It is, or easily becomes, slavery and obsession Enchained by covetousness, we lose our free spirit Covetousness can become a root of bitterness that kills off our joy in living Covetousness fills our mind with inappropriate thoughts and desires

> Covetousness is wrong because it is the seedbed in which evil, harmful acts are conceived and bear fruit But even if one does not directly act on it, a covetous attitude poisons relationships and the unseen atmosphere in which we and our neighbors live

and thus stifles our potential for healthy thoughts There is no room for what is good in our minds when we entertain evil Covetousness is a rotten tree, which cannot produce good fruit It is a poisoned spring, a

---

[18]Martin Buber, *On the Bible Eighteen Studies* (New York Schocken, 1968), pp 109-10

[19]Hybels, *Laws That Liberate,* p 128

seething cauldron of unquenched appetite, a terrible, frustrating way
to live

Chouraqui reminds us of Saul's attitude toward David Saul "conceived a great jealousy in his encounter with David From there, his behavior obeyed a logic of self-destruction that in the end cost him his
life This example shows how respecting the commandments is not just
good for society, but is equally linked to the psychological equilibrium
of those who respect them "[20]

Finally, covetousness is wrong because of the way it insults and of-
fends God Paul says that covetousness is idolatry When we fall prey to
covetousness, we sacrifice and bow down to the coveted object It
moves onto the throne of our life, where only God should sit But covetousness also manifests a lack of gratitude to God It "unmasks our
dissatisfaction with God's provision for us In our hearts we say, 'God,
you've not been fair with me I deserve a nicer wife, or a more lucrative
position, or a bigger house, or higher status You've shortchanged me
You owe me something better!'"[21]

With the tenth commandment we are also in the domain of God's
unseen Spirit This is the realm where God's quiet Spirit moves upon
us "Man looks on the outward appearance, but the LORD looks on the
heart" (1 Sam 16 7 RSV) According to Paul, all people have God's law
"written on their hearts, to which their own conscience also bears
witness" (Rom 2 15) As Jesus said in the Beatitudes, the "pure in
heart" will see God (Mt 5 8) *The
impure in heart cannot see God!*
Covetousness corrupts this spiritual domain with idols and vile
thoughts

> Covetousness insults God by making
> an idol of the coveted object and by
> rejecting God's provision in our lives
> as inadequate Covetousness enslaves
> the coveter and blocks God's
> communication to our interior—our
> conscience, our spirit and our heart

Covetousness blocks God's access to our spirit and our heart
Our conscience can be an interior
agent of God—an avenue by which
God speaks to us Yes, God causes
us to be born anew and plants

---

[20]Chouraqui, *Les Dix Commandements,* p 230
[21]Hybels, *Laws That Liberate,* p 128

within us a new heart But this renewal does not guarantee that we will never slide back into our old ways of covetousness, lust, greed, anger and envy We need to cultivate a pure heart, a spirit of gratitude for what we have, a spirit of contentment, and we need to fight off the spirit of ingratitude and discontent that so often becomes covetousness

The Culture of Covetousness

The commandment against covetousness really goes against the cultural flow and prohibits one of the central themes of modern life' Talk about swimming upstream We live in a world of total, constant advertising Junk mail and telemarketing calls often exceed the volume of our legitimate mail and phone calls, billboards assault us on every side as we travel, magazine and newspaper ads compose more than 50 percent of the publication space, television programs include growing chunks of volume-enhanced commercials, sports and entertainment events bombard those in even the most expensive seats with ads, team uniforms are covered with advertising logos, computer screens are filled with pop-up ads and spam—the deluge never ends And the common message is that you need to buy what is being sold in order to be happy, healthy, secure and good looking The message is simple the meaning of modern life consists in the abundance of things we possess—exactly the opposite of Jesus' message

Many people report that shopping is one of their favorite activities "Born to shop," the T-shirts brag What a pathetic excuse for a meaningful life—hanging out in the artificial world of shopping-mall zombies and robots instead of walking through a forest or having a friend over for coffee and conversation, baking bread, tending a garden or reading a good book It is not going to be easy to resist our desires in an environment like this

And many Christians have jumped right in, not just as consumers but as creators, endorsers and promoters of this culture of consumption Shouldn't followers of Jesus think twice about taking jobs where all of their energy and creativity are channeled into promoting greed and covetousness? Some televangelists flaunt their gaudily furnished stage sets, their expensive jewelry and their bouffant hairpieces, as though these had something to do with the gospel of Jesus Christ

"Name it and claim it!" they goad "Health and wealth for the followers of Jesus!"[22]

One side of this propaganda tries to make the stuff of the world as alluring as possible The other side tries to make us dissatisfied with ourselves—our cars, our houses, our clothes, our vacations, our bodies "You deserve more! Reach out and grab it!" Our society has whole industries dedicated to fanning our covetousness into action "Greed is good," we hear "Sexual fulfillment is your personal right Your desires are legitimate—all of them Fulfill yourself! Go for it!" We live in a culture of warped self-actualization and narcissism

Getting Back on Track: How to Overcome

How can we overcome a covetous attitude? First on many advisers' agendas is to pray for and practice self-control, deliberately choosing not to obsess and not to place ourselves in the way of temptation in areas where we know we are weak

> This Commandment goes to the root of all evil actions—the unholy instincts and impulses of predatory desire, which are the spring of nearly every sin against a neighbor   It commands self-control, for every man has it in his power to determine whether his desires are to master him or he is to master his desires Without such self-control, there can be no worthy human life, it alone is the measure of true manhood or womanhood "Who is strong?" ask the Rabbis "He who controls his passions," is their reply [23]

Luther once said that we cannot prevent the birds of the air from flying over our heads, but we can prevent them from building a nest in our hair That is part of the solution preventing what we see and experience from building a nest in our consciousness

---

[22]In the mid-1980s I visited a famous megachurch in Dallas, Texas, with my junior high school-age daughter, Jodie The famous pastor preached, in his great oratorical style, "God loves extravagance " Over and over he chanted that phrase, as we sat surrounded by wealthy, perfumed Christians in their costly furs and jewelry Thirty minutes into the sermon, my little girl leaned over and whispered to me, "Dad, I don't think these people need this message!"

[23]J H Hertz, ed , *The Pentateuch and Haftorahs Hebrew Text, English Translation and Commentary,* 2nd ed (London Soncino, 1988), p 300

Saying no can be a very freeing and empowering experience We can say no to some of the advertising that assaults us by rejecting it or throwing it away unopened, by asking to get off mailing lists, hanging up on telemarketers, zapping television ads and supporting political campaigns to restrict or penalize intrusive, resource-wasting advertising We can say no to unnecessary shopping, being much more selective and intentional when we go into stores We can practice setting boundaries and budgets We can question ourselves, *Have I ever been in a position where I wanted something and could buy it but chose not to? Or do I always indulge my appetites to the maximum I can afford?*

Not all consumption is based on covetousness We do not buy things only out of a desire for something that belongs to another But the attitude of always wanting more is a close relation of covetousness, and both need to be disciplined

But all of this is essentially negative saying no The old saying that "nature abhors a vacuum" is true Positive reinforcement changes behavior more profoundly than does negative avoidance It is a matter of what we love Joy Davidman writes, "There is, in the last analysis, only one way to stop covetousness and the destruction of body and soul that spring from covetousness, and that is to want God so much that we can't be bothered with inordinate wants for anything else "[24] Cultivating and unleashing a mad craving for God and a passion for his presence is the true antidote to covetousness Jesus taught, "Blessed are those who hunger and thirst for righteousness, for they will be filled" (Mt 5 6) "Strive first for the kingdom of God and his righteousness, and all these things will be given to you as well" (Mt 6 33) Paul encourages us to "pursue love and strive for ["covet earnestly," KJV] the spiritual gifts" (1 Cor 14 1)

As we pursue God, we need also to channel our appetites, desires and ambitions toward healthy, appropriate fulfillments If it is a desire for sex that drives you nuts, get married (carefully but then passionately), and love your mate intensely If it is a desire for a better house for your family or for using to serve others that you crave, don't waste time coveting other people's houses—go after your own

---

[24] Joy Davidman, *Smoke on the Mountain An Interpretation of the Ten Commandments* (Philadelphia Westminster Press, 1953), p 127

Part of the answer to the temptation to covet the spouse of another person involves learning to see people more holistically (not just as romantic, sexual objects) and relationally (not just as individuals) It is dangerous to build a close, admiring relationship to a married person without at the same time building a close, admiring relationship with their spouse If you can't do the latter, you should probably avoid the former Learn to see and relate to people as spiritual, intellectual and artistic beings, not just as sexual beings Focus on building a relationship as a brother or sister rather than as a nonfamily, unattached friend Treat others exactly as you would treat a precious sister or brother Learn how to *love* your neighbor and your neighbor's spouse The gospel is not simply the negation of covetousness, it is the introduction of a healthy, positive attitude toward your neighbor

Calvin argues that "any feeling of an adverse nature must be banished from our minds " Rather, "everything which we conceive, deliberate, will, or design, [should] be conjoined with the good and advantage of our neighbor "[25] Chouraqui eloquently describes this change of perspective

> Becoming aware of our irreducible specificity and of the fundamental otherness of the other can eradicate in us all covetousness and jealousy See the other in terms of complementarity and no more as competition Personalize the human When each one feels specific and irreplaceable, and considers the neighbor in the same way, covetousness no longer has a place to exist [26]

This way of thinking brings us back to the corollary of the first commandment, which teaches us to recognize the uniqueness of each person

Finally, even though covetousness is an unseen phenomenon, it is important to make it visible in a safe context Letting the objects of our covetousness know how we feel about them is extremely dangerous But sharing our feelings with some close, covenanted friends in a relationship of support and accountability is a very wise move We are most vulnerable when we struggle with covetousness all alone

The problem of covetous attitudes is placed in stark relief by Paul's famous statement to the Philippians "Let the same mind be in you that was in Christ Jesus, who, though he was in the form of God, did not re-

---

[25]Calvin Institutes of the Christian Religion 2 8 49
[26]Chouraqui, Les Dix Commandements, p 238

gard equality as something to be exploited, but emptied himself" (Phil 2 5-7) Christians follow a Lord who humbled himself, who gave himself for others, who could say to his heavenly Father, "Not my will but yours be done" (Lk 22 42) Having the mind of Christ as our own is the ultimate check to the spirit of greed and covetousness that dominates our era

Before leaving this discussion, let's take a brief look at four topics that relate to our ethical practice of the tenth principle

> Overcoming covetousness means developing self-control and learning to say no to temptation and to our appetites The best antidote to wrongly directed love and desire, however, is rightly directed love and desire, starting with our love and desire for God

If Your Eye Causes You to Offend

The first topic is how to apply some very radical biblical statements about lust and covetousness In the Sermon on the Mount, right after saying that "everyone who looks at a woman with lust has already committed adultery with her in his heart," Jesus gave the radical advice to tear out and throw away your right eye (or your right hand) if it causes you to sin (Mt 5 28-30) Apparently one of the early church fathers, Origen, thought (based on this text) that his testicles were the cause of his sexual lust, so he castrated himself! But is that the right way to interpret Jesus' advice?

Jesus sometimes spoke in stark, contrasting terms to make a point (e g , "whoever comes to me and does not hate father and mother," Lk 14 26) This is *hyperbole,* a manner of speaking that states an extreme in order to get across a decisive contrast Most of us do precisely *nothing* to improve our response to temptation, so Jesus says, essentially, we should hack off the cause of the problem The point is to take radical, decisive action to get rid of the true roots of our sin But think carefully it is *not* the eye, per se, that causes us to covet and lust It is the object of the eye's gaze The message is, don't play with fire Minimize, cut off or radically restructure your contact with the person or thing you cannot stop coveting and lusting after Cut off visual inputs, relationships or music that feed your attitude problems Act with courage and decisiveness to get rid of the causes of your temptation

A Christian Aesthetic

Could cultivating a discriminating taste for beauty be a Christian ethical practice? There is a somber, gray, utilitarian tradition in some parts of Christian history Stern, plain and grim, these believers were all business and seriousness about life and faith As a reaction to excesses in the opposite direction, this is perhaps understandable But the Bible offers a richer, more balanced perspective God's creation was both "good for" something (i e , useful) and "pleasant to the sight" (Gen 2 9) It is not possible or necessary in this context to review the long train of biblical evidence that God values beauty and that people are expected to do likewise But we can briefly recall that, as his own first miracle, Jesus turned water not into a utilitarian protein drink, but into the finest wine (Jn 2 1-11) He took note of beautiful birds and flowers and accepted precious ointment as a gift Jesus was radical and serious, but he shows us a life of beauty and joy as well Paul also urges a life that has room for beauty and an appreciation of excellence (Phil 4 8)

The relevance of a rediscovered Christian aesthetic to a discussion of the tenth commandment is that it trains us to appreciate and value beauty *without needing to possess it, use it or consume it* We need help to more fully observe and appreciate beauty Our aesthetic sense is either nonexistent or too narrow Like wine guzzlers who learn to become wine connoisseurs, we need to appreciate beauty more fully and enjoy it more deeply, but consume it with more restraint Let us be like food gourmands who enjoy smaller servings of wonderfully presented, delicious food, instead of like gluttons who shovel it in at all-you-can-eat buffets The consumer society promotes covetousness and excess, too often quantity wins over quality

> The relevance of a rediscovered Christian aesthetic to a discussion of the tenth commandment is that it trains us to appreciate and value beauty without needing to possess it, use it or consume it.

Similarly, let us learn from those who can view or listen to beautiful art or music or nature without needing to own it Learning how to enjoy and admire people and things without needing to control or possess them—this is our educational challenge This is learning how to love and admire, rather than covet, people and things The call for a renewed Christian aesthetic has nothing to do with snobbish luxury and pretension and everything to do with valuing the beauty of God's creation without yielding to covetous attitudes

Stumbling Blocks and Individual Liberty

Flaunting our possessions or our bodies in front of others can be like encouraging others to covet what we have Our own freedom to own or use something, or to dress and behave in one way or another, is to be worked out in our own serious interaction with our Lord "All things are lawful," Paul writes (1 Cor 10 23) "Why should my liberty be subject to the judgment of someone else's conscience? If I partake with thankfulness, why should I be denounced because of that for which I give thanks?" (1 Cor 10 29-30) It is dangerous to condemn someone for their choice of house or car or spouse or even clothes and makeup Especially for any mature, "strong" Christian, it is wrong to judge others or accuse them of intending to offend you and cause you to covet

The shoe is on the other foot when it comes to our responsibilities before so-called weaker, less mature Christians and seekers (1 Cor 8 9) " 'All things are lawful,' but not all things build up Do not seek your own advantage, but that of the other" (1 Cor 10 23-24) "Let us therefore no longer pass judgment on one another, but resolve instead never to put a stumbling block or hindrance in the way of another" (Rom 14 13) In a culture that promotes excess, vulgarity and covetousness, we need to exercise and enjoy our liberty responsibly before the Lord, taking into account the possible effect of our choices on others, especially the weak

Covetousness Engineering as a Career

Contrary to the propaganda generated by business leaders and their marketing staffs, the will to be rich and to accumulate an ever-increasing abundance of things is dangerous, according to Jesus and the whole of Scripture Take your pick whose disciple will you be? We must choose between nurturing the consumer mentality and nurturing the provider mentality Is our life's purpose to be found in accumulation and consumption? Or is it to be found in giving and providing for others? Jesus and Scripture teach us that it is in giving that we truly receive (e g , Acts 20 35) Those who will gain the whole world may lose their own souls in the process (e g , Lk 9 25)

How does this transvaluation of values play out in our lives? Certainly it should affect our personal and family lifestyle choices But Chouraqui argues that we should also reflect on the foundations of business and the economy "Individuals are less motivated by the desire to do better than by their peers, and want instead to possess We are watching a regression of the qualitative as the quantitative rises The market economy rests on covetousness "[27] The question is what our stance should be vis-à-vis the economy

Do we simply roll over and go along with business as usual? Or should we Christians resist jobs, occupations and careers that focus or depend on engineering covetousness? Should we take jobs in which our creativity and energy are directed toward creating and marketing consumer luxuries of doubtful value? For example, should a Christian artist use her gifts to attract more public participation in the state lotto? I think we should avoid, as much as possible, participating in or supporting enterprises that seek to foment covetousness

Ultimately, the battle against covetousness will not be won simply by saying no We stand at a crossroads, and we desperately need Christian entrepreneurs and business leaders to pioneer new ways of doing business that can be both economically successful and oriented toward providing goods and services that contribute to the life, health and happiness of people around the world, not just to investors' quarterly returns

It all comes back to our attitudes and desires

For Reflection and Discussion

1 How do you counteract the covetousness-producing messages of the media?

2 How do you differentiate appropriate ambition from corrupt covetousness or greed?

3 Have you ever had to act decisively and radically to cut off the cause

---

[27]Ibid , pp 236-37

of covetousness (of someone or something) in your life? Describe how you did it

4 Is it possible, in your view, to move from an attitude of coveting someone or something to a healthier more positive attitude? How did you do it? Or is it impossible to retreat once you have crossed the line?

Postscript
Doing Right in the Twenty-First Century

The Decalogue provides guidelines for ten arenas of life We searched for the core (area) principle in each commandment, which always comprised both a negative prohibition and a positive counsel, and which focused on both our neighbor and our God

---

Area Principle 1: Never allow anyone or anything to threaten God's central place in your life Rather, make it your top priority to value and cultivate your relationship with God

> *Corollary 1.1. Never treat any persons as though they are dispensable or without value Rather, regard and treat all people as unique individuals of great worth.*

> *Corollary 1.2· All ethical progress (reform, growth, maturity) depends on a clear and compelling vision of an end (purpose, mission)*

Area Principle 2· Never make, serve or worship any humanly made image or representation of God. Rather, honor and pursue the freedom, vitality and reality of the living Lord God

> *Corollary 2.1 Never view people through stereotypes and images or as fixed and unchangeable. Rather, do everything possible to guard their freedom and nurture their life and growth*

Corollary 2.2. Never think of, or act toward, anything you make as though it is sacred per se Rather, offer everything you make in service and tribute to God

Area Principle 3. Never use any of God's names in a trivial, negative or disrespectful way. Rather, speak to him by name daily, share his name with joy, and live up to the name that you bear

Corollary 3.1. Never use or impose a demeaning, trivializing or derogatory name on others Rather, learn the name they have chosen, use it respectfully, and initiate conversation

Area Principle 4. Set aside and guard regular sabbath time focused on being with God Give six days of creative and faithful work each week in service *for* God

Corollary 4.1· To care for any person (relative, friend, colleague, neighbor), we must invest focused, attentive time with them and work creatively and redemptively for them

Area Principle 5· Honor and care for those who are God's agents and representatives in your life Never treat God as though he relates directly to you without using any agents

Corollary 5 1. Show love to others by giving care and honor to their significant others, their agents

Area Principle 6 Never do anything that threatens or harms the life and health of another person Rather, regarding it as God's own creation, do whatever you can to protect that person's life and health and to promote peace and reconciliation.

Area Principle 7. Never act, think or communicate in any way, sexual or otherwise, that violates or threatens covenanted, committed relationships Rather, regarding such relationships as God's creation, do whatever you can to support fidelity, loyalty and commitment.

Area Principle 8 Never take or accept anything that belongs to others if it is necessary to their survival or if the means by which you acquire it are unjust

Rather, regarding yourself as a steward of God's possessions, work to care not only for yourself, your household and community, but also for the poor and needy of the world

Area Principle 9 Never communicate false or irrelevant information in a way that could harm someone's life or reputation. Rather, regarding truthfulness as an essential, core attribute of God's character and presence, communicate truthful information and wisdom that helps people and situations.

Area Principle 10 Never allow yourself to covet what belongs to someone else. Rather, regarding your thoughts and attitudes as belonging to God, cultivate gratitude for what you have and a positive appreciation for what your neighbors have

---

Patterns in the Decalogue

Life is often very complicated Ethics is often controversial and difficult In such circumstances it is important to step back and see the broad outlines, the general contours of both life and ethics We must learn how to see the forest, not just the trees Looking back at the Decalogue as a whole, what can we say about its architecture?

As we have seen, the most common view of the Decalogue is one that sees two tables (or tablets), the first concerning God, worship, religion and so on, and the second concerning our neighbor, community and ethics While some commentators (e g , Lew Smedes) have felt free to detach the "mere morality" of the second table from the "mere religion" of the first table, most disagree The common and obvious point is that ethics must be based on religion—for "our gods determine our goods"—and that our religion must be lived out in responsible, ethical relations with our neighbors

Another indisputable pattern is that commandments two through ten are elaborations and applications of the first, which stands above all the rest Each of the latter nine commandments is an implication of God's rule from his throne in our lives

The Jewish rabbis sometimes argued for another pattern within the Decalogue, one that reaches across the two tables Thus, command one is the companion to six, two is the companion to seven, three is the companion to eight and so on "*Melchilta* explains that when God gave the Ten Commandments He etched them on two matching tablets of stone—five commandments on each The second set of five corresponds to the first set The Sixth Commandment, You shall not kill, is parallel to the first commandment "[1]

Rabbi André Chouraqui explains

> In the Hebrew tradition, the ten fingers of the hands correspond to the Ten Commandments etched on the two Tables of the Law The five fingers of the right hand, the hand of mercy, represent the first five commandments regulating the relations of man to the creator of the heavens The five fingers of the left hand, the hand of severity represent the last five commandments regulating the relations among people

Chouraqui then tries to show how one relates to six, two to seven, and so on

> To murder another is to attack the One who created that other To bow down before other gods is to commit adultery vis-à-vis Adonai/YHWH Lifting up the name of God in vain corresponds to a theft Not to remember the Sabbath consists of lying to Adonai/YHWH Not to honor one's ancestors leads to coveting the goods of others [2]

Martin Buber sees instead *three* basic parts in the Decalogue, having to do with *God* (have no other gods, make no images, do not misuse the Name), *time* (remember the sabbath, honor parents) and *space* ("the with-one-another of the community") "There are four things above all that have to be protected, in order that the community may stand firm in itself They are life, marriage, property, and social honor "[3] Nevertheless, these four are not quite enough to protect the community, because

---

[1] Avroham Chaim Feuer, *Aseres Hadibros The Ten Commandments, A New Translation with a Commentary Anthologized from Talmudic, Midrashic and Rabbinic Sources* (Brooklyn, N Y Mesorah, 1981), p 54

[2] Andre Chouraqui, *Les Dix Commandements Aujourd'hui* (Paris Robert Laffont, 2000), pp 45-46 I like this concept, and I have read carefully both Chouraqui's and Feuer's arguments, but, try as I have, I cannot see any special relationship in these pairs It seems forced to me My own view of how the two tables relate follows below

[3] Martin Buber, *On the Bible Eighteen Studies* (New York Schocken, 1968), p 109

they deal only with actions Hence the last commandment prohibits the community-destroying *attitude* of covetousness, or envy

Walter Kaiser (following John J Owens) also sees three basic parts to the Decalogue, but for him they are determined by the three *positive* statements Thus the first part begins "I am the Lord your God" and guides "right relations with God" through the first three commands The second part begins "Remember the sabbath day" and guides "right relations with work" in the fourth commandment The third part begins "Honor your father and mother" and guides right relations with society in the fifth through tenth commandments [4] This is grammatically pleasing, perhaps, but it is impossible not to see the fourth and fifth commandments (equally with the first three) as explicit and essential components in "right relations to God " Their very language requires such a connection

These various interpretive schemes each have some merit, but my own conclusion is that the Ten Commandments beg for a holistic analysis that views them as one series of ten—not as two series of five or as three series For example, I would prefer to take all three of Kaiser's categories (right relations with God, work and society) and then read all ten commandments for insight into each of these three relations I would maintain that the first three commandments, for example, are as essential to a work ethic or social ethic as any of the later commands

One commentator who supports a more unified orientation is Jan Milič Lochman

> God and humanity cannot be divided, the ethic of the covenant presupposes the indivisible unity of the two tables of the Decalogue   These commandments of the First Table refused to stay up in the clouds, in heaven, they link up directly with the patterns of human behavior in all areas of life and are not merely concerned with cultic matters We must expect the same thing in reverse in the case of the commandments of the Second Table Here, of course, we shall be dealing with specific human relationships and conditions, but not in any spuriously concrete way, as if they could be considered theologically in and for themselves in

---

[4] Walter C Kaiser Jr , *Toward Old Testament Ethics* (Grand Rapids, Mich Zondervan, 1983), p 84

abstraction from their context in the history of the Exodus, with no reference to the Preamble to the Decalogue with its vision and presentation of the divine name and promise [5]

So let us review the Ten Commandments as all of these the *Ten Ways of Love* for both God and our neighbor, a *Ten-Part Code of Justice and Rights,* and a *Ten-Part Charter of Freedom* In the terminology I used earlier, this amounts to a reading of the Ten Commandments under the rubric of the four rules of the road, or cover principles Then we will look at the internal architecture of the "five axes" of the Ten Commandments

The Ten Ways of Love

How do we define *love*? What is true love? The Ten Commandments are a tenfold account of the ways to love God with all of our heart, soul, strength and mind and the ways to love our neighbor They are at the same time the ten ways that God loves us

The first movement in love is to guard the exclusive, unique place of the beloved in our life "You shall have no other gods before me" (Ex 20 3, cf Deut 5 7) This is the first way God wishes to be loved, but it is also the first way anyone (spouse, child, employee, etc) must be loved We cannot tolerate any rivals or threats to the unique place of the beloved in our lives It is the first way God loves us, too, for we are given a place in his family, at his table, that no one else can ever have

The second movement in love is to guard the dynamism and vitality of the beloved "You shall not make for yourself an idol" (Ex 20 4, cf Deut 5 8) Those whom we love—God and our neighbors—must not be confined to, or replaced by, any fixed image of our making Love guards their space for growth and change, love nurtures and rejoices in their vitality God loves us in this way also, always challenging us to grow, being ever patient and supportive, and accepting us as we go through changes

The third movement of love is to communicate to the other, to call out the name and initiate a conversation "You shall not make wrongful use of the name of the LORD your God" (Ex 20 7, cf Deut 5 11) Love

---

[5] Jan Milič Lochman, *Signposts to Freedom The Ten Commandments and Christian Ethics* (Minneapolis Augsburg, 1982), pp 73-74

makes sure the name is respected, not abused God knows our names and speaks to us in truth and love People may ignore or disrespect us, but God never will

The fourth movement of love has two parts "Remember the sabbath day, and keep it holy Six days you shall labor and do all your work" (Ex 20 8-9, cf Deut 5 12-13) First, love is expressed by spending special, focused time *with* the beloved Second, love is expressed by working *for* the beloved Both dimensions are critical God loves us by working *for* us and by meeting *with* us for focused time together

The fifth movement of love is to honor the agents and representatives of the beloved "Honor your father and your mother" (Ex 20 12, cf Deut 5 16) We love God by honoring and caring for the agents he has used to give us life and bring us truth More generally, any beloved must be loved in this manner—by honoring and caring for their significant others, their "agents " God honors and cares for our agents and loved ones as he loves us

The sixth movement of love is "life guarding" "You shall not murder" (Ex 20 13, cf Deut 5 17) We love God by protecting the human life he has created in his image and for his purposes We love our neighbors by protecting their lives from harm (even when the value of those lives is unclear to us) God loves us by protecting our life

The seventh movement of love is "commitment keeping" "You shall not commit adultery" (Ex 20 14, cf Deut 5 18) We love God by protecting and not "putting asunder" people he has joined together (even when we don't fully understand why they are together) We love our neighbors by supporting and protecting their relational commitments Such covenanted relationships are essential to life God creates and protects our relationships

The eighth movement of love is "stuff stewarding" "You shall not steal" (Ex 20 15, cf Deut 5 19) We love God by protecting his property from destruction and by respecting how he decides to allocate it (even when we don't fully understand why it has been distributed thus') We protect the material infrastructure of our neighbor's life God loves us by providing the material things necessary to our life and relationships

The ninth movement of love is "truth telling" "You shall not bear false witness" (Ex 20 16, cf Deut 5 20) We love God by guarding truth in the domain of words and communication This is God's domain, and all truth is God's truth We love our neighbors by protecting their reputations, a critical necessity in life God loves us by giving us his truth, his Spirit leads people to respect and guard our reputations

The tenth movement of love is "attitude aiding" "You shall not covet" what belongs to your neighbor (Ex 20 17, cf Deut 5 21) This is the realm of unseen attitudes and spiritual forces, the domain of the heart and the conscience This is God's domain, and we love him by guarding its purity We love our neighbors by not having covetous thoughts about members of their families or their possessions God loves us by only willing our best

The Ten-Part Code of Justice and Rights

The Ten Commandments must also be read as a tenfold code of justice and rights Each of the commandments expresses a "right" that God claims from us As our Creator and Redeemer, God has a right to be on the sacred throne of our life, not replaced by any idols or images He has a right to have his name used properly, to our sabbath time as well as our work time He has a right to demand that we honor our parents, his agents, that we protect life, relational commitments, property, truth and a good attitude These are not just grateful acts of love to God, they are at the same time obligations It is basic justice

But as we have seen, these same ten movements define how God relates to each of us They are an expression of the righteous will and character of God And they are the ten fundamental themes of justice and human rights for our neighbors around the world All human beings have rights to be treated as unique, living, growing individuals whose name and identity we respect All human beings have a right to sabbath time off and to the opportunity for productive work Parents have a right to be honored and cared for All humans have a right to life, to association, to property, to the truth and to an atmosphere free of predatory scheming by others This is basic human justice These are workers' as well as citizens' rights Women have these rights, as do children We are made in the image and likeness of God This account of justice not only flows from God's revealed Word, but conforms to our nature as God's creatures

The Ten-Part Charter of Freedom

The Ten Commandments are also a charter for freedom They are the
ten words of the God who delivered a people out of slavery and wishes
to keep them free The first commandment keeps us in relation to the
God of all the universe and all people It guards our freedom from sub-
mission to lesser, false gods It guards our neighbor's freedom when we
submit to the Creator of all, whereas a tribal god might not take an interest in our neighbor

The second commandment keeps our freedom alive in relation to
the living, dynamic God and preserves us from static, finite, fixed idols
The third commandment guards our freedom to communicate The
fourth guards our freedom from workaholism and for rest The fifth
preserves freedom across the generations by requiring that we honor
and care for our parents The remaining commands protect our freedom to live in safety, our freedom to associate and our freedom in
property, communication and spirit Those who respect these commands are creating zones of freedom for others And they are themselves freed from violence, relational corruption, materialism, lies and
gossip, and covetous obsessions

The Five Axes of the Moral Life

We have seen how the commands relate to each other in sequence,
from one to ten (and back) Is there another pattern? I am certain
there is

Several years ago I was asked by the Fellowship of Christian Librar-
ians and Information Specialists to give a speech at their annual meeting in San Francisco I was extremely busy at the time and was teaching the Ten Commandments in my ethics course So I proposed that I
would do it if I could do a talk on the two "communication/informa-
tion" commands among the ten The third commandment guides our
communication *to* someone, I argued, the ninth commandment guides
our communication *about* someone And in these two guidelines are
the fundamental principles of a communication/information ethic Kaiser (following Stephen A Kaufman) also notes (without developing the
point) that "there is a close association between the third and ninth
commandment the third prohibits swearing a false oath in the Lord's
name   and the ninth prohibits false witness between persons "[6]

A few weeks later I was asked to be a banquet speaker for MBA faculty and students at St Mary's College in Moraga, California I was still extremely busy and was still teaching the Ten Commandments So I proposed that I would do it if I could do a talk on the two "work/business" commands among the ten The fourth commandment guides our work and rest *process*, I argued, the eighth commandment guides our relation to the *products* of our work In these two guidelines are the fundamental principles of a work/business ethic

As a result of these talks, I saw two lines from three to nine and from four to eight I began calling the first of these the *communications axis* of the Decalogue and the second the *economic axis* It was not long before I saw that command one was related to command seven One guards the unique, exclusive place of God, seven guards the covenanted relationship One and seven form the *relational axis* of the Ten Commandments

> It is not accidental that throughout the Bible, the notions of adultery between people are paralleled with an estrangement of a people from God It is the sin of adultery that comes to symbolize the broken faith between God and people "How shall I pardon you for this? Your children have forsaken me and sworn by those that are not gods When I had fed them to the full, then they committed adultery" (Jer 5 7) [7]

Command two prohibits idols and images because they substitute a dead image for a living God Two and six are thus the *life axis* of the Ten Commandments Finally, command five deals with God's *external* agency in our lives, his work through other people, command ten deals with God's *interior* agency, his work through our conscience, heart, spirit and attitudes Thus, five and ten are the *agent axis*

Did God—or Moses or those who edited the Pentateuch—have this in mind when the commandments were written down? I have no idea I do not put much stock in the esoterica of biblical numerologists who see hidden patterns and meanings in everything I do not believe that the God we know in Jesus and Scripture hides behind cryptic messages,

---

[6] Kaiser, *Toward Old Testament Ethics*, p 132
[7] Laura Schlessinger and Stewart Vogel, *The Ten Commandments The Significance of God's Laws in Everyday Life* (New York HarperCollins, 1998), p 234

revealing himself only to those who discern magic formulas and codes

Nevertheless, at the least, we have to say that biblical revelation is not random It is thoughtful What does the order of presentation of these ideas imply, we justifiably ask? So the fivefold axis pattern I have described may not be a magic key that eluded the rabbis for centuries until this Berkeley boy finally figured it out But I think the pattern is there and makes sense and is helpful in guiding our lives

The Interior Architecture of the Decalogue

A The Relational Axis Commandments 1 and 7

B The Life Axis Commandments 2 and 6

C The Communications Axis Commandments 3 and 9

D The Economic Axis Commandments 4 and 8

E The Agent Axis Commandments 5 and 10

1 Have no other gods   6 Do not murder
                    A ✕ B
2 Worship no idols or images   7 Do not commit adultery

3 Do not misuse the Name   8 Do not steal
                    C ✕ D
4 Keep the sabbath, work six days   9 Do not witness falsely

5 Honor parents ———— E ———— 10 Do not covet

Doing Right in the Twenty-First Century

At the end of this rather long study, you may be as frustrated as I am that so many loose ends and questions remain, that so many ethical dilemmas have gone unsolved My discussions of specific issues—from capital punishment to profanity to censorship—are all, without exception, incomplete and inadequate For those confronted with hard ethical dilemmas at the moment, your work is just beginning

Our concern is to figure out how to do the right thing, the ethical thing. We want to do the right thing to please God, most of all, but also to be helpful to our neighbors (whether they recognize and appreciate it or not). And we would like to experience the blessing of God in our lives. We ask not for happiness and riches, but for God's blessing and presence in our lives. We believe the Bible teaches us that living righteously is a pathway to God's blessing.

The general themes are pretty clear. If we want to do right, we must seek to walk with God. That relationship is all-important. Knowing and loving God—understanding the teaching and example of Jesus Christ our Lord—is the foundation of doing right. We also need to study Holy Scripture and seek the guidance of the Holy Spirit. Our study of the Decalogue brought us ten powerful principles (and several corollaries) to illuminate and guide our decisions and actions. We did not apply these principles in detail to any of the dilemmas of our lives, but, first things first, we need to know these basic guidelines before we can apply them.

Two final requirements for doing the right thing are personal character and Christian community. In my earlier book *Becoming Good: Building Moral Character* (InterVarsity Press, 2000), I addressed the topic of building moral character in a biblical way. If we don't have the required strength of character, the best rules and principles will not be applied. There is no way around this. You need a new "you" before you can live out what you need to "do."

Community is the other essential. Christianity and its ethics are like a "team sport." I never get tired of reminding people that Jesus sent out his followers two by two, not one by one, and that God said "it is not good" for one to dwell alone. Together we bear the image and likeness of our Creator. Together we are the body of Christ—not alone and isolated but together with others. So if we really want to do the right thing, we must get serious and intentional not only about our relationship to God, but also about building relationships of support and accountability with a few other brothers and sisters.

Without these basic elements in place, we can neither become good people nor do the right thing. With them, life can unfold as an endless, meaningful adventure, even if we are pilgrims in an ethical wilderness.

Names Index

Scripture Index

David W Gill (Ph D , USC) is an ethics writer, educator and consultant He served as professor of Christian ethics at New College Berkeley (1978-1990) and professor of applied ethics at North Park University (1992-2001) He has often served as visiting or adjunct professor of Christian ethics at Fuller Theological Seminary (Northern California and Phoenix extensions) and Regent College (spring and summer schools) and of business ethics at Seattle Pacific University (School of Business) and San Jose State University (Professional Development Center) He is a member of the Society of Christian Ethics, Society of Business Ethics, and Association for Practical and Professional Ethics He is president of the International Jacques Ellul Society <www ellul org>

Gill is the author or editor of six books, including the two-volume introduction to Christian ethics, *Becoming Good Building Moral Character* (2000) and *Doing Right Practicing Ethical Principles* (2004) He often leads workshops, seminars and retreats for Christian students, faculty, professional and church groups <www DavidWGill org> and provides business ethics training and consulting services in the marketplace <www ethixbiz com> He is the husband of one, father of two and grandfather of six